Revolutionary Egypt in the Eyes of the Muslim Brotherhood

Revolutionary Egypt in the Eyes of the Muslim Brotherhood

A Framing Analysis of Ikhwanweb

Mohammed el-Nawawy and Mohamad Hamas Elmasry

ROWMAN & LITTLEFIELD
Lanham • Boulder • New York • London

Published by Rowman & Littlefield
An imprint of The Rowman & Littlefield Publishing Group, Inc.
4501 Forbes Boulevard, Suite 200, Lanham, Maryland 20706
www.rowman.com

Unit A, Whitacre Mews, 26-34 Stannary Street, London SE11 4AB

British Library Cataloguing in Publication Information Available

Library of Congress Cataloging-in-Publication Data
Names: El-Nawawy, Mohammed, 1968- author. | Elmasry, Mohamad Hamas, 1976-
    author.
Title: Revolutionary Egypt in the eyes of the Muslim Brotherhood : a framing
    analysis of Ikhwanweb / Mohammed el-Nawawy and Mohamad Hamas Elmasry.
Description: Lanham : Rowman & Littlefield, 2018. | Includes bibliographical
    references and index.
Identifiers: LCCN 2018028914 (print) | LCCN 2018029476 (ebook) | ISBN
    9781538100738 (electronic) | ISBN 9781538100721 (cloth)
    ISBN 9781538158265 (pbk)
Subjects: LCSH: Ikhwān al-Muslimūn—Public relations—Egypt. |
    Communication—Political aspects—Egypt. | Internet in public
    relations—Egypt. | Egypt—History—Protests, 2011-2013—Political
    aspects. | Egypt—Politics and government—2011-
Classification: LCC JA85.2.E3 (ebook) | LCC JA85.2.E3 E46 2018 (print) | DDC
    320.0140962090512—dc23
LC record available at https://lccn.loc.gov/2018028914

Table of Contents

Introduction

Since late in the last century, the Middle East in general and Egypt in particular have witnessed a type of political Islamic resurgence. Having made its political presence felt in several Arab Spring countries, the Muslim Brotherhood (MB) has been at the forefront of this revival. The movement, particularly in its native Egyptian formulation, has worked hard to create a more prominent media presence, ostensibly with the aim of reaching out to mass audiences and increasing its popularity within and outside the region. When a popular Egyptian uprising began to unfold in January 2011, the MB—the largest and most organized opposition movement under former Egyptian president Hosni Mubarak—quickly took center stage. Since that 2011 moment, the group has been front and center of both regional and global politics and political science and international affairs scholarship.

The MB emerged from the 2011 uprising as the early winner, having swept several elections and referenda in 2011 and 2012. In the summer of 2012, Mohamed Morsi, one of the group's key figures, became Egypt's first democratically elected civilian president. However, following a series of critical Morsi government missteps, a months-long counterrevolutionary movement aimed at ending his presidential term early, and a large anti-Brotherhood street protest movement organized in part by Mubarak regime elements, Morsi was forcibly removed from office by the military in July 2013.

Some observers noted that the Brotherhood was, at least in part, set up to fail by Egypt's "deep state" and other factions pursuing a political counterrevolution. These analysts noted some of the group's political contributions and hailed its moderation and apparent democratic aspirations (see Fadel, 2014; Hamid, 2014; Wickham, 2013). Other observers, however, argued that factors within the Brotherhood's control contributed to the group's quick political demise. Chief among these factors were the Brotherhood's political inexperience, narrowly cast agenda, unwarranted trust in the Egyptian military, and failure to achieve important objectives of the Egyptian uprising (see Monier & Ranko, 2013). Following Morsi's July 2013 removal, the Brotherhood's political party, the Freedom and Justice Party, was banned, and the group was violently suppressed and eliminated from Egyptian social and political life.

This book utilizes framing analysis to examine two years of content from the Egyptian Muslim Brotherhood's official English-language website, Ikhwanweb.com. The book's purpose is to shed light on the MB's positions on foundational political events in Egypt and, more importantly, to show how the group desired to be perceived by English-speaking audiences. Readers of this book should bear in mind that the book entails primarily a media study, not an analysis of the MB's policy positions. It was beyond the scope of this book to investigate the accuracy or fairness of claims made on the Brotherhood's English-language website.

Our analysis focused on ten events that took place between November 2010 and December 2012: the 2010 parliamentary elections, the 2011 revolution, the 2011 constitutional referendum, the Maspero Massacre, the Mohamed Mahmoud protests, the 2011 parliamentary elections, the Port Said Massacre, the 2012 presidential elections, Morsi's 2012 constitutional decree, and the 2012 constitutional referendum.

We have decided to limit our focus to these pivotal events because they arguably helped shape Egyptian politics and dictate the Brotherhood's agenda and destiny for the foreseeable future. Also, these events were so crucial and rich that they set the stage and provided important context for a nuanced reading of the dramatic political developments that took place in Egypt following the summer of 2013. The events that occurred in Egypt in 2013 and 2014, influential and admittedly important in their own right, should be the subject of another, separate project examining this stand-alone phase in Egypt's modern political history.

Many scholarly studies have been conducted on the Brotherhood's role within political Islam and place in contemporary Egyptian politics. Studies have examined the group's ideology (Abdo, 2000; Mitchell, 1993); activism (Al-Arian, 2014); history (Lia, 1998); relationship to the Egyptian state (Al-Awadi, 2004); and position on democracy (Baker, 2003; Bayat, 2007; Tadros, 2012), among other things. However, to date, very few studies have looked exclusively or primarily at the ways in which the MB has engaged modern mass media. This book attempts to fill this gap. Additionally, the book offers a key contribution to the literature on the timeframe of the 2011 Egyptian uprising and its aftermath—phases with which media and political scholars are continuing to grapple.

As mentioned above, all material that was subject to analysis in this study was taken from the MB's English-language website, www.ikhawanweb.com. Launched by the MB in 2005, Ikhwanweb was meant to serve as the group's "ideological platform for the Western world, and was primarily directed to the public, academics, researchers, media, think tanks and decision-making centers in the West" (Hamza, 2009). The site is considered "an official representative" of the MB and its policies (Hafiz, 2008). Ikhwanweb, as a term, is Arabic for "Brothers who have a Web presence" (Bardhan, 2014, p. 244). According to the "About Us" section of Ikhwanweb.com, the site's headquarters are located in London, and its mission is to "present the Muslim Brotherhood vision right from the source and rebut misconceptions about the movement in Western societies" (Ikwanweb.com).

As noted earlier, we used framing theory to qualitatively analyze posts dealing with the ten abovementioned events. Qualitative framing studies demand a close reading of texts to uncover underlying meanings of communicated messages (Pan & Kosicki, 1993). Framing has been used to study the specific ways in which communication is packaged for message recipients. Framing scholars pay close attention to word choice, syntax, placement, inclusion, exclusion, and sourcing, among other factors that can drive the interpretation of texts (Entman, 1993).

We used qualitative textual analysis as a method to discover meanings, inferences, implications, and associations from Ikhwanweb.com posts. Textual analysis is a type of "interdiscursive analysis" that sees "texts in terms of the different discourses, genres, and styles they draw upon and articulate together" (Fairclough, 2003, p. 3). Fairclough (1992) highlighted four factors that contribute to the importance of textual analysis. First among these factors is a theoretical approach that associates texts with social action. Second is a methodological approach that points to texts as rich foundations for the study of political and social ideologies and their underpinnings. Third is a historical dimension that views texts as important guides for cultural and social transformation within a given society. Finally, textual analysis is a worthwhile method because it is political and regards texts as venues through which social control is projected, experienced, and practiced.

Since the 1990s, the internet and new media have generated significant scholarly interest and, in particular, spawned a new generation of text and human subject studies focusing on interactivity and social identity, among other areas. In this context, Chouliaraki and Fairclough (2005) argued that, thanks to postmodern technologies, "traditional social structures are now replaced by information and communication structures and ... social identities are defined in terms of positions in and access to the mode of information rather than the mode of production" (p. 44). Along the same lines, Fairclough (2003) pointed to two features of online texts: "Multimodality," which exposes the user to various visual and linguistic modalities or structural components and interactivity, which provides the user with the ability to determine the type of material that he or she would like to look at and the duration of his or her exposure to it.

In the book, we examined posts that dealt directly with the events in question, including posts published in the lead-up to prescheduled events, such as the various elections and referenda, and periods immediately following both prescheduled events and unprompted ones, such as the Maspero and Port Said massacres. We examined all Ikhwanweb.com posts dealing principally with the ten events under study. Our advanced search of the website yielded a total of 375 posts, all of which were examined.

It is important to mention that textual analysis requires an in-depth and refined understanding of sociopolitical contexts and sociocultural subtleties (McKee, 2006). Here, our familiarity with both Brotherhood history and ideology, as well as our understanding of the Egyptian cultural landscape, were significant factors. Both of us have Egyptian origins, are fluent in written and spoken Arabic, and attended the massive protests that took place at Tahrir Square in Cairo in early 2011. We were also present in Egypt when most of the events under study took place. Our collective knowledge of the Brotherhood, and Egyptian culture and politics, then, informed our critical readings of Ikhwanweb.com texts. We used our repertoires of contextual knowledge to interpret messages embedded in website texts. Our approach to analyzing texts was to engage in individual close readings of individual posts and collectively discuss meanings, connotations, and implications. Our analysis sought to identify dominant frames through an examination of keywords, associations, sources, factual prominence, and narrative storylines.

This study showed—explicitly and unsurprisingly—that Ikhwanweb.com functions as an agent for the Brotherhood's social and political agendas. Under this function, the website is a critical platform through which the MB projects its political tenets and represents a manifestation of an articulate and consistent message of sympathy for the group's national cause and ambitions. On the one hand, the MB tended to frame both the Egyptian uprising and its role in it along positive lines; on the other hand, the group framed its political rivals, particularly the Mubarak regime, as profoundly immoral, corrupt, and abhorred by the public. In projecting these frames through Ikhwanweb.com, it was clear that the website serves not only as a venue through which the MB communicates with the outside, English-speaking world, but also as a tool of social capital that enables the group "to act together more effectively to pursue shared objectives" (Putnam, 1996).

Although the MB likely made decisions based on what it felt was in the best interests of the nation, there is no doubt that the MB, like all political factions, also made decisions based on calculations of self-interest. This was particularly evident in much of the positive framing of the Brotherhood that came in the context of elections, and which portrayed the group as a popular and legitimate representative of the Egyptian people. The MB also used Ikhwanweb.com to fend off allegations that it is a terrorist or extremist group. In this context, our analysis revealed the use of frames such as "Do Not Fear the Brotherhood," "The Brotherhood Is Peaceful," and "The Brotherhood Is Tolerant."

Framing was more complex and nuanced in the context of the Brotherhood's relationship with the military, which seemed to evolve over time. For instance, in its coverage of the March 2011 constitutional referendum, which occurred a month after Mubarak's ouster, Ikhwanweb.com projected relatively positive framing of the Egyptian military, mainly reflected in an "Embracing the Military Roadmap" frame. Soon after the referendum, however, Ikhwanweb.com's coverage of the military became more negative. This was reflected in blaming the military for the Maspero and Port Said massacres and the violence associated with the Mohamed Mahmoud protests. Ikhwanweb.com's critical framing of the military continued throughout the 2012 presidential election season.

Results of our analysis suggested that the MB was deeply concerned about how it was perceived in the West, particularly the United States. This reality was seen most clearly in attempts by Ikhwanweb.com to associate the Brotherhood with qualities that seem to be agreeable to Western governments, such as democracy, tolerance, and inclusivity. Importantly, this underscores that new media can serve an important function as political diplomacy tools for Islamists and other political groups who do not enjoy official participatory recognition or who may, for one reason or another, be unable to carry out traditional diplomatic communication.

The book is organized around six main chapters, in addition to a discussion. Chapter 1 ("Theory and Methodology") provides both the theoretical underpinnings for the analysis and a specific elucidation of the method used for data analysis. Framing theory is explained in a way that sheds light on how the approach informs the study, and qualitative textual analysis is explained in detail. The chapter also includes a brief background on the ten events chosen for analysis.

Chapter 2 ("The Egyptian Muslim Brotherhood: A Brief History") uses academic literature to provide a detailed overview of the Muslim Brotherhood as a political Islamic movement. The chapter delves into the MB's historical background and ideology; views on democracy and *Shari'a* (Canonical) law; relationship with the Egyptian state under former presidents Gamal Abdel Nasser, Anwar Sadat, and Hosni Mubarak; and role in the 2011 Egyptian revolution and its aftermath.

Chapter 3 ("The 2011 Egyptian Uprising") provides contextual background on the uprising that resulted in Mubarak's ouster. The chapter describes the lead-up to the uprising that started on January 25, 2011, and explains the protesters' motivations and objectives. The chapter also contextualizes the key revolutionary events, including the early days of the protests, the Friday of Anger, the Battle of the Camel, key Mubarak speeches delivered during the eighteen days of protest, and the day of Mubarak's resignation. The chapter also addresses the MB's role in key events during the anti-Mubarak protest period.

Chapter 4 ("From the 2010 Parliamentary Elections to the 2011 Constitutional Referendum") presents analysis of how Ikhwanweb.com framed the first three events in our analysis: the 2010 parliamentary elections, which were the last elections to take place under Mubarak, the 2011 Egyptian revolution, and the 2011 constitutional referendum.

Chapter 5 ("The Post-Uprising Era: Between Clashes and Parliamentary Elections") includes framing analysis of four major events treated by Ikhwanweb.com: The Maspero Massacre that took place in October 2011; the Mohamed Mahmoud protests staged on Mohamed Mahmoud Street in downtown Cairo in November 2011; the 2011 parliamentary elections, which were the first elections to take place after the revolution; and the Port Said Massacre, which took place in February 2012.

Chapter 6 ("From the 2012 Presidential Election to the 2012 Constitutional Referendum") presents analyses of Ikhwanweb.com frames of the last three events selected for study: Morsi's electoral victory, Morsi's November 2012 constitutional decree, and the December 2012 referendum on the constitution.

Chapter 7 ("Discussion") summarizes the main conclusions from the framing analysis. More significantly, the discussion explains underlying assumptions and implications of the analysis by examining Ikhwanweb.com's framing mechanisms, showing how frames developed and changed over time, and explaining inferences that can be gleaned from the dynamic framing process. The discussion also utilizes two theoretical approaches—rational choice and social capital—to understand how the MB's sociopolitical and religious networks were brought to bear on the group's support and/or opposition to individual entities, events, and policies. Here, attention was given to explaining how the Brotherhood communicates with the outside, English-speaking world. The discussion closes with some recommendations for future research into MB media.

Chapter 1

Theory and Methodology

FRAMING THEORY

Framing continues to be a dominant theoretical framework in journalism and media studies, among other social science disciplines. Scholars invoking the framing paradigm use it as a way of understanding the deep meanings of communicated texts, and also how audiences read and interpret communicated messages. To a meaningful extent, the framing paradigm has (in news studies) replaced the old "objective and bias" paradigm (Tankard, 2001). Tankard (2001) argued that "framing" is a more useful concept than "bias" because framing refers to an unintentional slant that can occur subtly, while "bias" implies intentionality, something that is usually difficult to pin down, particularly in journalism, a field dominated by notions of detachment and neutrality.

The framing process highlights the role of frames in communication, where frames can refer to either the "persistent selection, emphasis, and exclusion" (Gitlin, 1980, p. 7) contained within any communicated message, or the "central organizing idea or story line that provides meaning" (Gamson & Modigliani, 1987, p. 143) in any communicated text.

Tuchman (1978) and Goffman (1974) both argued that framing is a natural human phenomenon because it allows people to make sense of their experiences of the world by better organizing it. Goffman posited that frames allow people to "locate, perceive, identify, and label" (Goffman, 1974, p. 21). Tuchman, meanwhile, stated that a frame "organizes everyday reality" (1978, p. 193).

Media frames are similar to other frames but refer to a more specific journalism-related phenomenon. Valkenburg et al. (1999) argued that media frames are language shortcuts used specifically by journalists to tell a story efficiently and succinctly. For Valkenburg et al. (1999), framing is inevitable,

1

in part because journalists "have to tell a story within a limited time or space" (p. 550), and framing allows them to make events "accessible to a large audience" (p. 550). According to this basic definition, then, media frames "simplify and give meanings to events" and "maintain audience interest" (Valkenburg et al., 1999, p. 551). Both Chong and Druckman (2007) and Gitlin (1980) made similar arguments, with Chong and Druckman positing that media frames are "the key considerations in a [journalistic] speech act" (p. 106), and Gitlin noting that media frames are "devices that facilitate how journalists organize enormous amounts of information and package them effectively for their audiences" (p. 248).

There is general consensus in the media literature that framing is a process focusing fundamentally on selection, emphasis, exclusion, and, importantly, audience reception (see de Vreese, 2005; Chyi & McCombs, 2004; Entman, 1993; and others). De Vreese (2005) defined framing "as a process" (p. 51) of selection that involves both how frames emerge in communication contexts and the ways in which they are received, interpreted, and acted upon by audiences. Entman's (1993) comprehensive definition of the process, which highlighted both the communicator and receiver, remains the most cited in the literature. In a seminal paper, Entman wrote,

> Framing essentially involves selection and salience. To frame is to select some aspects of a perceived reality and make them more salient in a communicating text, in such a way as to promote a particular problem definition, causal inter- pretation, moral evaluation, and/or treatment recommendation for the item described. (1993, p. 52)

Framing occurs through the specific ways messages are packaged by communicators. According to Entman (1993), information selection and exclusion, keywords, placement, repetition, association, and sourcing can all dictate frames. Gamson and Modigliani (1989) argued that "metaphors, exemplars, catchphrases, depictions, and visual images" (p. 3) could drive and determine frames. For example, one study (Elmasry, 2009) posited that an act of killing could be alternatively framed as an act of aggression, an act of self-defense, or as an accident, depending on what pieces of information are highlighted, which words are chosen as descriptors, and which sources are referenced.

Pan and Kosicki (1993) developed a detailed conceptualization of news texts that includes framing as a central feature. The conceptualization centers on four dimensions—syntactical structures, script structures, thematic structures, and rhetorical structures. These are considered "framing devices" (1993, p. 59) in Pan and Kosicki's conceptualization. Syntactical structures are concerned with "the arrangement of words or phrases into sentences"

(p. 59), script structures are concerned with the "sequence of activities and components of an event" (p. 60), thematic structures refer to issue-focused news stories that focus on events and the "hypothesis-testing" nature of news stories (p. 60), and rhetorical structures refer to specific "stylistic choices" (p. 61), including choice of metaphors and visual images.

The oft-cited experiment by Tversky and Kahneman (1981) might be the one of clearest empirical examples of the power of framing. The authors presented subjects with a problem—a disease outbreak that was expected to kill six hundred people—and asked for their preferred treatment option. Two groups of experimental subjects were presented with a pair of treatment options each. Group 1 was offered treatment option A, which would lead to two hundred people being "saved," and treatment option B, which would leave a one-third chance that six hundred people would be "saved" and a two-thirds probability that no one would be "saved." Group 2 was offered treatment option C, which dictated that four hundred people would "die," and treatment D, which would lead to a one-third probability that nobody would "die" and a two-thirds probability that six hundred people would "die." The two groups of subjects were given effectively the same choices—the only difference was that group 1 was presented with a choice framed positively, in terms of lives "saved," while group 2 was presented with a choice framed negatively, in terms of people that would "die." As predicted, the difference in framing produced dramatic differences in perceptions and favorability. Although treatments A and C produced identical outcomes, 72 percent of subjects in group 1 preferred treatment A, which was framed positively, and only 22 percent of subjects in group 2 preferred treatment C, which was framed negatively.

Media framing can produce strong cognitive, attitudinal, and behavioral effects in part because of the way in which media frames interact with audience frames and societal frames. Entman (1993) argued that many frames are ubiquitous, taken for granted at the level of culture, and internalized at the level of the individual. Specifically, Entman argued that in any communication process, frames have four locations—"the communicator, the text, the receiver, and the culture" (p. 52). Valkenbug et al. (1999) said that media frames interact with audience frames, which are "schema of interpretations" that allow people to categorize and "make sense of incoming information" (p. 551). Chong and Druckman (2007) explained that, since "people draw their opinions from the set of available beliefs stored in memory" (p. 111), framing effects can only occur when communication frames interact and overlap with individual/audience frames. The authors noted that "[i]n order for a framing effect to occur, a given consideration ... needs to be stored in memory to be available for retrieval and use" (p. 110). Importantly, though, Chong and Druckman noted that framing doesn't always produce the same effects across individuals and groups and can sometimes have little or no effect on interpretation. In particular, framing effects can be moderated by values, topic-specific knowledge, and the strength of a frame (Chong & Druckman, 2007).

Differences in news framing of issues and events can be attributed to different editorial lines, or variations in individual or group ideology, among other things. Scheufele (1999) said that several factors can ultimately influence how an issue is framed by media persons, including "social norms and values, organizational pressures and constraints, pressures of interest groups, journalistic routines, and ideological or political orientations of journalists" (p. 109).

De Vreese (2005) suggested that there are often two types of frames at play in news reports—issue-specific frames pertain "only to specific topics or events" (p. 54), while generic frames "transcend thematic limitations" (p. 54), and can be found more generally in news coverage of a variety of different types of events. Iyengar (1991) argued that two other types of frames—"episodic" and "thematic"—dominate news coverage. Episodic framing focuses on specific cases and events, while thematic framing tends to tie topics back into society-wide issues.

Scholars have developed framing typologies, identifying common frames that are more or less ubiquitous in news content and which can be used as predetermined coding categories in content analyses that employ a deductive approach. For example, Valkenburg et al. (1999) argued that there are four dominant frames in news stories—conflict, human interest, responsibility, and economic consequences. Meanwhile, Semetko and Valkenburg (2000) presented a slightly expanded version that featured five dominant frames—conflict, human interest, economic consequences, morality, and responsibility. Most framing studies, however, employ an inductive approach, allowing frames to emerge naturally from raw data. Several inductive framing studies have examined coverage of the Muslim Brotherhood and other Islamists in various media contexts, and others have examined, more generally, framing of Islam or political events involving Muslims.

For example, studies by Guzman (2015), Pasha (2011), Golan (2013), and Allagui and Najjar (2011) studied framing of Islamists, including the Muslim Brotherhood, in a variety of media contexts, including American news media, Egyptian news media, European news media, and Egyptian entertainment media, respectively.

Guzman (2015) used both Orientalism and framing to study Fox News and CNN coverage of the 2011 Egyptian uprising. The study's results suggested that both Fox News and CNN framed the Muslim Brotherhood as both enemies of the United States and an irrational group, relying on Orientalist tropes in the process. The networks, meanwhile, framed other (non-Brotherhood) Egyptian protesters as both rational actors and friends of the United States.

Pasha (2011) studied how the Muslim Brotherhood is covered in Egypt's top state-run newspaper, *Al-Ahram*. The analysis suggests that the newspaper framed the Brotherhood negatively, often suggesting that the Egyptian government is "good" and the Brotherhood is "bad." More specifically, Pasha argues that *Al-Ahram* relied on Orientalist discourses to describe the Brotherhood, accusing the group of crimes it didn't commit and not allowing the group to describe itself or its actions.

An analysis of Egyptian cinema by Allagui and Najjar (2011) suggested that Egyptian films frame Islamists, including the Brotherhood, as backward, extreme, and fundamentally violent, and explained the presence of Islamism through references to poverty and government corruption.

Golan (2013) studied *International Herald Tribune* and European *Wall Street Journal* coverage of the 2011 Egyptian revolution, looking only at op-eds. According to Golan, the papers framed the Egyptian uprising in ways that privileged Western voices and silenced Arab perspectives. Both papers focused heavily on the Muslim Brotherhood, but the *International Herald Tribune* was more nuanced and balanced in its treatment of the group. Importantly, Golan argued that frames were dictated largely by the newspapers' choice of sources, nearly all of whom were American males.

A framing study by Hamdy and Gomaa (2012) didn't focus on the Brotherhood per se, but it did offer useful insights into Egyptian newspaper framing of the 2011 Egyptian revolution. The authors found stark differences in the ways government-owned and independent newspapers framed the uprising against Mubarak, with state-owned papers framing the protest movement as a conspiracy to destabilize the nation and independent papers employing a more favorable tone, often suggesting that the protests were a step in the direction of democracy and justice.

A handful of framing studies have also focused more generally on framing of Islam or political events involving Muslims. Ibrahim (2010) found that, in the aftermath of the September 11, 2011, terrorist attacks on the United States, frames of Islam on American network news both closely reflected official statements of the Bush administration and became considerably more positive than the previous norm. Islam was described as peaceful, stories often showed Muslims in everyday life situations, and more non-Arab Muslims were covered than the norm established in previous studies of American news coverage of Muslims. Ibrahim noted, however, that framing choices seemed to be more or less dictated by the Bush administration.

Melkote (2009) analyzed *New York Times* framing of the lead-up to the 2003 American invasion of Iraq, finding that the paper offered up subtle support for the impending U.S. invasion. Specifically, the paper generally avoided offering up inferences and judgments about the Bush administration and the U.S. armed forces, while framing Saddam Hussein negatively, playing up alleged Iraqi weapons of mass construction, and casting doubt on the United Nations and weapons inspections teams.

Ryan (2004) used framing theory to analyze "war against terrorism" editorials in America's ten largest newspapers immediately following the September 11, 2001, terrorist attacks against New York and Washington. Over the course of approximately one month, editorial writers at all sampled newspapers employed framing techniques that suggested strong support for American military action in Afghanistan. No editorials were published questioning the appropriateness of U.S. military intervention.

Carpenter's (2007) study employed a deductive approach and used framing theory and sourcing to compare elite and non-elite American newspapers' framing of America's war in Iraq. Elite newspapers were significantly more likely to rely on official sources than non-elite newspapers. Also, elite newspapers relied heavily on a "conflict frame" in their reporting, while non-elite newspapers relied heavily on a "human interest frame" in their coverage.

As is noted elsewhere in this book, very little research has been done on Islamist media framing—that is, how Islamist media frame issues and events. The analysis provided in chapters 4, 5, and 6 will be among the few that delves deeply into the issue of Islamist media framing.

TEXTUAL ANALYSIS

We used textual analysis as a method to extract meanings and explore connotations from Ikhwanweb.com posts dealing with the ten events analyzed for this book. Textual analysis is a qualitative method that expects researchers to immerse themselves in the text and engage in a close reading of its nuanced implications. By doing so, researchers can decipher the explicit and hidden meanings, inferences, and associations embedded in a text (Fursich, 2009). Van Dijk (1998) argued that textual analysis has its roots in linguistics, and that it "tends to deal more often with (abstract) structures of written discourse as a fixed object" (p. 23). Fairclough (2003) noted that textual analysis is not just a "linguistic analysis; it also includes ... interdiscursive analysis, that is, seeing texts in terms of the different discourses, genres and styles they draw upon and articulate together" (p. 3). McKee (2006) said that analyzing a text helps researchers "make an educated guess at some of the most likely interpretations that might be made of that text" (p. 1).

Our textual analysis examined Ikhwanweb.com coverage of ten Egyptian political events occurring between December 2010 and December 2012. In one sense, our study represents a type of "historical-diachronic analysis" because it examines "the course of social matters and their wider political, social and economic context" (Carvalho, 2016, p. 172). The ten events studied here were (1) the 2010 Parliamentary Elections, (2) the 2011 Egyptian Revolution, (3) the 2011 Constitutional Referendum, (4) the 2011 Maspero Massacre, (5) the 2011 Mohamed Mahmoud Protests, (6) the 2011/2012 Parliamentary Elections, (7) the 2012 Port Said Massacre, (8) the 2012 Presidential Elections, (9) the 2012 Constitutional Decree, and (10) the 2012 Constitutional Referendum. These ten events were selected because of their centrality to the Egyptian Revolution and its aftermath. Arguably, these ten political moments represent the most important of Egypt's tumultuous democratic transition.

Our strategy was to examine posts that dealt centrally with the events in question, including posts published in the lead-up to planned events, such as the various scheduled elections and referenda, and periods immediately following both planned events and spontaneous ones, such as the Maspero and Port Said massacres. We examined all Ikhwanweb.com posts dealing principally with the ten events under study. This strategy yielded a total of 375 posts, all of which were examined. The subsections that follow will detail the sampling strategies followed for all studied events.

SAMPLING

The 2010 Parliamentary Elections. We examined Ikhwanweb.com during the one-week lead-up to the first round of the 2010 parliamentary elections, which took place on November 28, 2010, and the day that followed the second and final round of voting, which took place on December 5, 2010. We examined a census of all posts dealing centrally with the elections. In all, sixty-five posts were studied.

The 2011 Egyptian Revolution. Regarding the 2011 Egyptian Revolution, our analysis considered posts published during the one-week lead-up to planned January 25, 2011, protests, during the entire eighteen-day uprising, and the day following Mubarak's decision to step down on February 11, 2011. We studied all posts dealing primarily with the protest movement—in all, 116 posts were analyzed. It is important to mention in this context that there was a gap in the Ikhwanweb coverage of the uprising between January 27 and February 2, 2012. This gap could possibly be attributed to the government's decision to cut off the internet services in the whole country during that timeframe.

The 2011 Constitutional Referendum. We studied Ikhwanweb.com posts during the one week prior to and the one week after the 2011 constitutional referendum, which took place on March 19, 2011. A total of sixty-four posts were examined.

The Maspero Massacre. The Maspero Massacre occurred on October 9 and 10, 2011. We studied the one-week period immediately following the massacre, which yielded eight posts.

The Mohamed Mahmoud Protests. Protests were staged on Mohamed Mahmoud Street in Cairo from November 19–21, 2011. We studied all fourteen Ikhwanweb.com posts published between November 20 and November 27.

The 2011 Parliamentary Elections. The 2011 parliamentary elections were held over multiple phases from late November 2011 until January 11, 2012. We examined the one-week lead-up to the first round of elections, and the one-week period following the last round of elections. We studied all posts dealing primarily with the elections. A total of twenty-eight posts were studied.

The Port Said Massacre. The Port Said Massacre occurred on February 1, 2012. We studied all thirteen Ikhwanweb.com posts about the massacre published in the week following the massacre.

The 2012 Presidential Elections. The 2012 presidential elections were staged over multiple rounds. Our analysis focused on all published posts between June 17, 2011, the day after the second round of voting, and June 30, 2011, the day of Morsi's swearing-in ceremony. In all, thirty-two posts were published, all of which were studied here.

Morsi's 2012 Constitutional Decree. We studied all twenty Ikhwanweb.com posts published about Morsi's decree in the one-week period immediately following its issuance on November 22, 2012.

The 2012 Constitutional Referendum. Egypt's 2012 constitutional referendum was held over two rounds on December 15, 2012, and December 22, 2012. We studied Ikhwanweb.com posts published from December 10, 2012, five days before the first round of voting, until December 25, 2012, three days after the conclusion of the second round of voting. In all, then, sixteen days of Ikhwanweb.com coverage were studied, and a total of fifteen posts were examined.

TEXTUAL ANALYSIS PROTOCOLS

Our strategy for examining Ikhwanweb.com texts was to engage in individual close readings of singular posts and convene to discuss meanings and implications. A text can lend itself to various readings, depending on how it is interpreted by the researcher(s). Given our familiarity with the literature and context, our readings and interpretations often converged. However, sometimes our interpretations differed. In these cases, we engaged in intensive discussions about the contested meanings of the text, always with reference to Brotherhood ideology, policy, and Egyptian political context. What emerged from these discussions was our shared, agreed-upon reading.

Importantly, textual analysis is predicated on strong understanding of sociopolitical and cultural contexts (McKee, 2006). Fairclough (1992) noted that textual analysis involves a type of "intertextual analysis [that] crucially mediates the connection between language and ... context" (p. 195). Here, our knowledge of both Brotherhood history and the Egyptian cultural landscape played important roles. Both of us are of Egyptian descent, are fluent in Arabic, and attended the mass Tahrir Square protests that led to Mubarak's ouster. Also, we were present in Egypt when most of the events under study took place. Our collective knowledge and familiarity with Egyptian culture and sociopolitics informed our critical readings of Ikhwanweb.com texts. We used our repertoires of contextual knowledge to decipher associations and connotations and understand layered meanings and ideological underpinnings of Ikhwanweb.com texts.

In the process of interpretation, researchers should not just rely on the elements that exist in the text, but also on the ones that are missing. This is because "silence can be as performative as discourse" (Carvalho, 2016, p. 171). Our analysis of Ikhwanweb.com posts grappled with the reality that the website frequently left important matters unsaid. For example, website editors chose not to critically interrogate Brotherhood policies and positions. Also, important debates held among Brotherhood leaders and members— about whether to participate in specific protests and elections—were kept out of Ikhwanweb.com content. Ikhwanweb.com's silence on these and other issues suggests that the webmasters wanted to project for English-speaking audiences an image of Brotherhood competence and unity.

Our textual analysis sought to identify dominant frames through an examination of keywords, associations, sources, factual prominence, and narrative storylines. Following Van Dijk (1988) and Entman (1993), we paid close attention to the specific terms that Ikhwanweb.com editors and writers used to describe people and events, and to how people and events were compared, contrasted, and otherwise implicitly associated. Also, we were interested in two kinds of sources that can drive frames—writers and individuals quoted or paraphrased in specific articles (or posts). As we'll explain later, Ikhwanweb. com editors' strategy was to draw from authoritative voices, but only when their views seemed to support the official Brotherhood line. Additionally, our analysis was concerned with how posts hinted at importance through placement and repetition. Here, we were especially interested in headlines and lead paragraphs. Lastly, we focused on how narratives about events and groups coalesced and/or changed over time.

EVENTS' BACKGROUND

Background on the 2010 Parliamentary Elections

Two rounds of voting were held for the 2010 parliamentary elections, on November 28 and December 5. Candidates competed for 508 seats in the Egyptian parliament, known as the People's Assembly ("Egypt Elections Set for November 28," 2010). Prior to the elections, several opposition parties called for a boycott of the polls, arguing that they would be rigged in favor of the ruling National Democratic Party (NDP). The Muslim Brotherhood (MB), however, decided to participate in the elections in hope that it would match or exceed its unprecedented and historic win of 88 seats—almost 20 percent of 444 seats—in the 2005 parliamentary elections ("Brotherhood to Run in Egypt Polls," 2010). In addition to the NDP and the MB, other parties that had decided to run in the 2010 parliamentary elections included the Progressive National Unionist Party and the Socialist Nasserist Party ("Q&A: Egypt's Parliamentary Election," 2010).

The MB nominated 107 candidates from among its members to run for elections. Since the MB was outlawed and not recognized as an official political party, its candidates were only allowed to participate in the elections as independents. However, their connection to the MB was publicized through extensive use of the group's slogan—"Islam is the solution"—on campaign materials. The days leading up to the first round of the elections witnessed the arrest and imprisonment of several MB leaders by the Mubarak government's security apparatus ("The Muslim Brotherhood in Flux," 2010).

Independent election monitors, as well as international human rights and professional groups, including Amnesty International and Reporters Without Borders, claimed that the 2010 parliamentary elections were held in an environment marred by fear, fraud, brutality, and bullying by the NDP and its supporters. Reports by several domestic and foreign journalists showed that violence erupted at a number of polling stations across the country. The NDP dismissed these allegations and argued that the elections were held in a transparent and open environment free from any government intimidation ("Egyptians Vote in Parliamentary Elections," 2010).

Unsurprisingly given the repressive environment, the NDP swept the elections by winning more than 80 percent of the 420 parliamentary seats. Also, independent candidates affiliated with the NDP won an additional 10 percent of the seats. The Al-Wafd Party won six seats, and the MB ended up with no seats. All opposition parties combined won fewer than 5 percent of contested seats. Members of the opposition accused the government of hijacking the elections, practicing unprecedented fraud, and "turning [the country] into a one-party state with a servile parliament" whose main job was to pave the way for a Mubarak victory in the presidential elections scheduled for 2011. Opposition leaders called on Mubarak to dissolve the newly elected parliament and call for new elections held under the watch of independent monitoring bodies ("Egypt Election," 2010).

Background on the 2011 Egyptian Uprising

In early January 2011, a call was made on social media, particularly Facebook and Twitter, by independent political activists and opposition groups to protest against police brutality, government corruption, and social injustices. The activists were inspired by the Tunisian revolution that led to the ousting of Tunisian president Zine El Abidine bin Ali on January 14, 2011. They called on the people to take to the streets on January 25, which is an Egyptian national holiday celebrating the police force.

January 25, 2011, witnessed massive protests, including tens of thousands of demonstrators at Tahrir Square in the center of Cairo. Other Egyptian cities witnessed similar protests, and police used water cannons, rubber bullets, and tear gas to disperse crowds. The Muslim Brotherhood, which was the largest opposition movement, did not officially support the protests, but did allow its members to participate in them ("Egypt Braces for Nationwide Protests," 2011).

After continued use of force on the part of police, the protesters' demands were escalated to include Mubarak's resignation. In response to the protests and calls for his resignation, Mubarak delivered a speech on January 28, in which he announced that he had dissolved his cabinet and appointed his chief of intelligence, Omar Suleiman, as vice president. These moves were not good enough for the protesters, however, who stood firm on their demands. In the meantime, the Mubarak regime took the unprecedented step of shutting down the internet and mobile phone systems for several days. In addition, the military was deployed to the streets and a countrywide curfew was implemented on January 28.

On February 1, Mubarak announced that he would not run for reelection, but he refused to succumb to the protesters' main demand of stepping down from office. Clashes between the police and protesters became more violent, particularly after some Mubarak supporters marched through the protesters at Tahrir Square on camels and horses and attacked them using clubs, knives, and swords. This event, which took place on February 2, came to be known as the "Battle of the Camel" ("Timeline," 2011).

The street demonstrations, which led to hundreds of deaths and injuries among the protesters, coincided with a sudden withdrawal of police forces from several key locations, including police stations, museums, shops, and prisons. This led to a massive wave of looting and ransacking of shopping malls and the escape of thousands of prisoners. Some political observers argued that the sudden withdrawal of police was orchestrated by the Mubarak regime to hold the protesters accountable for the deteriorating conditions of the country. As the protests continued to intensify, the MB started to increase their presence with the protesters, and they played a critical role in the negotiations that were called for by the new vice president (Shadid & Kirkpatrick, 2011).

On February 10, Mubarak announced during a televised speech that he would stay in power until September and then work on a "peaceful transition" of power. This announcement was met with anger by the protesters at Tahrir Square, who waved their shoes in the air to express their dissatisfaction and dismay. The situation had become more tense as thousands of protesters started marching toward the state television building and the presidential palace ("Timeline," 2011). On February 11, 2011, eighteen days after the start of the street protests, Vice President Suleiman stated during a brief televised announcement that Mubarak had decided to step down and yield power to the military. This announcement caused a great deal of elation and joy among the protesters at Tahrir Square and throughout the rest of the country. Chants of "God is Great" and "Egypt is free" were heard amid a display of fireworks at Egypt's main squares ("Egypt's Mubarak Resigns," 2011).

Background on the 2011 Constitutional Referendum

The Supreme Council of the Armed Forces (SCAF), which took over power in Egypt immediately following Mubarak's resignation on February 11, 2011, suspended the 1971 Constitution and formed a committee of eleven judicial experts to amend it. Nine constitutional amendments were drafted, the most prominent of which were limiting the number of years in office for the future president to two four-year terms; easing the qualification requirements for individuals who want to run for president; making it harder for the president to declare a state of emergency; guaranteeing judicial monitoring of elections; and making it mandatory for the president to appoint a vice president during his first month in office ("Q&A: Egypt's Constitutional Referendum," 2011).

SCAF then decided to hold a referendum on these amendments on March 19, 2011, to pave the way for the military's departure from the political scene and the subsequent holding of early parliamentary elections to be followed by presidential elections. Voters were asked to either agree to the package of all nine amendments or refuse them altogether. The main political parties had different positions regarding the logic of these amendments and the timing of the referendum. On the one hand, many independent activists and liberal politicians favored a new constitution rather than an amendment to the existing one. They also argued that expedited legislative elections would not allow them enough time to organize and play an effective political role. Moreover, they claimed that early parliamentary elections would primarily benefit the Muslim Brotherhood (MB), which was more prepared to run an effective campaign. On the other hand, the MB and other groups supported the referendum, arguing that the proposed amendments to the constitution would end military rule and expedite the formation of a civilian state (MacFarquhar, 2011).

Members of the MB organized an intensive campaign through which they distributed fliers and posted banners to encourage voters to participate in the referendum and vote "yes." Forty-one percent of the 45 million eligible voters cast their votes, according to official sources. Voters who participated in the referendum overwhelmingly agreed to the constitutional amendments, which passed with 77.2 percent approval (and 14 million "yes" votes). Around 4 million voters (22.8 percent) opposed the amendments (Michael, 2011). The voter turnout in the 2011 referendum was much higher than any votes in the Mubarak era, and youth turnout was especially high ("Egypt Referendum," 2011).

Background on the 2011 Maspero Massacre

On October 9, 2011, a large group of protesters, including members of Egypt's Coptic Christian minority, organized a street march in reaction to the September 30, 2011, burning of a Coptic church in Edfu, a city in the Aswan governorate in southern Egypt. The march started out peacefully in the Cairo neighborhood of Shubra, and then headed toward the Egyptian state radio and television building, known as Maspero, where protesters planned a sit-in. Participants in the march and sit-in demanded that the state protect existing churches and grant licenses to build new ones (Fahmy, 2011).

The Copts, who constitute a little over 10 percent of the Egyptian population, also accused the Supreme Council of the Armed Forces (SCAF) of not punishing those who had committed a series of offenses against the Coptic Christian minority. The protesters demanded the stepping down of the then SCAF chairman, Field Marshal Mohamed Tantawi. Clashes between protesters and members of the security forces ensued, and twenty-four protesters were killed in what a Human Rights Watch report said was "excessive force" used by military personnel against unarmed civilian protesters ("Egypt: Don't Cover up Military Killing of Copt Protesters," 2011). This massacre represented "the single bloodiest day since the [January 25 Revolution]" (Khalifa, 2014).

SCAF's official statement on the Maspero events cleared the soldiers of any wrongdoing. However, a Human Rights Watch report noted that "the military's … response [to the protesters] was disproportionate." The report called for an "independent and impartial investigation into the killing of unarmed protesters by military forces" ("Egypt: Don't Cover up Military Killing of Copt Protesters," 2011). Along the same lines, Amnesty International argued that "armed and security forces used excessive, including lethal, force against those not posing a threat to them or others" ("Egypt Copts Mark Massacre Anniversary," 2012).

A state-controlled television channel, in its coverage of the Maspero Massacres, argued that the violence was instigated by the protesters, not the soldiers. In fact, a news announcer on that channel argued that "Copts had put Egyptian soldiers in peril," and contended that there was a need for "all honorable citizens" to protect the military (Khalifa, 2014). In late 2012, a year after the massacre, three soldiers were accused of "involuntary manslaughter," and they received jail sentences ranging between two and three years in length (Ibrahim, 2012a). The Egyptian Initiative for Personal Rights described these sentences as "flimsy" ("Egypt Copts Mark Massacre Anniversary," 2012).

Background on the 2011 Protests of Mohamed Mahmoud

Mohamed Mahmoud Street, which runs between Tahrir Square and the old headquarters of the Ministry of Interior, had witnessed several clashes and confrontations—some of them bloody—between demonstrators and security forces during and after the 2011 uprising. One of the most violent clashes took place on November 19, 2011, following a police dispersal of a sit-in organized by the families of those killed and wounded during the 2011 uprising. Clashes during that sit-in lasted for six days and led to the killing of more than fifty people. Eyewitnesses said they saw tear gas fired by riot police and snipers aiming at the protesters' eyes (Khalil, 2012). In return, protesters threw rocks, canisters of Molotov cocktails, and homemade bombs at the security forces (Ryzova, 2011).

Official reports from the Egyptian Ministry of Health noted that the violent clashes had resulted in tens of deaths and 1,700 injuries. Nearly all of the victims were protesters. The injured protesters were transported via motorbikes to a nearby field hospital staffed with volunteer doctors and nurses (Shenker, 2011). A Human Rights Watch report urged the Public Prosecutor to "conduct a transparent investigation into the use of lethal force and military involvement in the abuses, and military command and control over the riot police" ("Egypt: Protesters' Blood," 2011). According to the report, "Law enforcement officers have the right to use proportionate force where strictly necessary, but the use of firearms is only permitted against an imminent threat of death or serious injury, and where less extreme means are insufficient" ("Egypt: Protesters' Blood," 2011).

According to a (2013) Human Rights Watch Report, only one police officer was prosecuted and sentenced (to just three years in prison) for his role in killing several protesters on Mohamed Mahmoud Street. The report said that "the public prosecutor has not prosecuted any other police officer for the death of 51 [Mohamed Mahmoud] protesters" ("Egypt: No Acknowledgment or Justice," 2013).

The clashes took place at a time when the country was preparing for the first parliamentary elections after the 2011 uprising. Many protesters expressed their dismay at the the military's performance during the post-uprising transition. Some Mohamed Mahmoud protesters chanted specific-ally against the Supreme Council of the Armed Forces (SCAF), which was running the country during the transition (Eissa, 2015). Several political factions participated in the Mohamed Mahmoud sit-in; however, the Muslim Brotherhood and its recently founded Freedom and Justice Party (FJP) decided not to participate. Instead, the MB was involved in preparations for the parliamentary elections that were scheduled to start on November 28, 2011. Some political observers argued that the MB "feared that mounting violence and chaos ... [in the Mohamed Mahmoud sit-in] could lead to the postponement—or downright cancelation—of the scheduled parliamen-tary polls, in which the group hoped to achieve substantial electoral gains" (Ibrahim, 2012b).

In this context, the MB leadership—as reflected in the FJP's news-paper on November 21, 2011—was skeptical of the protesters at Mohamed Mahmoud, and described the skirmishes as "the work of thugs ... [whose] goal [is to] delay the elections" (Ketchley, 2017, p. 98). However, some Brotherhood members, including leader Mohamed Beltagy, were supportive of the Mohamed Mahmoud protests. Beltagy tried to join the protests, but was pushed out by protesters, "who accused the Brothers of selling out their fellow revolutionaries for electoral gain" (Ketchley, 2017, p. 98).

Background on the 2011 Parliamentary Elections

Elections to choose members of the Egyptian parliament (People's Assembly) were held in three phases over a six-week period between November 28, 2011, and January 11, 2012. This was the first election held after the January 25, 2011, uprising, and was "arguably the first free and fair vote since Egypt's experiment with parliamentary democracy in the 1920s" ("Interactive: Full Egypt Election Results," 2012).

The new parliament would include 498 elected members, in addition to ten members who were to be appointed by the Supreme Council of the Armed Forces (SCAF). Two-thirds of the elected parliamentary seats were designated for party list candidates, while the remaining one-third was to be subject to direct voting for independent candidates who did not have party affiliation ("Egypt's Islamist Parties Win Elections to Parliament," 2012). Approximately forty political parties and six thousand candidates were to compete for parliamentary seats. The elections were held in a tense environment in which polarization and lack of security were common ("Q&A: Egypt's Parliamentary Elections," 2011).

In these elections, the Muslim Brotherhood's Freedom and Justice Party (FJP) won 235 seats (47.2 percent), followed by the ultraconservative, Salafi-affiliated Nour (Light) Party, which won 121 seats (24.3 percent). The New Wafd Party came in a distant third with only 38 seats (7.6 percent). The FJP nominated one of its senior members, Saad El-Katatni, to be the assembly's speaker ("Egypt's Islamist Parties Win Elections to Parliament," 2012).

With more than 70 percent of the parliamentary seats under their belt, the two Islamist blocs (the Muslim Brotherhood and the Salafis) were set to form a strong conservative coalition inside parliament. However, the two groups had major differences in their political approaches and social agendas. While the MB prioritized socioeconomic issues, the Salafis wanted to work on new legislation for Islamic moral matters (Kirkpatrick, 2012a). Despite these differences between Islamists, Egypt's liberal and secularist parties were concerned about the increasing role of Islamists in the country's legislative system ("Q&A: Egypt's Parliamentary Elections," 2011).

Although SCAF had announced that it would "keep [the then newly elected] Parliament in a subordinate role with little real power until the ratification of a constitution and the election of a president," the parliament was expected to play a critical role in selecting the one hundred members of a constituent assembly whose task was to draft a new constitution (Kirkpatrick, 2012a). This constitution, in turn, would have a great impact on the country's immediate future ("Q&A: Egypt's Parliamentary Elections," 2011).

Background on the Port Said Massacre

On February 1, 2012, immediately following a soccer match between Al-Ahly and Al-Masry, a massacre was carried out against soccer fans of the Al-Ahly club. Al-Ahly is a popular Cairo-based club, and Al-Masry is the home team of the Mediterranean coastal city of Port Said. In all, more than 70 fans were killed and 248 injured, marking this "the deadliest single incident since Egypt's [2011] revolution ... and one of the worst sports-related tragedies in decades" (Bradley, 2012).

The massacre took place after the referee's final whistle at Port Said stadium. Importantly, the killings were carried out under the watch of police officers, who, according to eyewitnesses, did little to try to stop the bloodshed. Thousands of Al-Masry fans left their seats inside the stadium's terraces and ran angrily toward the field, despite their team's 3–1 victory over Al-Ahly. They started beating Al-Ahly players and fans, using rocks, canes, and knives. Sports officials indefinitely suspended the country's soccer premier league competition, and the then prime minister, Kamal El-Ganzouri, suspended Port Said's governor, security chief, and head of police. Victims' families held the military, which was running the country, accountable for the lack of security, and they gathered outside the stadium, chanting "down to military rule." Members of the newly elected parliament condemned the bloody incident and called for an emergency session to deliberate over its causes and repercussions (Fahmy, 2012). A fact-finding committee set up by the newly elected parliament and led by a member of the Brotherhood's Freedom and Justice Party "put the blame for the calamity on the shoulders of the security apparatus, [Al]-Masry Football Club and the Port Said Stadium governing body" ("Fact Finding Committee," 2012).

The Ministry of Interior claimed that its officers had taken every step within their means to secure the fans but were taken over by the crowd's "intentional hostility." The ministry blamed the sudden fans' rushing of the field for the high number of deaths. Several of the fans who were killed at Port Said stadium belonged to an organized soccer fan group known as the Al-Ahly "Ultras." Members of this group had been involved in violent clashes with the military and police forces since the end of the 2011 uprising and had called for an end to military rule. Some members of parliament argued that the security forces might have deliberately allowed the violence to escalate at the stadium to take revenge on the Ultras (Bradley, 2012). A senior Muslim Brotherhood member, Mohamed Beltagy, accused the military of orchestrating "a deliberate ploy ... to build support for an extension of [its] power" (Kirkpatrick, 2012b).

In an attempt to absorb public anger over the massive loss of life, the Supreme Council of the Armed Forces (SCAF) issued travel bans against several senior police officers in the Ministry of Interior and promised to initiate a wide-scale investigation. In addition, SCAF issued a statement encouraging Egyptians to "confront the attempts at escalation by foreign and domestic parties" (Kirkpatrick, 2012b).

Several arrests were made in relation to the massacre, and in June 2015 an Egyptian court sentenced ten defendants to death on murder-related charges. Later, in February 2017, an appeals court upheld the death sentences. The defendants were condemned for "premeditated murder and attempted murder of Al-Ahly fans, thuggery, vandalism and theft." Forty other defendants received jail sentences ranging between five and fifteen years ("Two Dozen Protesters Against Death Sentences," 2017).

Background on the 2012 Presidential Elections

Two rounds of elections were held on May 23–24, 2012, and June 16–17, 2012, to choose a president from a ballot that initially included thirteen qualified candidates. This was the first presidential election held after the ousting of Mubarak on February 11, 2011. The election was held in the immediate aftermath of a court ruling, in April 2012, that suspended the constituent assembly that was tasked with drafting a new constitution. The court ruled that assembly members did not represent the population at large but was viewed by critics as improper and politicized. This ruling had implications on the president who was to be elected, as he would not have defined constitutional powers as the head of the executive branch (Wedeman & Greene, 2012).

During the presidential election campaign season, a high court also dissolved the parliament, arguing that the parliamentary elections that were held in November 2011 were unconstitutional. This ruling also had an impact on the incoming president, since it meant he would not be subject to parliamentary oversight ("Celebration in Egypt as Morsi declared winner," 2012). Analysts widely interpreted these legal maneuverings as attempts by Egypt's "deep state" to engage in a counterrevolution (Wickham, 2013).

None of the candidates won more than half of the votes in the first round to win the presidency outright, but two candidates won enough votes to proceed to the second round for a run-off: Mohamed Morsi, a senior member of the Muslim Brotherhood and FJP chairman, and Ahmed Shafiq, the last prime minister under Mubarak. Morsi won 24.3 percent of the votes in the first round and Shafiq won 23.3 percent (Fayed & Zayed, 2012). Two days before the polls closed in the run-off, the Supreme Council of the Armed Forces (SCAF) issued an interim decree that granted it "legislative powers and reinforced [its] role in the drafting of a permanent constitution" (Abdelhadi, 2012). The decree also took away the majority of the incoming president's powers and reinstated martial law in the country (Kirkpatrick, 2012c).

On June 23, 2012, the electoral commission announced that Morsi had won the election run-off, in which he secured 51.7 percent of the vote to become Egypt's fifth president. As president-elect, Morsi delivered a televised victory speech in which he thanked the voters and promised the Egyptian people that he would "restore their rights" ("Celebration in Egypt as Morsi declared winner," 2012). Morsi, who resigned from the MB and the FJP as per his campaign promise, also vowed that he would be "a president for all Egyptians." Morsi had become the first Islamist to win the Egyptian presidency, the first Egyptian president to come from outside the military establishment, and the first democratically elected president in Egypt's history (Kirkpatrick, 2012c). Soon after taking office, Morsi reversed earlier SCAF constitutional decrees, to the delight of Egypt's revolutionary forces (Hussein, 2012).

Background on Morsi's 2012 Constitutional Decree

On November 22, 2012, Morsi issued a constitutional decree that granted him broad powers and shielded him from judiciary oversight or challenges. The decree appointed a new public prosecutor to replace the existing one, extended the functioning of the Islamist-dominated constituent assembly that was working on drafting a new constitution, and prevented the judiciary from disbanding the upper house of parliament, known as the *Shura* (Consultative) Council. The decree also called for the retrial of all political figures accused of killing protesters during the January 25 uprising, including Mubarak (Abou Bakr, 2012). Mubarak was, at the time, serving a life in prison sentence after a court indicted him for killing protesters, but several of his officials had been acquitted in trials held after the uprising. Morsi's decree also immunized any laws that Morsi had issued since taking over as president by making them final and not subject to appeal. So, in a way, this decree granted Morsi judicial and legislative powers, in addition to the executive powers that he already held as president (Fahmy & Hanna, 2012).

Morsi defended his decree, which he said was necessary to safeguard the goals and achievements of the 2011 revolution and to expedite the country's move toward democracy ("Egypt's Morsi Assumes Wide Powers," 2012). Morsi also noted that the decree was temporary and aimed at securing the process of ratifying a new constitution by preventing the judiciary from dissolving the constituent assembly. His spokesman, Yasser Ali, referred to the decree as "an attempt to end the transitional period as soon as possible." However, Morsi's political opponents, particularly the liberal and secularist factions, accused him of hijacking the country's transition to democracy, and they called for massive protests against the decree, which they described as a "setback for the revolution" (Kirkpatrick & El Sheikh, 2012). Several judges also expressed their dismay at the decree, saying that it was "an assault on the legislative and judicial system" (Fahmy & Hanna, 2012). The national lawyers' association and the Judges Club called on the courts to go on strike to express their total opposition to Morsi's decree (Kirkpatrick, 2012d). Additionally, several international organizations expressed concern about the controversial decree. For example, a spokesman for the UN human rights commissioner said, "We are very concerned about the possible huge ramifications of this declaration on human rights and the rule of law in Egypt" ("Protests Erupt across Egypt after Presidential Decree," 2012). Some political scientists defended Morsi, however, arguing that the decree was necessary to combat attempts by Egypt's deep state—which included repressive judges appointed by Mubarak—to stifle moves toward a truly democratic state (see Ashour, 2012; Fadel, 2014; Feldman, 2012).

Following Morsi's decree, thousands of demonstrators headed back to Tahrir Square, and violent clashes erupted between the secularist and Islamist crowds. Some protesters uttered the same chant heard during the 2011 uprising—"The people want to bring down the regime." Security forces fired tear gas at protesters. Opponents to the decree also set ablaze the offices of the Freedom and Justice Party in several cities, including Cairo, Suez, and Port Said. Morsi criticized the protesters who were engaged in violent acts and accused them of conspiring with the Mubarak regime to derail the accomplishments of the 2011 revolution. Morsi supporters also organized a massive rally outside the gates of the presidential palace ("Protests Erupt across Egypt after Presidential Decree," 2012).

On December 8, 2012, Morsi decided to make some concessions by rescinding several articles of his decree, but he insisted on holding a referendum on the newly drafted constitution on time ("Q&A, Egypt Constitutional Crisis," 2012).

Background on the 2012 Constitutional Referendum

A referendum on a constitution that was drafted by the constituent assembly took place in two voting rounds on December 15 and 22, 2012. The referendum was held amid tense circumstances resulting from violent confrontations between Islamists and secularists following the controversial constitutional decree issued by Morsi in November 2012 (Lyon & Elyan, 2012).

The draft of the constitution was written over a period of about six months by a hundred-member constituent assembly formed by the parliament (which had been freely elected in January 2012 and later disbanded by SCAF). The draft constitution was shrouded in controversy, in part over its content and in part because of complaints by secular liberal political factions about the composition of the constituent assembly (Fadel, 2014).

Because Islamists dominated the parliament, they ended up comprising a disproportionate number of seats in the constituent assembly, something that displeased liberal and secular politicians. Ultimately, and as work on the draft was near completion, several assembly members representing secular, liberal, and Coptic Christian sociopolitical causes decided to withdraw from the assembly, citing concerns about its Islamist character and specific articles.

With respect to the assembly's composition, there were two prevailing views. First, from the perspective of some secular and liberal politicians, the assembly had an unfair Islamist bent, owing to the fact that a majority of the assembly's members could be faithfully characterized as Islamists (Fadel, 2014; Kirkpatrick & Fahim, 2012). According to this view, the fact that Islamists won a majority of seats in the 2012 parliamentary elections should not have had much, if any, bearing on the composition of the constituent assembly. Second, from the perspective of individuals who did not withdraw, the configuration of the assembly was fair and included sufficient and proportionate representation of secularists, liberals, state representatives, and Coptic church figures. Proponents of this view pointed to the fact that all the membership numbers were agreed upon prior to the assembly beginning work, with a formal agreement signed by all twenty-two represented Egyptian political factions in June 2012.

In terms of content, there is a general, if imperfect, consensus among experts that the 2012 constitution represented a meaningful democratic move forward for Egypt—particularly when the document is compared with the 1971 (Mubarak era) constitution—but also that the 2012 document contained significant flaws. Experts noted, for example, that the document limited a president to two four-year terms, allowed for a relatively powerful prime minister (who could not be dismissed by the president), and imposed stringent rules about the declaration of states of emergency, among other democratic provisions (see Fadel, 2014). On the other hand, experts criticized the document on the basis that it included "broad statements about Egyptian identity … [and] loopholes regarding the protection of rights" (Kirkpatrick & Fahim, 2012), with other critics arguing that it was biased in favor of Islamists and did not account for the rights of minorities, particularly Coptic Christians and women. At the time, Human Rights Watch wrote, "[T]he draft provid[ed] for basic protections against arbitrary detention and torture, but fail[ed] to end military trials of civilians or to protect freedom of expression and religion" ("Q&A, Egypt Constitutional Crisis," 2012).

A referendum was held in December 2012, with 10 million (or 63.8 percent) voters saying "yes" to the new constitution, and 6 million (or 36.2 percent) voting "no" ("Egypt Voters Back New Constitution," 2012). Although the turnout was relatively low (32.9 percent of Egypt's 52 million eligible voters), it still was a "turning point" for Egypt's democratic transition (Kirkpatrick & Fahim, 2012). However, opponents of the newly drafted constitution refused to acknowledge the results of the referendum and called for a wide-scale investigation into voter fraud and other violations.

A day after the announcement of the referendum results, Morsi signed the new constitution into law. He also delivered a speech to the nation in which he urged all political factions to act in unison for the sake of moving the democratic process forward. Morsi said, "We don't want to return to an era of one opinion and fake, manufactured majorities. The maturity and consciousness of voters heralds that Egypt has set on a path of democracy with no return."

Morsi also swore in new members of the upper house of parliament known as the *Shura* (Consultative Council). The *Shura* Council, which was immunized against dissolution by Morsi's constitutional decree, included 270 members. This council was expected to serve as the legislative body until the election of the lower house of parliament ("Mohamed Morsi Signs Egypt's New Constitution into Law," 2012). Additionally, Morsi acknowledged flaws with the newly approved constitution, and formed a committee of legal experts to revise it according to concerns raised by secular and liberal opponents (Shalaby, 2013).

Chapter 2

The Egyptian Muslim Brotherhood

A Brief History

The Muslim Brotherhood is the largest Islamist movement in the world and widely considered to be the father of political Islam. Unsurprisingly—especially given the group's prominence and importance—scholars from political science, sociology, history, and media studies, among other disciplines, have generated large bodies of literature about the Brotherhood. Literature has focused on the group's founding, ideology, internal dynamics, and place in Egyptian society (and other Arab and Muslim societies to which the group has spread). Navigating the literature is difficult, in part, because much of it is plagued, arguably, by problematic underlying assumptions and sweeping generalizations about political Islam in general and the Brotherhood in particular (Wickham, 2013).

Wickham (2013) argued cogently that Islamist movements should be studied on their own terms, with groups as large as the Brotherhood treated as diverse, complex, dynamic entities, rather than static monoliths. In particular, Wickham sought to demonstrate how the Brotherhood changed over time. Importantly, she argued that demonstrable changes haven't simply been the product of strategic thinking, as some analysts and scholars have alleged. Rather, members of the Brotherhood have changed ideologically over time, sometimes evolving as a result of political experiences, and sometimes growing discontent with at least some aspects of Brotherhood belief and practice. Wickham argued that "new forms of political engagement can … produce self-conscious shifts in the commitments of political actors as a result of new experiences and/or exposure to new information and ideas" (2013, p. 12).

Wickham also pointed to the numerous debates and contestations held between members of the Brotherhood—about "movement goals, strategies, and practices" (2013, p. ix)—during significant historical moments. She contended that groups like the Brotherhood "are not monolithic entities whose members think and act in lockstep" (2013, p. 2), and cautioned against "exaggerating the extent of the ideological and behavioral uniformity within" the Brotherhood (2013, p. 6).

Al-Arian (2014), meanwhile, argued that too much of the literature on political Islam focuses on Islamist militancy, often finding (or assuming) violence, even when there is none. Specifically, regarding the literature on the Brotherhood, Al-Arian noted that "the bulk of the scholarship ... [focuses] on the group of only a few thousand radicals, as opposed to the hundreds of thousands of self-declared Muslim Brothers" (2014, p. 10).

Although the Egyptian Muslim Brotherhood ultimately produced offshoots in a multitude of countries in the Muslim-majority world, each chapter is so uniquely distinct—organizationally, philosophically, and politically—as to constitute an entirely separate organization (see Al-Arian, 2014; Fahmy, 2016; Hamid, 2014; Wickham, 2013). In line with the focus of this book, this chapter specifically discusses the Egyptian Muslim Brotherhood. In the pages that follow, a brief history of the Brotherhood will be provided, with attention to important figures, and key aspects of the group's basic philosophy and vision for Egyptian society.

THE BROTHERHOOD'S HISTORICAL TRAJECTORY

In 1928, Hassan Al-Banna, a school teacher and religious preacher, founded the Muslim Brotherhood in Ismailia, Egypt, as a "religious and charitable society" (Wickham, 2013, p. 20). The context of the Brotherhood's founding is relevant—by the late 1920s, the once mighty Muslim world had witnessed several hundred years of steady global decline, including the 1924 collapse of the Ottoman Empire. Al-Banna founded the Brotherhood as a type of Islamic revival movement, emphasizing that Muslims could return to past glory if they returned to the basic principles of their religious tradition (Husaini, 1984). Hamid (2014) wrote that Al-Banna's goal "was nothing less than the revival of Islam and Islamic civilization in an age of secularization" (p. 15). Other scholars have argued that the Brotherhood's founding was, at least in part, a reaction to both modernity and sociopolitical conditions inside Egypt and the Arab world, including the British occupation of Egypt and the Zionist movement's occupation of Palestine (see Harris, 1964; Mitchell, 1993; and Sullivan & Abed-Kotob, 1999).

Al-Banna's initial focus was on "preaching, education, and recruiting new members in a hostile environment" (Hamid, 2014, p. 9). One of the more debatable aspects of Al-Banna's teachings—and one which seemed to appeal to new members of the Brotherhood—was his claim that Islam represented a complete, totalizing way of life. For Al-Banna, Islamic morality, spirituality, law, and politics were deeply intertwined, practically inseparable. Al-Banna called for the implementation of Islamic (*Shari'a*) law, and he openly opposed the adoption of Western laws, which, according to him, "had poisoned Muslim society" (Sullivan & Abed-Kotob, 1999, p. 42).

Mitchell (1993) said that Al-Banna sought to establish "a total reform of the political, economic, and social life of the country" (p. 260). Critics, who included some Muslim scholars, argued that the Brotherhood's early focus on politics and society came at the expense of core aspects of Islam, such as spirituality. Al-Banna's messages, however, also focused heavily on Islamic spirituality, meditation, and *tarbiyyah*, or individual character development (Lia, 1998; Al-Arian, 2014).

The group's initial popularity was aided by the fact that it organized a successful stream of social and welfare programs, often in areas the Egyptian government had been failing. Importantly, the Brotherhood's message also caught on because of an "ideological appeal" that attracted "disenchanted young men who had been alienated" by both the Egyptian government and British occupation forces (Lia, 1998, p. 280). Lia argued that the Muslim Brothers' early successes allowed the group to become "the first non-elite political force to challenge the ruling class in Egypt" (p. 280).

THE BROTHERHOOD AND THE EGYPTIAN ESTABLISHMENT

The Brotherhood has experienced high degrees of political ambivalence vis-à-vis successive authoritarian Egyptian governments. The group's relationships with the King Farouk, Gamal Abdel Nasser, Anwar Sadat, and Hosni Mubarak regimes were often topsy-turvy, featuring both extended periods of severe repression and brief openings and short periods of relatively amicable relations.

Regime repression has been a consistent reality for the Brotherhood, regardless of which regime has been in power. Scholars generally agree that Egyptian "regime repression has played a significant role in shaping the Brotherhood's internal dynamics and organization" (Al-Anani, 2016, p. 10). Hamid (2014) contended that living through authoritarianism has forced the Brotherhood to "put aside … their dream of an Islamic state" (p. 4) and instilled in the group "an almost obsessive commitment to gradualism" (p. 4). Hamid (2014) also argued that authoritarian repression forced the Brotherhood to modernize and democratize its "internal organizational structures" and create "new channels of cooperation with secular parties" (p. 4). Pargeter (2013), meanwhile, contended that one basic problem for the

Brotherhood has been the group's dilemma of "how best to engage the political process without selling out on the movement's core Islamic principles" (p. 54). Pargeter's analysis suggested that the group has been unable to resolve this basic dilemma.

The King Farouk Period. Al-Banna's relationship with the Egyptian state under King Farouk was characterized by inconsistencies. On the one hand, Al-Banna opposed political parties and the Egyptian political establishment in general. On the other hand, however, he demonstrated an inclination to join forces with the political establishment when he thought it may help the Brotherhood's growth (Pargeter, 2013).

In the late 1930s, Al-Banna established the "Special Apparatus," a type of military wing designed to defend Muslims against aggressors, including Zionists and British occupation forces (Pargeter, 2013). However, the Special Apparatus spun out of control, with some vigilante members carrying out acts of violence apparently not sanctioned by Al-Banna (Pargeter, 2013). Specifically, Brotherhood members or former members carried out multiple acts of violence targeting figures representing the Egyptian political establishment. Al-Banna distanced himself and the group from the violence. After the 1948 assassination of Prime Minister Mahmoud Nuqrashi and a bomb attack on a Cairo courthouse by young members of the Brotherhood, Al-Banna famously declared that the perpetrators were "neither [Muslim] Brothers, nor are they Muslims" (Pargeter, 2013, p. 30). Pargeter (2013), however, argued that Al-Banna was not hard enough on violent Brotherhood members, noting that some violent members were not excommunicated from the group.

Importantly, the King Farouk period also featured the formal disbanding of the Brotherhood by the Egyptian government (in 1948), and the 1949 assassination of Al-Banna by the government security apparatus. Two years after Al-Banna's assassination, in 1951, Hassan Al-Hodaibi was named the organization's second General Guide. The year 1951 also witnessed the lifting of the ban that was imposed on the Brotherhood three years earlier (Sullivan & Abed-Kotob, 1999).

The Nasser Period. Shortly after Al-Hodaibi took over as the Brotherhood's new General Guide, Nasser helped carry out the 1952 Free Officer's revolution against the King Farouk monarchy. The revolution led ultimately to the end of the British occupation of Egypt in 1954 (Vatikiotis, 1991). The Brotherhood supported the revolution and hoped that the Free Officers would allow them to participate in the newly formed government (Sullivan & Abed-Kotob, 1999).

The Brotherhood's relationship with Nasser (officially Egypt's president from 1956 to 1970) began on a relatively positive note, with the Brotherhood expressing hope that the new Egyptian regime would move toward Islamic reform. After an assassination attempt on Nasser while delivering a speech in

Alexandria in 1954, however, the dynamic shifted. Although the Brotherhood denounced the assassination attempt and there was no evidence linking them to it (Pargeter, 2013), Nasser initiated a harsh anti-Brotherhood campaign of repression, which included mass arrests and several executions.

The Nasser era was foundational for the Brotherhood, which, during this period, solidified its intellectual positions on a number of important issues. Al-Hodaibi, who served as General Guide from 1951 to 1972, is largely credited with cementing important Brotherhood ideas about the role of Islam in governance, Islamic law, modernity, and political violence (see Al-Arian, 2014; Pargeter, 2013).

Al-Hodaibi authored an important text, *Preachers Not Judges*, as a response to Sayyid Qutb, an important Brotherhood figure and one of the group's few well-known intellectuals. Qutb, who was imprisoned and subsequently executed by Nasser, wrote a controversial text, *Milestones*, that argued that contemporary Muslim governments were in a state of *jahaliya*, or pre-Islamic ignorance. Qutb gained hardline followers, some of whom interpreted his words as a call to arms against Muslim governments. Some of Qutb's followers went on to found extremist groups, including *al-takfir wal-hijrah*.

Al-Hodaibi's book provided a systematic rebuttal of Qutb's hardline ideas. In the years that followed the publication of *Preachers Not Judges*, the Brotherhood successfully "consolidated its intellectual position vis-à-vis the rising militant fringe" (Al-Arian, 2014, p. 15). Al-Arian (2014) considers the Al-Hodaibi period to be a formal "reassertion of the original Muslim Brotherhood" message (p. 13). Modern-day members of the Brotherhood consider Al-Hodaibi's foundational text as evidence that the group is essentially nonviolent (Pargeter, 2013). Al-Hodaibi also took steps to bring the Special Apparatus under official Brotherhood control and expel violent members. Some expelled Brotherhood members went on to join extremist groups like *al-takfir wal-hijrah*.

The Sadat Period. Sadat ruled Egypt from 1970 to 1981. For most of the Sadat period, a reformer, Umar Al-Tilmisani, served as the Brotherhood's General Guide (Pargeter, 2013). Officially, Tilmisani served as General Guide from 1972 to 1986, overseeing a significant period in the Brotherhood's history.

One of Sadat's first moves as president was to free political prisoners, including members of the Brotherhood. Importantly, Sadat also worked to privatize the Egyptian economy and liberalize Egyptian politics. He championed an *infitah* (or opening up) policy, which allowed for some increased freedoms (Beattie, 2000).

The political opening of the 1970s triggered unprecedented activism on Egyptian college campuses (Pargeter, 2013). A significant number of college activists had Islamist predilections. Over time, the Brotherhood successfully merged key student leaders with the Islamic movement (Al-Arian, 2014). The Brotherhood and other young Muslim activists were particularly active during the Sadat years. The Brotherhood changed its political strategy under Sadat to "become one of accommodation of, not struggle against, the political system, of course with an eye toward reforming the system" (Sullivan & Abed-Kotob, 1999, pp. 44–45).

During the 1970s, "the Muslim Brotherhood and religious student groups published books, periodicals, and wall magazines, and produced pamphlets, cassette tapes, and banners, all of which reflected the group's mission and ideological outlook" (Al-Arian, 2014, p. 8). Brotherhood writings during this period served to lay out both the group's Islamic philosophy and vision for Egypt.

For a number of years during the Sadat era, the Brotherhood worked with the regime against extremist groups (Wickham, 2013). Importantly, Sadat allowed the group to have some influence in politics and shape the state. A major factor behind Sadat's toleration, and even support of expanding the Brotherhood's role in politics, was to curtail the presence of socialist activists, particularly on university campuses (Abdo, 2000).

The Brotherhood emphasized nonviolence and gradualism during this period and benefited greatly from Sadat's relatively progressive policy program. Sadat shifted course, however, in 1981, when he began a wide-ranging campaign of repression that targeted important parts of Egypt's political opposition, including the Brotherhood (Wickham, 2013). Sadat's repressive campaign was one of the factors that led to his dramatic assassination in October 1981 (Abdo, 2000).

A handful of jihadist, takfiri groups were established in the 1970s and 1980s. They became rivals of the Brotherhood. These groups "condemned the gradualist approach advocated by the Brothers' senior leadership" (Wickham, 2013, pp. 33–34). Wickham noted that "[w]hile the jihadists denounced the Brotherhood's conciliatory methods, the Brotherhood condemned the jihadists' depiction of ordinary Muslims as infidels and portrayed their resort to violence against the state as a futile exercise that would only end up damaging the movement itself" (Wickham, 2013, p. 34).

The Mubarak Era. Mubarak took over as Egypt's president in 1981, ruling until his ouster following a 2011 mass uprising. During the Mubarak period, the regime "maintained a strategic relationship with the Brotherhood" (Fahmy, 2016, p. 77). The Brotherhood under Mubarak was "considered the single largest and most organized opposition group in Egypt" (Noueihed & Warren, 2013, p. 103).

The Brotherhood was allowed to carry out charitable and social programs in exchange for its tacit acceptance of Mubarak rule. Still, the Egyptian constitution prohibited the formation of religious parties, which made it unfeasible for the Brotherhood to officially field its own candidates in parliamentary elections. That was why the Brotherhood—in an attempt to take part in the electoral process—had to either field candidates as independents or form political coalitions with authorized opposition parties. The consequence of this basic restriction was that the Brotherhood's "ability to campaign openly for their ideas was restricted and their success limited" (Abdo, 2000, p. 80).

The Mubarak period featured several distinct phases. The early period was characterized by appeasement, with Mubarak letting key Brotherhood figures (who had been jailed under Sadat) out of prison. But when the Brotherhood formally entered politics in 1984—forming an alliance with the liberal Wafd Party—the regime reexamined its position regarding the Brotherhood. In the 1984 parliamentary elections, which were the first to take place under Mubarak, the Brotherhood-Wafd alliance won 58 out of 448 seats, including eight Brotherhood seats. In 1987, the Brotherhood formed a successful alliance with the Liberal Party and the Liberal Socialist Party that resulted in securing 36 parliamentary seats in that year's elections (Fahmy, 2016). During this period, the Brotherhood became, for the first time in its history, "the largest opposition group in parliament" (Al-Awadi, 2004, p. 114). This fact prompted the regime to start undermining the Islamist movement by claiming it had links to extremist groups (Fahmy, 2016).

The Brotherhood gained popularity throughout the 1990s, particularly as it stepped in to provide social services that the Mubarak regime was unable, or unwilling, to provide (Fahmy, 2016). In this context, Al-Awadi (2004) argued that the Brotherhood's social contributions had three main features: "First, a legitimacy gained from the social services; second, an organized network enabling such services to be delivered effectively; and third, the politicization of this legitimacy" (p. 21).

In addition to its charitable and social welfare programs, the Brotherhood continued its foray into formal politics. In fact, the Brotherhood was able to have several of its candidates compete in the 1995 parliamentary elections, despite the severe restrictions that were imposed by the regime on the movement's political participation (Sullivan & Abed-Kotob, 1999).

In an attempt to get around the regime's restrictions on the political and electoral fronts, the Brotherhood worked hard to intensify its presence and involvement in professional syndicates. During the 1990s, the movement gained control of the majority of seats in several prominent syndicates, including the doctors, pharmacists, dentists, lawyers, and engineers syndicates (Mitchell, 1993; Sullivan & Abed-Kotob, 1999). The Brotherhood's success in this area prompted the regime to draft a new law allowing the judiciary "to intervene in syndicate elections" (Sullivan & Abed-Kotob, 1999, p. 55).

In addition to its control of the syndicates, the Brotherhood made its presence felt on various university campuses. The group won student union elections at major universities in Cairo, Alexandria, and Zaqaziq. The group's popularity across student bodies was due to its "ability to provide students with services which transcended political and ideological rhetoric and which therefore appealed to broader sectors of students" (Al-Awadi, 2004, pp. 122–23).

The Brotherhood's success at the social and syndicate levels was driven mainly by the group's reform agenda that aimed at effective participation in an open, democratic environment. In this context, Fahmy (2016) argued that, during the thirty-year Mubarak era, the Muslim Brothers made a conscious decision to move away from pressing for Islamic law and toward political reform and formal political competition. Several Brotherhood General Guides—Muhammad Hamid Abu Al-Nasr (1986–1996), Mustafa Mashhur (1996–2002), Mamun Al-Hodaibi (2002–2004), and Mohammed Mahdi Akef (2004–2010)—oversaw the Brotherhood's political reform focus. In 2004, the Brotherhood published a document that laid out the group's commitment to basic democratic principles and outlined their ideas for social reform in Egypt (Pargeter, 2013).

In a stunning political development, and despite the repressive tactics adopted by the regime's security apparatus, the Brotherhood won eighty-eight seats in the 2005 Egyptian parliamentary elections. This represented almost "ten times the number of seats (nine) won by all of the country's legal opposition parties combined. Even more telling, the Brotherhood won roughly two-thirds of the seats they contested" (Wickham, 2013, p. 118).

Beyond simply shocking the Mubarak government and Egyptian society at large, the Brotherhood arguably had a real, positive effect on Egyptian politics. Fahmy (2016) argued that Brotherhood parliamentarians forced members of Mubarak's National Democratic Party (NDP) to show up for work and vote on key legislation. Importantly, Brotherhood parliamentarians had a reform-minded agenda, and worked to reach out to their constituents, something that NDP members were notorious for not doing. As a result of the Brotherhood's efforts, the Mubarak government decided to stop airing parliamentary sessions on live television—Fahmy (2016) argued that this decision was made because the government didn't want the public to see how Brotherhood parliamentarians were performing. The Mubarak government responded to Brotherhood advances with a massive crackdown against the group in 2007. Al-Anani (2016) contended that the Brotherhood sought to leverage this period of repression "to gain public support and [also] to maintain cohesiveness and solidarity among its members" (p. 10).

The Brotherhood put out a critical document in 2007 outlining their political program. The document projected the Brotherhood "as a civil party with an Islamic frame of reference" (Wickham, 2013, p. 124). Pargeter (2013) argued that the group "shot themselves in the foot" (p. 58) by demonstrating their illiberal predilections. The most controversial elements in the document stated that women and non-Muslims, while equal citizens, should not be allowed to become president of Egypt. The controversial components of this document represented an attempt on the part of the Brotherhood's conservative wing to assert its power over the group's reformist, more liberal wing. The group's conservative members "acted unilaterally and inserted these more controversial elements into the agreed document at the last moment, something that sparked fierce internal wrangling within the ... [group]" (Pargeter, 2013, p. 58).

The Brotherhood's electoral success in the 2005 parliamentary elections was not repeated in the 2010 elections, which were the last to be held under Mubarak. In these elections, which are discussed at length in this book (as one of the ten events under study), the Mubarak regime suppressed all factions of the opposition. The ruling National Democratic Party ultimately won over 80 percent of the seats, amid widespread fraud allegations (Tadros, 2012). Most of the remaining 20 percent of seats went to independents affiliated with the ruling party (Tadros, 2012; Hassan, 2015). These elections also witnessed a strong clampdown on the Brotherhood, including the arrest of more than 1,200 of the group's members and the assault of several of its key figures (Wickham, 2013).

The Egyptian Uprising. As we've noted elsewhere, the Muslim Brotherhood did not formally endorse the first of the January 25, 2011, protests against the Mubarak government, but it did allow its members to attend demonstrations as private citizens (Wickham, 2013). On the uprising's fourth day, the group formally joined the protest movement. Wickham said the Brotherhood exercised "pragmatic self-restraint" (p. 11) during the uprising's early stages because, as the largest and most organized of Egypt's opposition groups, it stood the most to lose from a failed protest movement. The Brotherhood did not save any effort in assuring the Egyptian public that the group "did not seek to lead or control the uprising" (Wickham, 2013, p. 167). Wickham noted that the group also highlighted that it "did not seek to establish a religious state akin to the Islamic republic of Iran but [rather] 'a civil state and an Islamic democracy, where people are the source of authority and sovereignty'" (Wickham, 2013, p. 167).

Importantly, during the post-Mubarak transition period, the Brotherhood decided to formally enter Egyptian politics as real contenders for power. Shortly after Mubarak's removal from power, the Brotherhood succeeded in institutionalizing its participation by forming the Freedom and Justice Party. The party had approximately nine thousand founding members (Ketchley, 2017; Wickham, 2013).

Hamid (2014) argued that the Brotherhood "pushed to the side" (p. 4) their normally cautious approach to political involvement for a chance to have a major say in Egypt's political future. Hamid considered this decision to be a mistake, arguing that the group should have chosen a backseat instead of striving for power. Hamid's analysis suggested that the prospect of real political power proved to be too "tempting" for the Brotherhood to resist.

In 2012, longtime Brotherhood leader Mohamed Morsi became Egypt's first-ever democratically elected president. His presidency was characterized, on the one hand, by a counterrevolutionary movement designed to undermine both his presidency and Egypt's democratic turn (Elmasry, 2013; Fadel, 2014), and, on the other hand, a series of significant missteps by Morsi and the Brotherhood (Fahmy, 2016). Although Morsi pursed some progressive policies and tried to move against entrenched state corruption, some of his policies likely contributed to a sense that the Brotherhood was trying to dominate politics or roll back gains made by the revolution, or both (Fahmy, 2016). Adding to this, Morsi's "association with the more conservative wing of the … [Brotherhood] and his rigid public persona arguably limited his crossover appeal" (Wickham, 2013, p. 257). Following anti-Morsi protests in Cairo and several other governorates in late June and early July 2013, Morsi was removed from office by the Egyptian military. His ouster came exactly one year into his first term in office.

The post-2013 period has proven to be the harshest in the Brotherhood's ninety-year history. The new Egyptian government, led by Morsi's former defense minister, Abdelfattah Al-Sisi, moved quickly to ban the Brotherhood's Freedom and Justice Party, declare the group a terrorist organization, and pass draconian legislation designed to ensure the Brotherhood's complete elimination from Egyptian politics and public life. More ominously, the regime carried out, in the summer of 2013, a series of mass killings and mass arrests against Brotherhood members and supporters (Human Rights Watch, 2014).

Chapter 3

The 2011 Egyptian Uprising

GLOOMY ENVIRONMENT UNDER MUBARAK

Although the massive protests that erupted in Egypt on January 25, 2011, took the Mubarak regime by surprise, they were the culmination of a handful of major political, economic, and social problems that were the source of suffering for many Egyptians for at least two decades.

The political environment at the end of the Mubarak era was characterized by high levels of government repression. Mubarak allowed for a multiparty system, but the ruling National Democratic Party (NDP) had almost complete control over several rounds of fraudulent presidential and parliamentary elections. Political parties were marginalized, and the Muslim Brotherhood (MB), which was the most popular and well-coordinated opposition group in the country despite an official ban on it, suffered from widespread torture, imprisonment, and other modes of repression (Noueihed & Warren, 2013). According to MB sources, around thirty-five thousand Brotherhood members were arrested throughout Mubarak's thirty-year reign. This caused the MB to practice caution and limit participation in public activities. The MB's "large size and influence made it more vulnerable to repression [by Mubarak], and hence more reluctant to cross the red line and mobilize its supporters into the street" (Wickham, 2011, pp. 211–12). This basic reality is one reason why the Brotherhood was cautious at the start of anti-Mubarak protests in January 2011.

The surfacing of Mubarak's younger son, Gamal, on the political scene in the mid-1990s, as well as his grooming to succeed his father, contributed to increasing public frustrations with the regime. These frustrations were reflected in a Gallup poll conducted right before the uprising. Around 53 percent of one thousand randomly polled Egyptians expressed dissatisfaction with the lack of freedoms in Egypt. The emergency law, which was in effect throughout Mubarak's time in power, was a major source of public anger. The law allowed the regime to coerce political dissidents and yield tremendous powers over various facets of Egyptian life (Noueihed & Warren, 2013; Hassan, 2015).

Under Mubarak, Egypt also witnessed consistent human rights abuses, including at police stations and prisons, where police officers carried out torture against detainees and prisoners. Most of the officers who committed these violations were not prosecuted or punished. In fact, several "prosecutors had become tools of the executive, and the judiciary was no longer a reliable avenue of redress for the many victims, who numbered in the tens of thousands" (Bassiouni, 2017, p. 19). The presence of state security was strongly felt at university campuses, mosques, churches, and even coffeehouses. The regime also tried to control the functioning of nongovernmental organizations (NGOs) overseen by the Ministry of Social Affairs. Several laws were passed to control NGO bylaws, budgets, boards of directors, and even fundraising activities (Lesch, 2012).

Economically, Egypt suffered from high rates of unemployment and harsh economic conditions in the years leading up to the 2011 uprising. This caused many young Egyptians, who were desperate and jobless, to attempt to emigrate to Europe and North America through both legal and illegal channels. A 2008 report by the Egyptian Organization for Human Rights showed that the first seven years of the new millennium witnessed the illegal immigration of approximately half a million Egyptians to Europe (Osman, 2013). Another report by Egypt's Central Agency for Mobilization and Statistics showed that in 2008 more than 21 percent of Egyptians lived below the poverty line and over 2.5 million people earned less than $1.25 daily. According to the International Monetary Fund's World Economic Outlook database, Egypt's inflation was at 11.7 percent at the onset of the revolution—the dramatic price increases for basic goods led to a wide gap between rich and poor. The wealth gap was exacerbated by the fact that members of the upper class moved to gated communities in the wealthy suburbs of Cairo, leaving behind the poor, who were crammed into randomly built neighborhoods characterized by unsanitary conditions and a lack of basic living necessities (Noueihed & Warren, 2013; Lesch, 2012).

Corruption, nepotism, and favoritism were rampant under the Mubarak government, which allowed ministers in successive governments, senior NDP delegates, as well as Mubarak family members to organize and participate in projects that exclusively served their interests. A 2008 Corruption Perceptions Index by the Berlin-based Transparency International organization ranked Egypt 115th among 180 countries with regard to corruption level. Institutionalized and systematic corruption led to a feeling of socioeconomic inequality and total dejection among the Egyptian lower classes (Osman, 2013). Several ministers gave away government land to members of their families and friends. Officials also struck illegal commercial deals with business people for extremely high commissions (Lesch, 2012).

Prominent Egyptian economist Galal Amin summed up the state of despair and suffering of Egypt's lower-class youth during the Mubarak era, writing, "The Egyptian government, after thirty years of highly reckless and selfish policies, had reduced a considerable proportion of the Egyptian population to a standard of living not fit for human beings. It did this by starving a large number of Egyptians, neglecting to educate them, and failing to provide them with rewarding jobs, to build houses that were fit for human habitation and that would enable them to marry and settle down, provide public transport that they could use with dignity, and so on" (Amin, 2013, p. 15). According to Amin, the Mubarak regime showed a total lack of concern toward people's problems and feelings. This sense of "indifference toward and gross contempt for the people and their wishes" was one of the main factors that led the people to revolt (Amin, 2013, p. 108).

OFFLINE AND ONLINE ACTIVISM UNDER MUBARAK

Despite the repressive tactics of the Mubarak regime, there was room for collective action, including online and street activism, particularly during the decade preceding the 2011 revolution (El-Ghobashy, 2012). "Bottom-up" activist movements and public mobilization emanating from the grassroots of Egyptian civil society took various forms and paved the way for the revolution (Korany & El-Mahdi, 2012, p. 9).

A case in point was the "Egyptian Movement for Change" that came to be known as *Kefaya* (Arabic for *enough*). This movement was formed in 2004 to raise awareness about corruption, human rights violations, and lack of political transparency. The movement also called on Mubarak to step down and was opposed to the succession plan for his son Gamal. *Kefaya* included activists, intellectuals, and civil society leaders representing various political and ideological backgrounds, such as liberalism, socialism, and Islamism. Members of *Kefaya* held various public protests and rallies that attracted members of the general public. Many of these protests were suppressed by the authorities. While the movement was not successful at creating drastic political or social change, it triggered public debate about critical issues and generated some movement in the stagnant sociopolitical environment. According to one of the movement's leaders, George Ishak, "we achieved three things: we broke the culture of fear, we obtained the right to demonstrate without permit, and we obtained the right to criticize the president" (Gunning & Baron, 2014, p. 50).

The *Kefaya* movement encouraged political activists to launch hundreds of blogs that revitalized the political public sphere by creating an alternative virtual platform for the public to express their views and air their grievances about the regime. Many bloggers planted the seeds that led to the eruption of the 2011 uprising. Street activities carried out by *Kefaya* gradually decreased until they totally disappeared by the end of 2006, due primarily to a government crackdown and internal conflicts within the movement. The movement, however, continued to be active online and on satellite channels (Lim, 2012).

Another activist group that played a prominent role in raising awareness about workers' rights was the "April 6 Youth Movement," which emerged out of calls for a national strike made through a Facebook page on April 6, 2008, as a show of support for underpaid workers in the industrial city Mahalla El-Kubra. The online call was initiated by two activists, Israa Abdel Fattah and Ahmed Maher, and attracted hundreds of other activists representing various political leanings. This blew life into the labor union movement in Egypt, as tens of thousands of people joined the strike in a move that was shocking to the authorities, who were unprepared for such a tactic (Gunning & Baron, 2014). By 2009, the April 6 Facebook page had more than seventy thousand members, but the movement's street activities were more limited than *Kefaya*'s (Lim, 2012).

Another Facebook page that played a critical role in mobilizing the public was called "We are all Khaled Said." This page was tied to an incident that took place in the coastal city of Alexandria on June 6, 2010, approximately six months before the 2011 revolution. On that day, two undercover police officers arrested a young activist named Khaled Said at a cyber café; they beat him to death and left his body on the street nearby. The authorities claimed that Said died as a result of swallowing a pack of marijuana, but his family and fellow activists claimed he was targeted for uploading a video showing police officers dividing up the gains of a drug bust. An activist named Wael Ghoneim created a Facebook page that showed two mugshots of Said: one showed his smiling face and the other displayed his deformed face after his beating and death (Gunning & Baron, 2014). Ghoneim, whose identity was revealed during the revolution, wrote the following: "The 'We are all Khaled Said' page expressed my feelings perfectly. Khaled Said was a young man just like me, and what happened to him could have happened to me. All young Egyptians had long been oppressed, enjoying no rights in our own homeland" (Ghoneim, 2012, p. 60). The Khaled Said photos went viral in the virtual world, and his page was effective in mobilizing the public for five silent protests held during the month following Said's death. The photos created a feeling of "shared victimization" among Egyptian youth and succeeded in widening the scale of both online and offline activism against police brutality and state suppression (Lim, 2012).

Another movement that was effective in mobilizing the Egyptian public in the lead-up to the 2011 revolution was the National Association for Change (NAC), which was formed in February 2010 by Nobel Laureate and former head of the International Atomic Energy Agency, Mohammed El-Baradei. El-Baradei, an Egyptian national who returned to Egypt in 2010, announced that he would run for president in 2011. His expected bid for president and his launch of the NAC renewed the youth's hopes for a real political transformation. The NAC included representation from various parties and movements, such as the Muslim Brotherhood, April 6 Movement, the Democratic Front Party, and Al-Ghad Party. NAC members developed a manifesto for political change that obtained more than one million signatures (Gunning & Baron, 2014).

Importantly, the Muslim Brotherhood's political participation and activism, which included anti-Mubarak regime agitation and opposition in parliament and organizing hundreds of anti-regime protests, also contributed to the general political atmosphere of opposition in the months and years directly preceding the 2011 uprising (Fahmy, 2016).

The Egyptian youth represented the core of most of the abovementioned movements. According to Dina Shehata, a senior researcher at the Al-Ahram Center for Political and Strategic Studies, these movements shared various characteristics: They united Egyptians through an "action-oriented" approach that called for bottom-up political change; they had an inclusive and diverse nature that made them open to members from various ideological and political backgrounds; they prioritized their dedication to democracy and human rights over ideological differences; and they utilized communication technology, such as Facebook, Twitter, and blogs, in mobilizing the public (Shehata, 2012).

THE TUNISIAN REVOLUTION TRIGGER

The Tunisian protests that began on December 17, 2010, were ignited by the self-immolation of a young street vendor named Mohamed Bouazizi after he was humiliated by the Tunisian police. The protests led to the escape of longtime Tunisian dictator Zin El Abedine Ben Ali to Saudi Arabia on January 14, 2011, just eleven days before the start of the Egyptian revolution. What came to be known as Tunisia's "Jasmine revolution" was the first in a series of popular revolts in different Arab countries, and it was a source of inspiration for the young Egyptians who took to the streets on January 25, 2011 (Hassan, 2015). While the Ben Ali regime was harsher than the Mubarak regime in dealing with opposition, "Egyptians had more reason to be angry than the Tunisians because the average income in Egypt was about half what it was in Tunisia, and the proportion of people below the poverty line ... in Egypt was seven times what it was in Tunisia" (Amin, 2013, p. 103).

THE EGYPTIAN REVOLUTION AND
THE FALL OF MUBARAK

The mounting frustrations with the Mubarak regime led a group of youth activists from several movements, including April 6, the Revolutionary Socialist Movement, the National Association for Change, and the Democratic Front Party, to call for wide-scale protests on January 25, 2011. The call was made through the "We are all Khaled Said" Facebook page (Duboc, 2015). The call was accompanied by a video blog that was posted on January 18, 2011, featuring a female activist and member of April 6 movement, Asmaa Mahfouz, who blamed the regime for the self-immolation cases that had taken place in the months preceding the uprising. Mahfouz encouraged Egyptians to take to the streets and end what she described as the corruption of the regime (Herrera, 2014). January 25 was selected as it commemorated National Police Day. So, the activists wanted to take a stand against police brutality on the day that revered police forces (Ghoneim, 2012).

Groups of protesters took to the streets in a spontaneous and leaderless fashion, chanting "freedom, bread, social justice and human dignity." The protests started out in Cairo, Alexandria, and Suez, and they unexpectedly caught momentum in a way that was shocking, even to the organizers. Protesters carried posters that were critical of the security forces and called for the firing of the minister of interior, Habib El-Adly. Protesters also demanded an end to the emergency law and setting a presidential term limit. In Cairo, thousands of protesters convened in several neighborhoods, breaking through police barricades and marching toward Tahrir Square in the heart of the city (Momani & Mohamed, 2016, p. 1; Lesch, 2012; Hellyer, 2016). The Muslim Brotherhood did not officially endorse the protests, something that, as will be discussed below, angered some protest organizers. The MB did, however, encourage individual members to participate, and Brotherhood leaders and youth members were visible during the initial days of protest (Ketchley, 2017).

The choice of Tahrir Square as a central location for the protests bestowed on it a symbolic image as an ideal or "utopian space" representing an era of hope, egalitarianism, and free speech in the "New Egypt" (Peterson, 2015, p. 75), and as "a counter ... deviant, diverted space which had managed to escape the control of the established order" (Aboelezz, 2014, p. 609).

In his description of the structure, size, and goals of the protests, the Egyptian economist Galal Amin argued that several unique phenomena characterized the protests. First, he said that the vast number of protesters—mobilized to achieve the same goal—was unparalleled in Egypt's modern history. Second, the simultaneous eruption of protests in various Egyptian governorates and cities was also an unusual phenomenon in Egypt's history of political activism. Third, the protests witnessed notable participation from the educated members of the middle and upper classes—a remarkable happening in a country that has relatively high illiteracy and poverty rates. Fourth, unlike Egypt's previous revolutions, which had either an economic or political focus, the protesters in the 2011 uprising had both political *and* economic demands. Finally, according to Amin, the 2011 uprising was leaderless, something that pointed to the collective vigor and communal energy that characterized the movement (Amin, 2013).

Despite collective chants of "Peaceful! Peaceful!" from protesters, police tried to violently disperse the crowds using tear gas, water cannons, and rubber bullets. This confrontation provoked the protesters, who tried to march toward the Ministry of Interior, which was located in the immediate vicinity of the square. Ultimately, and as an apparent response to the viciousness of the security forces, protester demands were escalated to include the stepping down of Mubarak (Lesch, 2012, p. 18). For a time on January 25, the security forces were able to temporarily evacuate the square, but the evacuation did not last long. Protesters used various tactics to escape police, reorganize, and regroup back in the square, where they held onto their positions and set up tents for camping (Hellyer, 2016). On January 26–27, the protesters continued their marches and sit-ins, albeit in smaller numbers due to the increasingly violent responses of the security forces, who were able to temporarily contain the protests' intensity and magnitude (Ketchley, 2017).

The protesters, however, used an innovative tactic called "flash mobs" for deciding on meeting points for demonstrations. With this tactic, clusters of protesters would spring up randomly and simultaneously at different locations in a way that made it hard for the security forces to find and suppress the protest sites. The protesters used Twitter, Facebook, and text messaging to help them communicate and exchange fast and short messages about the timings and locations of demonstration points. So, social media played a strategic mobilization role that contributed to the protests' effectiveness during the course of the uprising (Gunning & Baron, 2014; el-Nawawy & Khamis, 2013). It was for this reason that the Mubarak regime decided to implement a five-day shut-down on both the internet and mobile services on January 27, 2011 (Herrera, 2014).

By January 27, however, it was seemingly too late for the regime to rein in the protests or regain control over the situation on the ground. Switching off the internet and communication services ultimately backfired on the regime, as online activists who were sitting behind their computer screens had left their homes and taken to the streets (Ketchley, 2017). On January 28, 2011, a day that was described as the "Friday of Rage," protesters called for large protests in Cairo's main streets and squares following the Friday Muslim prayers. This call attracted a huge following from among members of various political movements, as well as average Egyptians, who left their homes to join the protests. In response, the regime beefed up security around the major squares and set up checkpoints throughout Cairo neighborhoods. Security forces also closed down several mosques to prevent potential gatherings after the prayers and arrested thousands of activists representing different ideological backgrounds. These measures, however, did not stop the protesters from marching, and violent clashes ultimately ensued between the security forces and protesters, leading to the death and injury of hundreds of protesters at the hands of the police. Protesters also set the headquarters of the NDP in downtown Cairo ablaze. For many of them, the NDP building symbolized the corruption and repression of the regime and its ruling party. The massive protests on January 28 shocked the regime, which seemed unprepared to face the magnitude of the protests (Ketchley, 2017; Albrecht, 2012).

It is worth mentioning in this context that, on January 25 and 26, the regime accused the MB of orchestrating the January 25 protests and arrested some of its members. In fact, state television, based on direct instructions from the then minister of information, Anas El-Fiqqi, claimed that the MB "and other subversive elements had infiltrated protests with the goal of destabilizing the country and bringing about chaos" (Hassan, 2015, p. 40).

As mentioned above, the MB didn't initially endorse the protest movement, but they did encourage individual members to participate. The group did officially endorse the protests beginning on January 28, the "Friday of Rage." According to one view about the Brotherhood's initial reluctance, the group, having officially endorsed the protests only after they had already begun, were "opportunistic latecomers" (Ketchley, 2017, p. 83) to the revolution, seeking to take credit for the achievements of non-MB protesters and then ride the wave of the revolution to power. In this context, Hellyer (2016) argued that Egypt's "[liberal] revolutionary camp claimed a monopoly on the uprising and claimed that the MB only joined in after it became clear that it could plausibly serve the MB's own partisan interests" (p. 41). According to another view, however, the group's early reticence about fully endorsing the protests—along with the group's decision to support the protesters' basic demands and allow individual MB members to participate—were the products of "special circumstances [the MB] faced as the largest and best-organized sector of the opposition" (Wickham, 2013, p. 161). As Wickham described, "The Brotherhood's decision to support the general demands of the protest and permit its members to participate in it as individuals, without granting the event their official endorsement, reflected such conflicting priorities" (p. 161).

In this context, MB sources claimed that the group's reluctance to endorse and fully participate in the protests during their initial stages was the result of a meeting that took place between the state security and MB leadership on January 24, 2011. During that meeting, the state security "threatened to suppress the movement if it called its members out into the streets" (Ketchley, 2017, p. 83).

In light of the abovementioned circumstances, the MB faced a serious quandary during the first three days of protest: if the group decided to openly and officially endorse the protests, it would have encountered a heavy backlash from security forces, and if it decided to distance itself from the protests, it would have been seen as letting down activists on the ground. The MB issued a statement on January 19, 2011, in which it called for peace and stability and urged the regime to allow for some political reforms. The statement stopped short of endorsing the national protests. The group, however, allowed its members to participate in the protests in their individual capacities. When, on the eve of January 28, clashes between the security forces and protesters gained more intensity, the MB announced its official endorsement of the protests (El Houdaiby, 2012; Al-Awadi, 2013; Gunning & Baron, 2014). The MB's decision to endorse the protests narrowed the gap that existed between the group's "risk-averse, conservative old guard," who were cautious about participation in street activism and the group's younger generations, who were "bolder and more ready for change" (Gunning & Baron, 2014, p. 96; Al-Awadi, 2013, p. 542).

The security forces were stunned by the scale and extent of the protests on January 28, and this led to the complete breakdown of the security apparatus. Many streets were filled with police armored vehicles that were abandoned and burned. There was a sudden and almost complete withdrawal of the police forces from the streets of Cairo. The police withdrawal caused a security void that led to looting of public and private property, as well as the escape of a number of inmates from the unguarded prisons and police stations. Civilians set up neighborhood watches and checkpoints at the entrances of their buildings to protect themselves and their neighbors against intruders. Also on January 28, Mubarak deployed the military onto the Egyptian streets (Hellyer, 2016; Ketchley, 2017; Shokr, 2012). While the protesters were overjoyed to see the police disappear from the scene, they felt apprehensive about the military deployment. Some protesters chanted, "The people and the army are one hand," while others took photos of themselves with military tanks (Ketchley, 2017, p. 58).

The military neither antagonized the protesters nor stood with them, possibly out of fear that a violent confrontation could lead to further escalation and destabilization of the country (Hellyer, 2016). The military released an official statement toward the end of January, in which it recognized the protesters' right to express their frustrations with the regime. This statement reassured the protesters that the military would not try to suppress them or support the regime against them (Bassiouni, 2017).

On the evening of January 29, Mubarak delivered his first speech to the nation since the start of the uprising. He announced that he had reshuffled his cabinet and appointed his intelligence chief, Omar Suleiman, as vice president. In the speech, Mubarak said, "I will not hesitate in taking any decision to preserve for every Egyptian their safety and security and I will defend the security and stability of Egypt. That is the responsibility for which I swore an oath before God and the people." Immediately after his appointment, Suleiman called for an open dialogue with the leaders of political movements and opposition parties, including the MB. The protesters, however, expressed their dissatisfaction with Mubarak's moves and insisted on his departure from power (Hassan, 2015, p. 53; Gardner, 2011).

During the last three days in January, the MB utilized its skills in on-the-ground mobilization and coordination, which it had gained from its involvement in the civil society under Mubarak. The group tasked several of its members at Tahrir Square to guard the square's main entrances and exits and to keep an eye on the daily activities within the square to protect the protesters' safety. Moreover, MB representatives worked on providing the protesters with food, blankets, and other basic supplies that they needed during their stay at the square (Wickham, 2013).

Activists from other groups also contributed to daily activities inside the square. In his book about the revolution, Wael Ghoneim described the division of labor among the protesters: "The number of tents increased many times over with the arrival of participants from every corner of the nation. The sit-in participants were organized and divided duties among themselves. … Some groups were responsible for cleaning litter from the square, while others took care of securing the entrances and searching people coming into Tahrir. Doctors who were protesting established a field hospital in one of the square's small shops. … Plumbers brilliantly converted a few of the now dysfunctional armored vehicles into public bathrooms for those taking part in the sit-in. Other people created a lost-and-found desk to help people locate their missing belongings" (Ghoneim, 2012, p. 225).

On the evening of February 1, Mubarak delivered his second speech since the start of the protests. In this speech, he stated that he would not run for reelection in September 2011, but made no reference to his stepping down before then. He also reflected on his career and spoke in a mollifying tone, as if he was appeasing the protesters. He said, "Hosni Mubarak who speaks to you today is proud of his many years spent in the service of Egypt and its people. This dear country is my homeland, just as it is for every Egyptian man and woman. In this country I have lived. I have fought for it. I have defended its territory, sovereignty, and interests. On this land I will die and history will judge me and others, either for us or against us." Mubarak's words had a positive impact on many Egyptians, but the protesters at Tahrir Square again rejected his appeal and vowed that they were not leaving their posts at the square until his ouster (Hassan, 2015, p. 60).

On February 2, 2011, several pro-regime thugs in plainclothes stormed Tahrir Square on camels and horses, attacking protesters using clubs, knives, and swords. They also threw rocks at protesters and destroyed a podium that was set up in the middle of the square. Most of the thugs came to the square from the direction of the Great Pyramids, where they offered camel rides to tourists. During this episode, which came to be known as the "Battle of the Camel," protesters were taken aback by the unexpected attacks. Activists from various movements, including the MB, regrouped and engaged in intense clashes with the attackers. The event, which marked the most violent and bloody day since the start of the uprising, resulted in the death and injury of many protesters. Several thugs were eventually pulled off the horses and camels and beaten up by the protesters, while others were handed over to the military units at the square. After these clashes, more barricades were set up around the square, and the military beefed up its presence at checkpoints leading to the square. The losses among the protesters increased their resilience and insistence on Mubarak's resignation (Ketchley, 2017; Bassiouni, 2017).

On February 6, Vice President Suleiman invited members of the opposition groups to the Presidential Palace to engage in negotiations about the country's political future. The meeting was widely attended, and the MB sent two of its leaders, Mohamed Morsi and Saad El-Katatni. Covering the meeting for the *New York Times*, David Kirkpatrick and David Sanger wrote that the meeting was attended by "a group of about 50 prominent Egyptians and opposition figures, including officials of the small, recognized opposition parties, as well as a handful of young people who helped start the protest movement" (Kirkpatrick & Sanger, 2011). During the meeting, Suleiman proposed that Mubarak would stay in power while a committee would be formed to draft constitutional amendments. Some revolutionary youth expressed their disapproval of negotiating with the regime and accused the parties that attended the meeting of straying away from the revolution's goals. Participants in that meeting announced that they would not engage in further negotiations with the regime, and the MB's Guidance Office issued a statement on February 7 that called on Mubarak to step down (Hassan, 2015).

Collective chants calling on Mubarak to leave power continued to be heard at Tahrir Square and its surroundings, and on February 8, tens of thousands of demonstrators started marching from the square in the direction of the nearby parliament building. On February 10, the military made a televised statement reassuring the protesters that their demands were "legitimate" and informing them that the Supreme Council of the Armed Forces (SCAF) was "in continuous session" to discuss the "procedures and measures that may be taken to protect the nation, and the achievements and aspirations of the great people of Egypt" (Hassan, 2015, p. 71).

Amid anticipation that he would announce his resignation, Mubarak appeared for his third and final televised speech on the evening of February 10. In the speech, Mubarak expressed his sorrow for the loss of lives during the uprising by saying, "I tell the families of the innocent victims that I am suffering, as you are. My heart is hurt by what happened to them, as your hearts hurt." He also reiterated his intention not to run for reelection and to delegate some of his powers to his vice president. He also said that the state of emergency would continue until conditions return to normal. Protesters at Tahrir rejected the speech, waving their shoes in the air as a sign of their disappointment and anger. They also threatened that they would march toward the radio and television building (Maspero) and the Presidential Palace in the Cairo neighborhood of Heliopolis (Hassan, 2015, p. 72).

On the evening of February 11, 2011, Vice President Suleiman appeared on state television to deliver a thirty-second statement that read, "In the name of God, most gracious, most merciful. My fellow citizens, in the difficult circumstances our country is experiencing, President Muhammad Hosni Mubarak has decided to give up the office of the president of the republic and instructed the Supreme Council of the Armed Forces to manage the affairs of the country. May God guide our steps" (Ghoneim, 2012, p. 289). Hearing this news, protesters at Tahrir Square were elated, and began celebrating what they considered to be a great achievement sparked by eighteen days of continuous protest (Hassan, 2015).

On February 17, MB General Guide Mohamed Badie argued that "the revolution must be a starting point for Egypt to take up its place in the world again, through recognizing the importance of our responsibilities toward our nations and defending them and their legitimate demands" (Hamid, 2011, p. 46). Following Mubarak's ouster, all eyes were focused on the MB, which was "by far the most organized and disciplined" political group during that time (Osman, 2013, p. 119). The group's social capital, which it had gained by providing social services and carrying out grassroots activities in civil society throughout the Mubarak period, could be invested in the political arena. On April 30, 2011, the MB officially launched its Freedom and Justice Party (FJP) to allow the group to participate in future parliamentary elections (Hellyer, 2016; Ketchley, 2017). After decades of acting as an underground, banned, and outlawed group, the MB was in a position to play a key "above ground" role in Egypt's post-Mubarak political arena (Shehata & Stacher, 2012, p. 176).

OVERJOY AND ELATION VS. TRIALS AND TRIBULATIONS

There was a strong sense of fulfillment and nationalism among the young revolutionaries for their success in deposing a longtime dictator and standing strong in the face of a ferocious state security apparatus. Feelings of emancipation and empowerment extended to the Egyptian public in general, which was looking forward to a better and more promising future. These feelings were reflected in a national survey that was conducted by *Al-Shorouk*, an independent Egyptian daily newspaper, following the fall of Mubarak. Around 88 percent of the those surveyed felt uninhibited in expressing their opinions, and 93 percent were proud of their Egyptian identity (Korany, 2012).

The Youth Coalition that was formed during the uprising tried to stay active after the regime's fall by pressuring SCAF to fulfill revolutionary demands. The coalition called for prosecuting officials responsible for protester deaths during the revolution, putting Mubarak and his government on trial, releasing political prisoners, including MB members, and forming a civilian government to run the country during the transitional phase. The Youth Coalition, however, was not strong enough to achieve these demands, and it was further weakened by divisions among its members regarding political direction and overall vision (Shehata, 2012).

Several political challenges faced the country during the weeks and months that followed the ousting of Mubarak. Most of the ministers who served in the cabinet that Mubarak had appointed at the start of the protests (at the end of January 2011) remained in office. The Ministry of Interior, whose restructuring was among the protesters' primary demands, remained largely unscathed. More importantly, the ruling power in the country was transferred to SCAF, which issued a constitutional declaration that suspended the constitution and dissolved the Parliament's two chambers on February 13, 2011 (Hassan, 2015).

SCAF ended up staying in power for almost eighteen months (February 12, 2011, to June 29, 2012), during which time the country went through several political confrontations and tribulations. During this time, the MB witnessed "major splits" within the group, the most notable of which was the expulsion of Abdel Moneim Aboul Fotouh, who was ousted from the group after he declared his intention to run for president. Moreover, the group expelled several of its young members, who went ahead and formed a new party called the Egyptian Current (El Houdaiby, 2012, p. 125).

The Brotherhood chalked up several political wins, starting with their successful campaign to mobilize the public to vote "yes" on a March 2011 referendum about constitutional amendments. This referendum was part of SCAF's roadmap aimed at expediting parliamentary and presidential elections. The MB's support of this roadmap was met with criticism from some revolutionaries, who accused the MB of being "unprincipled opportunists" and prioritizing the group's interests over the country's well-being (Ketchley, 2017, p. 99). In this context, Shenker (2016) argued that the MB's agenda was set on getting closer to power. Thus, the group subscribed "to 'a transition plan' that would revolve around a series of elections … which only the well-organized Brotherhood were ever likely to win." Another view, however, defended the MB's adoption of the roadmap, as "it provided assurance that the ousted president's partisans would be excluded," and it set a clear timeframe for the country's move away from military control and toward democracy (Rougier & Lacroix, 2016, p. 5).

The March 2011 referendum was followed by the MB's winning 40 percent of the votes in the parliamentary elections that took place between November 2011 and January 2012. The highlight of the MB's political achievements was having one of its leaders, Mohamed Morsi, win the June 2012 presidential election. The MB had initially decided not to have one of its figures run for president. However, this decision was changed after "a narrow vote in the MB's Guidance Council, the [group's] top executive authority" (Hellyer, 2016, p. 57).

Following his election, Morsi had several standoffs with SCAF and with members of the judiciary (Osman, 2013). Morsi's first few months in office were extremely challenging and tumultuous, as they witnessed hundreds of public demonstrations and sit-ins (Al-Awadi, 2013). The MB's rise to power might have "caused much resentment among the existing military-bureaucratic caste, who had always viewed senior Brotherhood leaders as mortal enemies" (Shenker, 2016, p. 258).

Morsi was isolated politically during his time in office, in part because of mutual distrust between the MB and some of its secular and liberal opponents. The quick disappearance of the MB-affiliated revolutionaries from the post-Mubarak street scene had a negative impact on the Youth Coalition, which reached its peak in mass mobilization when all factions, including the MB, were acting in unison during the eighteen-day uprising. The MB's retreat from the coalition and its "uncoordinated demobilization meant that the movement had few allies willing to defend Egypt's newly elected democratic institutions against old regime holdovers opposed to new forms of elected civilian authority" (Ketchley, 2017, p. 158).

Chapter 4

From the 2010 Parliamentary Elections to the 2011 Constitutional Referendum

This chapter is the first of three chapters presenting results of our framing analysis of the Brotherhood's English-language website, Ikhwanweb.com. The chapters are presented chronologically—that is, results are presented on studied events in the order in which they occurred—and follow the theoretical framework and methodological protocols presented in chapter 1 ("Theory and Methodology"). Specifically, we employ textual analysis driven by framing theory to carry out our examination of the texts. The present chapter analyzes three events—the 2010 parliamentary elections, the 2011 revolution, and the March 2011 referendum on constitutional amendments.

THE 2010 PARLIAMENTARY ELECTIONS

The Muslim Brotherhood's English-language website devoted significant attention to Egypt's 2010 parliamentary elections, which the Islamist group viewed as an opportunity to build on its 2005 electoral success. Our analysis studied all sixty-five articles posted about the elections between November 21, 2010—exactly one week prior to the first round of voting—and December 6, 2010, the day after the second and final round of voting. Perhaps unsurprisingly, the Brotherhood's English-language posts served to legitimate the group and their political positions and denounce their political rivals. Most of the posts were articles written by staff writers at Ikhwanweb.com, but, importantly, the Muslim Brotherhood (MB) also sometimes posted articles from other sites. The articles from external sources always supported the Brotherhood's positions, making the MB's political arguments about the elections and the Mubarak government for them.

Four dominant frames emerged from our close reading of the texts: The 2010 Parliamentary Elections Are Rigged; The MB Is Peaceful and Democratic; The MB Is a Popular Savior (while the Mubarak government is, in contrast, illegitimate and unpopular); and MB Victimization. The MB Is Peaceful and Democratic frame included subframes. The pages that follow will discuss each of these four frames in turn.

The 2010 Parliamentary Elections Are Rigged Frame

Muslim Brotherhood English-language posts about the 2010 parliamentary elections consistently delegitimated the electoral process as flawed and rigged. The MB's negative framing of the elections began in the lead-up to the elections, well prior to the first day of voting. The Elections Are Rigged Frame was driven by both topical emphasis and sourcing. The Brotherhood chose to write intensively about alleged Mubarak regime violations, and strategically selected local and external sources and quotes that supported the election-rigging position.

For example, several articles published on November 21, 2010, the first day of our sample period, denounced the elections as deeply flawed. The MB's first post on November 21, 2010, documented "1044 Arbitrary Arrests in [the lead-up] to Egypt's Polls." The second article posted on that day cited an article published by Michael Jansen in *The Gulf Today*, in which Jansen argued that the elections would prove to be farcical, with the Mubarak regime using heavy-handed measures to limit the number of opposition victories and retain near-complete control over parliament. The article also noted that "Egyptians ... do not believe their votes count," highlighting one citizen who said, "I never voted in my life."

Also on November 21, 2010, Ikhwanweb.com posted the "Muslim Brotherhood's Statement on Rigging of Parliamentary Election." The statement was ostensibly written by the MB's general guide, Mohamed Badie, whose picture was placed immediately below the article's title. The statement described, in some detail, what it considered Mubarak government abuses of the political process and election "rigging," called on Egyptians to resist government tyranny, and promised that the MB would continue to fight for "usurped rights" and to "achieve the desired reform and restore Egypt to its great status among the nations." The statement described Egypt's system of governance as "totalitarian" and described government abuses and election "rigging" and attempts to "falsify the election results and tighten its grip around MB candidates." Alleged abuses included mass arrests, state-sponsored violence, and shutting down businesses and confiscating property, among other alleged abuses. The statement asked, "How can a corrupt and tyrannical system keep its promises or respect people's will?"

Several November 22, 2010, posts referenced specific alleged Mubarak regime abuses, including arrests of Brotherhood leaders and "hostilities against the political opposition." A November 23, 2010, article highlighted comments made by Abdel Moneim Abul Fotouh, a "leading Brotherhood figure." Abul Fotouh's remarks predicted that the forthcoming elections would be "rigged." He was quoted as saying, "Unfortunately, the elections—in the eyes of the ruling party—are not a peaceful political struggle that is subject to the people's will and the ballot boxes, but a guerilla war in every sense of the word." The article spoke of "poll rigging" and the need to "preserve the integrity of the ballot boxes," warned against government "propaganda campaigns" and "falsifying the election results," and called for a committee to monitor the elections "for the benefit of Egypt." Another November 23, 2010, post made repeated references to election "rigging" and described an attempt by Egypt's Kefaya Movement to organize a reelection at the conclusion of the electoral process. Other November 23, 2010, posts described specific restrictions imposed by the Egyptian government, including a "ban on filming, photograph[y], and engaging in any campaigning," and poked holes at the government's claim that the electoral process would be free and fair.

On November 24, 2010, the MB drew attention to obstacles faced by journalists covering elections in Egypt, quoting a statement issued by BBC Arabic and the Arab Forum for Alternatives (AFA), which said that there is "no hope for fair, equal and neutral media coverage" of the parliamentary election. The article specifically highlighted "the need for a permit to film in the streets ... police harassment, and sources refusing to cooperate, as well as public fear to speak out." A long editorial written on November 25, 2010, by a Muslim Brotherhood webpage staff writer argued that the elections would be rigged. The article justified, however, the MB's continued participation in the electoral process, suggesting that participation would make clear the far-cical nature of the elections.

Several November 26, 27, and 28 (2010) Ikhwanweb.com posts relied on external Western sources to emphasize points—the elections will be rigged, and the Mubarak regime is authoritarian—that the MB had already made. For example, a November 26, 2010, post summarized an article published in the *Washington Post* describing the Mubarak regime as a dictatorship and questioning the legitimacy of the electoral process. It also described how the election results would be used to justify Mubarak's handing over the Egyptian presidency to his son, Gamal. Another November 26, 2010, post cited a report by Amnesty International urging free and fair elections and highlighted Egyptian government abuses in the run-up to the polls. A third November 26, 2010, post summarized a Reporters Without Borders report that condemned the Mubarak regime for measures taken to restrict freedom of expression and freedom of the press during the campaign season. The post also alluded to the government's intimidation of journalists covering the run-up to the elections. A November 27, 2010, post cited an article published in *The Economist* arguing that the Egyptian government intended to rig the parliamentary elections. On November 28, 2010, Ikhwanweb.com borrowed an editorial written by Shadi Hamid in the *Huffington Post*, in which he discredited the electoral process. In all these posts, then, the Brotherhood strategically selected credible Western sources to argue points that the group had already been making, effectively (arguably) strengthening the group's position.

After voting began, the MB continued to press the election-rigging issue. On November 29, 2010, the MB presented alleged evidence of election rigging. For instance, "the vast majority of opposition candidates and their delegates were beaten, and forcibly prevented from entering polling centers to monitor voting." The post documented "ballot stuffing" and the use of "tear gas," and "[gun]fire to disperse the crowds." The post also documented twelve killings and the alleged physical and verbal assaults of "a large number of MB candidates." Moreover, the post alluded to the blocking of the MB website by the Egyptian government in what was described as "an attempt to hinder the monitoring of electoral violations."

Another November 29, 2010, post described the election process as "heavily rigged"; a November 30, 2010, post wrote that "massive fraud" characterized the voting process; and a separate November 30, 2010, post argued that the Mubarak government's blatant election tampering proved that it "does not respect the people's will, the law or the constitution."

From December 1, 2010, to December 3, 2010, Ikhwanweb.com relied extensively on prominent external sources to demonstrate its argument—that the elections were rigged. One article documented an Amnesty International report calling on Egypt to "fully investigate" violence carried out against members and supporters of the political opposition, as well as numerous arbitrary arrests. The report also noted irregularities, including the closing of several polling stations for hours. Another December 1, 2010, article, written by American scholar Michele Dunne and published originally by the Carnegie Endowment, argued that the elections would provide "little credibility either inside or outside the country due to the total lack of transparency and the widespread irregularities and violence that characterized the voting and counting processes." A third December 1, 2010, article, written by Haroon Siddiqui and published originally in the *Toronto Star*, posited that the "authoritarian" Mubarak government engaged in widespread "electoral fraud." In another December 1 post, the Brotherhood wrote that U.S. president Barack Obama criticized Egypt's elections and called out specific irregularities.

On December 3 and December 6, 2010, more alleged evidence of election rigging was provided, and again the Brotherhood relied on external sources as authorities. One post discussed a report by the Human Rights Association of Egypt documenting more than one thousand violations, including "134 cases of violence." A second December 3, 2010, Ikhwanweb.com post again mentioned the United States. The post read, in part, "Everyone, from the voter on the street in Egypt, to the U.S. government, acknowledges that Egypt's parliamentary elections in 2010 were rigged." The post continued, "Even the U.S. has expressed its dismay at reports of intimidation of voters and MB candidates." A third December 3, 2010, post cited the protest resignation of a prominent Egyptian judge, who mentioned voting irregularities as his reason for resignation; and another Carnegie Endowment article, written by Egyptian scholar Amy Hamzawy, also decried the alleged vote rigging and authoritarian nature of the Mubarak government. On December 6, 2010, the Brotherhood's English-language website again referenced the United States: "even the U.S. acknowledged the NDP's ballot box stuffing, vote rigging, and intimidation of voters."

The MB Is Peaceful and Democratic Frame

During the 2010 parliamentary election period, Ikhwanweb.com framed the Muslim Brotherhood as a peaceful and democratic group that stood in stark contrast to what the website portrayed as the brutal and authoritarian Mubarak government. This frame was dominant and was often supported by a type of direct, explicit comparison between claims the Brotherhood made about itself and claims it made about the Mubarak regime. A subframe emerged from this analysis—Mubarak Is Brutal and Authoritarian.

Importantly, the MB often appeared to be addressing the government of the United States, which was sometimes invoked directly by the group's posts. The Brotherhood made multiple appeals to the American administration to use its leverage to pressure the Egyptian government to abide by basic rules of democracy. Brotherhood posts during this period also spoke to the group's self-proclaimed moderate religious nature, arguing both that the MB is committed to equality for Egypt's Coptic Christian minority and that the group could be a bulwark against Muslim extremism. These messages of claimed moderation can be seen as addressing American government concerns about Islamists.

In several posts, the Brotherhood claimed to be peaceful and democratic. At the same time, the group repeatedly argued that the Mubarak government was brutal and authoritarian.

In a November 25, 2010 post, Ikhwanweb.com summarized an interview by the Brotherhood's general guide, Mohamed Badie, on Al-Jazeera. In the interview, Badie argued for democracy in Egypt and implied that the Brotherhood is both essentially democratic and peaceful. He said the MB refuses "to shed the blood of any Egyptian" and that the group "has chosen the path of elections to bring about peaceful change." He also noted that the Brotherhood "will not choose a different path despite the violations [carried out against it]." Also, in what amounted to a claim that the Mubarak government is authoritarian, Badie maintained that Egyptians are as entitled to democracy as other nations that have "changed [their] tyrannical regimes." He also contended that the Brotherhood fundamentally rejects the notion of tawreeth al-sulta (inheriting power), something that was of concern to many Egyptians in light of suggestions that Mubarak would hand over power to his son, Gamal, in 2011.

A November 25, 2010, post summarized an interview given on the Al-Arabiya Satellite News Network by Mohamad Morsi, the Brotherhood's then spokesperson. In the interview, Morsi said that the "MB will accept whoever comes to power according to the will of the nation without [elections] being rigged, even if [the Brotherhood] does not believe he is suitable." He also said that the group would "never" accept a leader "who comes to power despite the will of the people." Morsi also argued that the Brotherhood is an essentially democratic organization, noting that he believes that "free and fair elections in which the nation is the source of authority" constitute the proper direction for Egypt, and that "the internal affairs of the MB are run with great transparency, democracy and freedom of choice."

A November 26, 2010, post suggested that the Brotherhood advocates democracy. The post cited a senior MB member who argued that the group endorses "a civil state based on Islamic Law which respects all citizens regardless of religion, color, or creed." A November 28, 2010, post again cited Morsi's views, which implied that the Brotherhood believes that a democratic system would help solve Egypt's problems. Specifically, Morsi said that a "civil political party" and a "multi-party system" would alleviate the nation's difficulties. The post also said that the MB "does not want to cause riots in the streets."

On November 30, 2010, an Ikhwanweb.com staff writer wrote that the Brotherhood would not be dragged into violence despite pressure from the Mubarak administration. The post read, "Despite the regime's broken promises to conduct free and fair elections, the MB—the best-organized and largest opposition group in the country—refuses to resort to violence" and has limited its activities to "protests, rallies and awareness raising in a bid to successfully enter the next phase."

The Brotherhood "vowed its determination to continue the movement of peaceful change through legal processes" in a December 3, 2010, post. A December 5, 2010, Ikhwanweb.com post said that Mubarak government repression would "not deter" the MB from "calling for peaceful reform." The post emphasized that the group would remain peaceful and work "for the country and the people calling for reform through only peaceful means."

A December 6, 2010, post positioned the MB as true democrats, noting that they would come together with other opposition politicians to form a "parallel parliament" to counter the Mubarak parliament, which the post suggested was illegitimate.

In contrast to the Brotherhood's claimed peacefulness and democratic nature, the group denounced Mubarak as brutal and dictatorial. As mentioned previously, Mubarak Is Brutal and Authoritarian is a subframe of the MB Is Peaceful and Democratic frame. For example, a November 21, 2010, article documented abuses by Mubarak's security forces, noting that they had "brutally attempted to stop peaceful campaign rallies by MB MP candidates." A photo showed Central Security Forces raising clubs at protesters. Another November 21, 2010, post referred to Egypt's system of governance as "totalitarian" and described alleged government abuses, including mass arrests and violence. The post asked, "How can a corrupt and tyrannical system keep its promises or respect people's will?"

A November 22, 2010, post again painted the Mubarak regime as ruthless, describing "security forces backed by thugs" and "swords, bladed weapons, tear gas, and live bullets" used against protesters. A November 23, 2010, post documented an Amnesty International report that noted violent government abuses, while a separate November 23, 2010, post described a violent assault on Saad El-Katatni, an MB candidate for parliament. El-Ketatni was quoted as saying, "Assaults on me by thugs were [carried out] with the approval of the Ministry of Interior."

In framing themselves as "Peaceful and Democratic" the Brotherhood addressed the United States in several posts, appearing to attempt to allay fears that the Obama administration held about Islamists. Some posts called on the United States to urge the Mubarak government to abide by democratic norms. For example, on November 24, 2010, Ikhwanweb.com ran an article that summarized the views of Project on Middle East Democracy (POMED) director Stephen McInerney, who argued that the United States should persuade Egypt to hold free and fair elections. Also, on November 26, 2010, a post rejected a claim made by Mubarak regime leader Fathi Sorour suggesting that the Brotherhood desired to establish a "religious state" in Egypt. Sorour had alleged that the United States was wrong to push aggressively for democratic reforms in Egypt because doing so could lead to the establishment of "an Islamic state" in the country. The post cited a senior MB member responding directly to Sorour's allegations. He said the MB endorses "a civil state based on Islamic Law which respects all citizens regardless of religion, color, or creed." The post also went on to assert that the Brotherhood supports political and religious tolerance and that the Mubarak government had used the Brotherhood "as a scapegoat to continue in its repression."

In a December 1, 2010 post, the Brotherhood called directly on the U.S. government to apply pressure on the Mubarak government. In this direct appeal, the Brotherhood made several recommendations to the American administration, including "to call [Mubarak regime] violations by their names and describe the situation [in Egypt] as it is."

A December 3, 2010, post titled "The Muslim Brotherhood Bows Out Graciously" noted that the Brotherhood's position is "hardly an extremist stance" and that the group "will continue to monitor and expose" the Egyptian government. The reference to "extremism" is significant given well-known American concerns about Islamist extremism and terrorism. The post continued in a type of challenge to the United States to stay true to its stated democratic principles: "It's unlikely the U.S. would celebrate the idea of the Muslim Brotherhood taking control of Egypt, but in a true democracy their opinion would not matter; as it would be the Egyptians themselves who would decide." This December 3, 2010, post continued, arguing that "the credibility of the Muslim Brotherhood will increase." This statement can arguably be seen as an attempt to project themselves as a viable alternative to Mubarak. The statement can also be seen as a proclamation to the United States because it declares the seeming inevitability of the Brotherhood's rise and suggests that the United States will have to deal with the group at some point.

A December 6, 2010, post, "Election Victory with No Glory," was perhaps the most direct appeal to the United States. The post said, "The moderate voice of the Brotherhood has been largely drowned out by the riotous indecent behavior of the regime, who, determined to avoid anything resembling an Islamic state, has foolishly, perhaps inadvertently, opened the door for militants to emerge." This statement is meaningful because it notes the MB's allegedly "moderate" nature, and also claims, importantly, that the Mubarak government's alleged authoritarianism could lead "inadvertently" to radicalization. This is a message that could resonate with the United States and other Western nations concerned with Muslim radicalization. Toward the end of the post, the Brotherhood website staff writer noted, "the best way to change the system is from within." This final statement can be seen as a response to extremist groups who argue that governments in the Muslim world should be overtaken forcefully.

In another discourse that is targeting the West, and in particular the United States, Ikhwanweb.com also sought to assuage fears that Brotherhood rule would repress Egypt's Coptic Christian minority. For instance, a November 25, 2010, post spoke of the need to strike deals with Coptic Christians, and noted that "deals [between the Brotherhood and Copts] have in fact been made … in the past." A separate November 25, 2010, post—the aforementioned article that summarized Morsi's Al-Arabiya interview—highlighted the

Brotherhood's alleged belief in an Islam that respects and honors Christians. The post noted that Morsi "confirmed the rights to Christians, saying that their rights are obligations and duties we have in our religion which does not require a campaign to stress on it. He explained that texts in the Noble Qur'an order us to look after the Christians, our fellow citizens, on the humanitarian level, and to accept, love and be just with them. He noted that Christians have the same rights in the country [as] Muslims, as mentioned in the Qur'an and the teachings of Islam."

The MB Is a Popular Savior Frame

Another frame emerging from our analysis of Ikhwanweb.com suggested that the MB is a popular group and a savior for Egyptian society. The "The MB Is Popular" frame was not as prominent as the two previously discussed frames, but its employment was nonetheless notable. In addition to suggesting that the Brotherhood is popular and a savior for Egyptian society, Ikhwanweb .com posts also suggested that the Mubarak government is illegitimate and unpopular.

A November 22, 2010, post suggested that the ruling National Democratic Party would soon falter and that the popular Brotherhood could be there to step in in its place. The post implied that the MB is the only serious opposition to the unpopular NDP and that their maneuverings would put them in position to "attract broad support for the moment the ailing National Democratic Party (NDP) will fall." Meanwhile, a November 23, 2010, post called the MB "the most potent force against President Hosni Mubarak's ruling National Democratic Party."

Results of an informal internet news poll were published on Ikhwanweb .com on November 23, 2010. The poll results, taken from the Masrawy website, showed the Brotherhood as the most popular political group in Egypt among those polled and the NDP as deeply unpopular. MB candidates for parliament were supported by 42 percent of those polled, while NDP candidates were supported by just 16 percent. A November 23, 2010, post says that the Mubarak government is "not at all popular" in Egypt and suggests that the Brotherhood would win a free and fair election in a landslide. A November 25, 2010, post cited a Muslim Brotherhood leader's claim that the MB "would secure at least 75 [parliamentary] seats if there was no rigging." A separate November 25, 2010, post cast doubt on the legitimacy of the ruling NDP, while a November 26, 2010, post implied that the Mubarak government was illegitimate.

A November 30, 2010, editorial by an Ikhwanweb.com staff writer claimed that the MB enjoys "popular support," and a separate post published on the same day maintained that the Mubarak government's corruption had caused it to "lose its legitimacy." The December 1, 2010, post written by Haroon Siddiqui discussed the MB's widespread influence and popularity in Egypt, and a December 3, 2010, post said both that the "Egyptian population is looking to [the MB] for their next move" and that the group had experienced "increasing popularity."

In addition to describing itself as widely popular, the Muslim Brotherhood also described itself as a type of savior for Egyptians. For example, a December 2, 2010, post relied on an authority figure to proclaim the group's status as savior. The post quotes an Egyptian judge as saying that the MB's decision to boycott the second round of the parliamentary elections effectively "saves Egypt's dignity," which had been "wasted by [electoral] fraud." The post also mentioned that "[t]he MB announced that it is against fraud and aims at combatting corruption and tyranny."

A December 3, 2010, post suggested that the Brotherhood's bravery and wisdom were saving Egypt from mass civil unrest and violence. In the post, an Ikhwanweb.com staff writer wrote, "The Muslim Brotherhood's role of taking on the regime legally and politically and exposing its irregularities is vital amid the economic dissatisfaction, police brutality and torture, and public safety problems that are souring the attitudes of Egyptians." The post continued, "It could be argued that without the presence and influence of the MB, the internal situation of Egypt would be difficult to keep at a simmer, and could easily boil over in to even more violence and civil unrest."

MB Victimization

Ikhwanweb.com's coverage of the 2010 parliamentary elections also framed the Muslim Brotherhood as victims of Mubarak regime political repression. This frame dovetailed nicely with the aforementioned frames that described the elections as rigged and the Mubarak regime as brutal and authoritarian. Overall, and as noted in a November 22, 2010, post about alleged election rigging, the website suggested that the Brotherhood was the sacrificial lamb of a "regime ... bent on rigging the elections" and carrying out other abuses.

A November 23, 2010, post titled "MB Press Conference: Despite Violence and Oppression, We Will Continue" described a Muslim Brotherhood press conference and highlighted the group's status as victims of Mubarak regime violence. The post said that "the country [had] witnessed all kinds of violence and oppression against any individual remotely affiliated with the Muslim Brotherhood group." The post also called attention to alleged "arbitrary arrests, thug attacks and intimidating of" Brotherhood members and others in the political opposition and mentioned that "more than 1200 members of the [Brotherhood] have been detained since it announced it would vie for seats in parliament."

The November 23, 2010, editorial by Hamzawy discussed attempts to intimidate and harass members of the MB, while a November 26, 2010, post alluded to Egyptian court rulings calling for reinstating members of the Brotherhood and other opposition members into the parliamentary election competition. That post also described how some rulings were either overturned or ignored by the High Elections Commission as a way of dismissing "the country's strongest opposition, the Muslim Brotherhood."

A November 28, 2010, post described "systematic violence against MB candidates" and specifically detailed an alleged assassination attempt on Saad El-Katatni, a senior Brotherhood member. The post also documented other alleged government abuses carried out against members of the group. On November 30, 2010, in a post that hailed the Brotherhood's decision to participate in the elections, an Ikhwanweb.com staff interviewed a former Brotherhood member of parliament, who spoke of a sense of collective victimization. The former MP said that "the regime has excluded prominent figures of the opposition including the MB and other parties and political powers." He also said that the unprecedented political exclusion of opposition figures in Egypt "should be registered in the Guinness Book of World Records." A prominent Egyptian politician, former Minister of Foreign Affairs Abdallah Al-Ashal, was quoted on December 2, 2010: "There is a political decision [in Egypt] to exclude the MB." A December 5, 2010, post argued that Brotherhood members in both Egypt and Jordan are victims of government tyranny. The article said that "the regimes ... have both targeted the Muslim Brotherhood opposition in their parliamentary elections." The post continued, "The MB ... faced the fiercest crackdown."

The 2011 Egyptian Uprising

Of the ten events studied as part of this research, the 2011 Egyptian uprising garnered the most attention by Ikhwanweb.com. The Brotherhood's framing of the mass protests offers insights into how the group viewed its role inside Egypt, the Mubarak government, other members of Egypt's political opposition, and the West (including the United States). Importantly, there were four main objects of the Brotherhood's framing of this event: the Muslim Brotherhood itself, the Mubarak government, the West, and Egypt's protesters, whom Ikhwanweb.com considered revolutionaries.

In all, a total of 116 Ikhwanweb.com posts were devoted to the uprising from January 18, 2011, one week prior to scheduled protests, and February 12, 2011, one day following Mubarak's decision to step down from the presidency.

Initially, the Brotherhood's posts struck a supportive but cautious tone toward the planned protests, but as the protest movement generated steam, posts became more openly and bluntly supportive of the movement. Many posts seemed to address Western audiences, with the Brotherhood attempting to allay common Western fears about political Islam in general and the MB in particular.

Ten distinct frames emerged from our analysis, all centering on the four aforementioned objects: Do Not Fear the Brotherhood; Mubarak Is Evil; Revolution; Blame the West; Hope; Despair; MB as Savior; MB as a Superior Alternative to Mubarak; MB Victimization; and MB as Part of the Egyptian Fabric.

The frames emerging here represent partial continuity of frames emerging from our analysis of the 2010 parliamentary elections. Specifically, the MB Victimization and MB as Savior frames appeared in analyses of both events. Also, the MB Is Peaceful and Democratic frame continued, but as two distinct subframes subsumed by the much larger, more dominant Do Not Fear the Brotherhood frame. The previous Mubarak Is Brutal and Authoritarian subframe continued to be a subframe, but subsumed under a larger, more dominant frame—Mubarak Is Evil.

Do Not Fear the Brotherhood Frame

The Do Not Fear the Brotherhood frame emerged prominently from our analysis of MB posts about the 2011 Egyptian uprising. Overall, many Ikhwanweb.com posts appeared to address Western audiences, attempting to allay common fears about political Islam and the Muslim Brothers. Brotherhood posts differentiated the MB from Muslim extremist groups like Al-Qaeda, and described the MB as essentially peaceful, democratic, and inclusive. Specifically, the Do Not Fear the Brotherhood frame included four subframes: the MB Is Not an Extremist Group; the MB Is Peaceful; the MB Is Democratic; and the MB Is Inclusive.

The MB Is Not an Extremist Group Subframe. Ikhwanweb.com posts went to some lengths to distance the Brotherhood from Muslim groups and governments that the West considers to be extremist. For example, a February 4, 2011, post quoted Mohamed El-Baradei: "The Muslim Brotherhood has nothing to do with the Iranian movement, has nothing to do with extremism as we have seen it in Afghanistan and other places." A separate February 4, 2011, post said that "[f]ear of the Muslim Brotherhood is grossly overdone," and noted that the group had "no desire for leadership or even a place in the interim government. ... [T]he Brotherhood is the level-headed voice in Egypt." Also, a February 8, 2011, post decried America's "policy of paranoia" vis-à-vis Islamists. The post continued, "In recent times in Egypt, a large part of America's discussion and analysis has centered around whether or not it is an 'Islamic' revolution, even though there has been no word about jihad or terrorism." The post argued that "a new frame of thought is required" for examining the Brotherhood.

A February 9, 2011, post declared that the "MB denounces Al-Qaeda's call to Egypt's protesters to wage Jihad." The post implies a clear difference between Al-Qaeda and the MB, which was said to have "condemned statements by jihadist groups affiliated with Al-Qaeda." Another February 9, 2011, post suggested that one of the "impediments" to understanding the Egyptian uprising was the persistent "fear" that a successful revolution would lead to "a repressive form of Islamic rule." The same post later mentioned that the "international community is … paranoid about the Brotherhood and anything that faintly resembles 'Islam.'"

A February 10, 2011, post written by then Brotherhood member Abdel Moneim Abou el-Fotouh was even more explicit. The post was titled "Democracy Supporters Should Not Fear the Muslim Brotherhood," called the MB a "nonviolent Islamic movement," and referred to "patent falsehoods, fear mongering and propaganda … against us." Abou el-Fotouh also wrote, "Contrary to fear-mongering reports, the West and the Muslim Brotherhood are not enemies. It is a false dichotomy to post, as some alarmists are suggesting, that Egypt's choices are either the status quo … or a takeover by 'Islamic extremist.'"

Another February 10, 2011, post written by Khaled Hamza, the Ikhwanweb .com web editor, decried alleged "paranoia" surrounding the MB and said that the group has "firm stances against Al-Qaeda" and "terrorism." The post also called the Brotherhood a "much-needed moderate voice in the Islamic world." A February 11, 2011, post celebrating Mubarak's removal from power took a jab at Al-Qaeda. The post read, "The peaceful protests across Egypt have been blessed with success! Demonstrations marked by nonviolent behavior that constituted a national uprising in Egypt, to remove oppression by tyranny, have achieved more in 18 days than Al-Qaeda-like terrorism has done in decades." The post also described the MB as "the voice of moderate, insightful, peaceful Islam." A separate February 11, 2011, post written by a senior Brotherhood official said that the MB's "principles … affirm an unequivocal position against violence." A February 12, 2011, piece argued that Western "fears of a Muslim nation are unfounded."

The MB Is Peaceful Subframe. In covering the mass protests, Ikhwanweb .com regularly framed the Muslim Brotherhood as a peaceful group that applies exclusively peaceful methods of reform. In many ways, this subframe can be seen as an attempt to speak directly to Western audiences, which have sometimes conflated political Islam with violence.

In the lead-up to scheduled January 25, 2011, protests, the MB stressed peacefulness as a necessary requirement for social change. For example, a January 22, 2011, post summarized a statement released by then Brotherhood

general guide Mohamed Badie. Badie's statement said that "peaceful perseverance" would lead ultimately to "peace." Badie argued that "all Muslims
should rise and voice their dissent," emphasizing that only "peaceful and
tolerant methods" should be employed. A pair of January 23, 2011, posts
clarified the Brotherhood position on social change. One post said that the
group believes "reform and stability" can be accomplished "only through
peaceful methods." The other post noted that the group "advocates reform
only through peaceful methods."

Once the protests started, the MB consistently drew attention to the
alleged peaceful nature of the protesters, including Brotherhood protesters.
For example, a February 3, 2011, post referred to the Mubarak opposition
as "peaceful protesters" and argued that "the [Egyptian] streets remain filled
with peaceful, determined protesters." A February 4, 2011, post again referred
to "peaceful protesters" and emphasized that the MB, as part of Egypt's larger
political opposition, called for "peaceful political reform." On February 9,
2011, the MB's English-language web editor said that the "revolution is
peaceful." Another February 9, 2011, post said that the Brotherhood "continues to share their demands that a peaceful transfer of power is carried out
immediately." A February 11, 2011, post praising the uprising's apparent victory said that the Egyptian people have produced an "unprecedented peaceful,
positive and successful uprising." A February 12, 2011, post said that "[t]he
overall peaceful behavior of the protesters was based on Islamic teachings
concerning ethics and behavior."

The MB Is Democratic Subframe. Ikhwanweb.com discussed the idea
of democracy prominently in its coverage of the 2011 Egyptian uprising.
Posts generally spoke favorably of democracy, criticized the authoritarianism
of Arab states, accused Western governments of deterring democracy in the
Muslim world (something that will be discussed later), and talked about the
2011 Egyptian protest movement as a democratic one. Some posts claimed
that the Brotherhood is an essentially democratic group.

For example, a February 4, 2011, post seemed to indicate the Brotherhood's
preference for democratic forms of government. The post read, in part, "[t]he
alternative to democracy is dead end." Another February 4, 2011, post subtly
argued that the Brotherhood's understanding of Islam is consistent with
notions of citizenship, democracy, freedom, and equal rights. The post said,
"The MB will continue to call for the constitutional rights of men, women,
Muslims and Christians alike calling for a civil state based on Islamic democracy which respects the freedom of judiciary; freedom of speech; freedom
of media."

A February 9, 2011, post was even more explicit about the Brotherhood's
claimed democratic nature. Specifically, the post lamented that the "international community" consistently "fails to see the pro-democracy trend of the

Brotherhood." A February 8, 2011, post referred to the MB as representatives of "a new generation of Islamist democracy."

Several posts attempted to allay fears that the MB might attempt to monopolize Egyptian power or implement an authoritarian form of Islamic governance. For instance, a February 7, 2011, post argued that the Brotherhood does "not have a special agenda," and claimed that the group was "not seeking power or position" and would "not nominate anyone to run for presidency."

A February 9, 2011, post written by a Middle East expert, Paul Woodward, implied that the MB has more in common with secularists than with hardline Islamist governance. The post said that the group was "more interested in expressing its solidarity with its secular co-revolutionaries than its Iranian co-religionists."

A separate February 9, 2011, article, written by a senior Brotherhood official, claimed that the MB wasn't trying to take over Egypt. "Accusations that we aim to dominate or hegemonize the political system could not be further from the truth," the post read. Another February 9, 2011, post summarized an MB press conference, noting that "the MB reiterated that they are not seeking power nor do they have any intentions of fielding any of the group's members for presidency."

A February 10, 2011, post seemed to speak to Western governments and corporations concerned about the effects of the MB's possible rise to power. The post read, "The MB has consistently reiterated its firm stances regarding its position in Egypt which includes its respect for international treaties and the global economy."

A February 11, 2011, article written by a senior Brotherhood official and titled "What the Muslim Brothers Want" claimed that the MB did "not intend to take a dominant role in the forthcoming political transition."

The MB Is Inclusive Subframe. The final part of the "Do Not Fear the Brotherhood" frame—the MB Is Inclusive subframe—constituted an important part of Ikhwanweb.com's attempt to assuage fears of the group. This subframe emphasized the MB's self-proclaimed respect for all people, including non-Muslims.

A February 4, 2011, post stressed the importance of unity between Muslims and Christians in Egypt. The post, titled "Muslims and Christians United in the Battle for Tahrir Square," seemed to attempt to deflect accusations that the MB is exclusionary by implying that the group welcomes solidarity with Christians. "In the past days of unrest, as Muslims prayed in Tahrir Square during the protests, Egyptian Christians protected them from pro-Mubarak thugs in a moving scene of solidarity and humanity."

A February 5, 2011, post suggested that the MB "welcomes constructive and equal dialogue with all Egypt's political opposition and respects all sects, demanding that all be treated equally." A February 9, 2011, post documented an MB press conference, noting that the group's "major concern is the well-being of all Egyptians regardless of religion, political trend and sect." A February 10, 2011, post struck a similar tone, remarking that "the MB works openly and in cooperation with Egyptians from all walks of life, religions, sects and political leanings."

The aforementioned February 11, 2011, post, titled "What the Muslim Brothers Want," said that the MB aimed "to achieve reform and rights for all: not just for the Muslim Brotherhood, not just for Muslims, but for all Egyptians."

A February 12, 2011, post titled "The West's Debt to Egypt" praised the Egyptian uprising for having "embraced all elements of society ... [and] seeking universal values—the most important of which is freedom."

Mubarak Is Evil Frame

Throughout its coverage of the anti-Mubarak protests, the MB positioned itself as antagonistic to and opposite of the Mubarak government. Consistently, the MB suggested that Mubarak was an illegitimate, despised, and criminal ruler, unwanted by the overwhelming majority of Egyptians. This frame, which we have called "Mubarak Is Evil," was highly pervasive, and encompassed four subframes: Mubarak Is Treasonous, Mubarak Is Corrupt, Mubarak Is Brutal, and Mubarak Must Go. Some of these subframes bear resemblance to Ikhwanweb.com's coverage of the 2010 parliamentary elections, which positioned Mubarak as corrupt, brutal, authoritarian, and deeply unpopular.

Mubarak Is Treasonous Subframe. Several Ikhwanweb.com posts suggested that Mubarak was a treasonous leader, more loyal to foreign enemies of Egypt than Egypt itself. For instance, a February 2, 2011, post claimed "Mubarak has actively sought, and in agreement with our enemies, to destroy our nation internally and externally." The post continued as a sort of warning to Egyptians: "Do not let the one who is deceiving himself, thinking that he is still the president; and do not let the regime, assistants, or those who manage and control [it] from abroad, deceive you internally or externally." A separate February 2, 2011, post played on widespread Egyptian dislike for the Israeli government, suggesting that Mubarak was "favored by Israel."

A February 3, 2011, post implies that Mubarak is a friend of both Israel and the United States—also distrusted by many Egyptians—and that an Islamist government would be more antagonistic to Israeli and American interests in the region. The post read, "America and Israel fear that the post-Mubarak era would shift Egypt toward democracy and that free elections would bring the Muslim Brotherhood to power. After supporting the Egyptian dictatorship for almost 30 years, [Israel and the United States would] hate to see an Islamist government on the borders of Israel."

A February 4, 2011, post builds on the notion that Mubarak is treasonous, arguing that "the U.S. tolerated and abetted Mubarak's repressive rule for three decades because he has cooperated with U.S. strategy on issues ranging from Israel to Iran." The post also described Mubarak as a "key ally" to the United States.

Mubarak Is Corrupt Subframe. Numerous Ikhwanweb.com posts claimed that the Mubarak government was corrupt, and, specifically, guilty of stealing money from the Egyptian people. A week prior to the start of protests, on January 18, 2011, a post suggested that the government was hiding stolen wealth both inside and outside of Egypt. A January 22, 2011, post documented a statement by Brotherhood general guide Mohamed Badie, in which he encouraged "all Muslims ... [to] rise and voice their dissent against the widespread corruption" of the Mubarak government. On January 24, 2011, the MB published a post claiming that the Mubarak government was guilty of "plundering public funds." Meanwhile, a January 25, 2011, post referred to Mubarak as "the corrupt, despotic, and failing Mubarak," and a January 27, 2011, post said that "corruption is rife" in Egypt. A February 2, 2011, post referred to "the corrupt Mubarak government."

A February 6, 2011, article titled "The Mubarak Family's Wealth" claimed that the Mubarak family had embezzled billions of dollars of Egyptian wealth. Specifically, the article argued that Mubarak's son, Gamal, had amassed "17 billion dollars ... in banks in Switzerland, Germany, the U.S. and the United Kingdom." The post also claimed that Mubarak's wife, Suzanne, was also a billionaire with properties "in London, Frankfurt, Madrid, Paris, and Dubai," and that Mubarak's other son, Alaa, was also worth billions of dollars. As for Mubarak himself, the article, which called him a "corrupt dictator," claimed that he was "worth no less than 40 billion [Egyptian] pounds."

A February 7, 2011, post said that Mubarak's rule had been characterized by "corruption and dictatorship," and a February 8, 2011, post called the government a "corrupt regime." A February 9, 2011, post posited that "money that has been looted by businessmen [affiliated with the Mubarak government] is sufficient to pay off all Egypt's debts and built [sic] a strong economy." A February 10, 2011, post titled "Public Figures Demand Immediate Investigation into Mubarak's Ill-Gotten Fortune" implied that the Mubarak family had embezzled billions of dollars of Egyptian wealth. A post published just after Mubarak stepped down, on February 12, 2011, claimed to document Egyptian financial losses resulting directly from Mubarak era corruption. The post specifically claimed that the Mubarak government had been guilty of widespread tax evasion and that, overall, corruption cost "Egypt $6 billion annually."

Mubarak Is Brutal Subframe. One of the more widespread subframes of the "Mubarak Is Evil" frame suggested that Mubarak government policy was characterized by ruthless disregard for the most basic human rights. Mubarak regime brutality was highlighted by keywords noting alleged government "tyranny" and "brutality," and frequent mentions of government-perpetrated violence and political repression. In particular, Ikhwanweb.com documented cases of alleged police brutality against Egyptians participating in mass demonstrations against the government.

A post published on January 23, 2011, during the lead-up to scheduled January 25, 2011, protests, highlighted alleged government "tyranny" and noted that Muslim Brotherhood leaders had been summoned "to security headquarters" and threatened "with arrests, violence and detention" if they attended planned protests. A January 24, 2011, post described "the regime's repression and horrifying crimes against the Egyptian people especially with regard to Islamic law [and] disregard for human rights."

On January 25, 2011, Ikhwanweb.com quoted a Muslim Brotherhood leader, Saad Al-Husseini, who argued that "the reason for Egypt's suffering is due to the state of tyranny in the country." A separate January 25, 2011, post said that Mubarak's police are "known to break up protests with violence" and refers to the "police brutality" associated with Khaled Said, who is described as "a symbol of [government] torture and repression."

Once protests began on January 25, 2011, Ikhwanweb.com posts featured steady commentary on alleged government-perpetrated violence against protesters. For example, a January 26, 2011, post referred to the "brutality practiced by Egyptian authorities against tens of thousands of protesters" and noted that the government "blocked ... popular social networking site, Facebook." The post also claimed that "Egyptian police beat protesters and used live bullets" at multiple protest sites across the country. A January 27, 2011, post relied on an authority, the Arabic Network for Human Rights information (ANHR), to make the Brotherhood's point about alleged police violence. ANHR claimed that "excessive use of force was deployed" against protesters and that "Habib Al-Adli, Minister of Interior, bears the blood of them all." Another January 27, 2011, post said that Mubarak's "security forces are known for brutality." Several other posts highlighted alleged acts of police violence, including a February 2, 2011, post that claimed that "police opened fire on protesters [at one protest]" and that "security police began shooting at our brothers held as political prisoners in Abu Zaabal." The same post decried the "brutality, repression and torture that have plagued Mubarak's reign."

On February 3, 2011, Ikhwanweb.com published a review post, which referenced "Mubarak and his thugs" and claimed that the government had "acted violently" and used "water cannons, rubber bullets, tear gas canisters as well as live bullets" on peaceful protesters. A February 4, 2011, post claimed that the government had forcibly disappeared human rights activists, while a separate February 4, 2011, statement by Badie said that "[government] thugs have taken to the streets attacking peaceful protesters and raiding press and media headquarters." Badie also argued that "[t]he regime imposes only violence and does not understand the concept of mature and civilized democracy."

A February 5, 2011, post documents a statement by the Egyptian Organization for Human Rights (EOHR), which expressed its concern over the well-being of protesters and held the government responsible for violations against protesters, journalists, and human rights activists. A February 6, 2011, post documented complaints by ANHR. The post decried what it called "criminal [government] gangs [attacking] ... protesters with weapons ... [and how] the militias of the NDP and the police force were attacking and killing journalists on the streets." A post published on February 6, 2011, referred to Mubarak government "baltagies," or thugs, and claimed that they "were armed with clubs, machetes, razors, knives, or other sharp objects."

Three February 9, 2011, posts called for legal accountability for Mubarak regime figures responsible for illegal violence against Egyptian citizens. The first post called for trials for Mubarak regime officials "responsible for the bloodshed that marred the peaceful protests," while the second post highlighted a demand by ANHR for an end to impunity for "torturers." The third post, a Muslim Brotherhood press release, suggested legal accountability for Mubarak himself, while asking a rhetorical question: "Is not Mubarak personally responsible for the missing people who have been detained, tortured and killed under his regime?" On the day following Mubarak's resignation, February 12, 2011, Ikhwanweb.com published a post following the same theme of legal accountability. The post said that "Mubarak and his regime [will] ... inevitably be prosecuted," and noted that a fact-finding committee was formulated to examine alleged crimes committed during Mubarak's thirty-year rule.

Mubarak Must Go Subframe. Another pervasive subtheme suggested that Mubarak had lost his legitimacy to govern Egypt and should follow protesters' demands to step down immediately. Importantly, this subframe did not emerge until about one week into the protests. The first evidence of the "Mubarak Must Go" frame appeared in several February 2, 2011, posts, which followed a five-day gap in Ikhwanweb.com coverage. The gap may have been the result of regime pressure and restriction.

One February 2, 2011, Ikhwanweb.com article, written by senior Brotherhood member Ashraf Abdel Ghaffar, was blunt about the Brotherhood's desire to see Mubarak leave office. Abdel Ghaffar argued that Egyptians should "be wary of Mubarak's promises of reform" and continue protests "until the goal has been obtained: the end of Mubarak's reign." Apparently referring to a Mubarak speech promising reforms, the article cautioned Egyptians not to be swayed by emotional appeals. The article said, "Does [Mubarak] really believe that power still resides in his hands? Has he not heard the calls of the Egyptian people? Power lies with the people of Egypt." A separate February 2, 2011, post said that "Mubarak has to decide whether to save his country from violence and bloodshed and step down, or remain in power surrounded by disdain, anarchy and the stubbornness that seems to characterize elderly Arab rulers." Another February 2, 2011, post said that the "MB rejects Mubarak's attempt to stay on until the end of his term."

February 3, 2011, and February 4, 2011, posts continued on the same line, suggesting that the MB believed there was no room for negotiating on Mubarak's presidency. "The Muslim Brotherhood group has demanded an immediate resignation by President Hosni Mubarak and the creation of a unity government including all opposition groups," the February 3, 2011, post read. The February 4, 2011, post said that the Brotherhood "considers the regime's legitimacy as invalid and confirms that it will not engage in any dialogue until Mubarak leaves."

On February 6, 2011, the MB published a post including a list of eleven demands addressed to the Egyptian regime. The most notable demand was for Mubarak to step down. Three February 7, 2011, posts reiterated the basic demand. One post said, "Protesters have made it clear they have no intentions of compromising and insist that President Mubarak step down immediately." A second post declared, "The MB has not changed its stance for an end to President Hosni Mubarak's 30 years in power." The final February 7, 2011, post noted that the Brotherhood's "immediate priority is to ensure that President Hosni Mubarak steps down."

Several other posts from February 8, 2011, and February 9, 2011, highlighted the demand for an end to Mubarak's rule, with one February 9, 2011, post suggesting that the demand was unanimous among Egyptians. The post said, "The Muslim Brotherhood along with the whole nation is unrelenting in its demand that President Hosni Mubarak stands down immediately." A February 9, 2011, Muslim Brotherhood press release called Mubarak "the illegal president" and said, "Attempts by Mubarak to remain in power [are] not welcomed by the people, and those who are allegedly keen on his dignity as Egypt's president [should] convince him to leave for the sake of the country's supreme interests."

Other posts from February 9, 2011, and February 10, 2011, wrote of a transitional government, suggesting that Mubarak's departure may be imminent. When Mubarak surprised protesters on February 10, 2011, by announcing that he would stay on until September (2011), Ikhwanweb.com wrote, "Roars of anger rang out of Tahrir Square after Mubarak announced he would not leave until September. Protesters waved their shoes at Mubarak as a carnival-like atmosphere turned to rage."

Revolution Frame

The Muslim Brotherhood's English-language website framed Egypt's mass protest movement as a national uprising, or revolution. This frame was apparent even before the start of January 25, 2011, protests, and in spite of the fact that the MB did not officially announce their decision to participate in the protests until later. During the one-week lead-up to the scheduled January 25 protests, the Brotherhood published a number of reports drawing associations between Tunisia's Jasmine Revolution and Egypt's scheduled protest movement. These reports implied that Egyptians would, following Tunisians, successfully overthrow their government. Importantly, these posts were written in a favorable tone, suggesting that an overthrow of the Mubarak government would be a good thing for Egypt.

Posts that framed events in Egypt as a revolution tended to go beyond simple descriptions of mass protests, and, instead, explicitly describe demonstrations as a "revolution" or "uprising." Also, many of these posts claimed that the Mubarak regime was on the verge of collapse.

The "Revolution Frame" included several subframes about the revolutionaries and the Muslim Brotherhood's role in the protest movement. One subframe, "The MB Is Part of the Revolution," made clear that the MB felt it was an integral part of Egypt's national uprising. Another subframe, "Praising the Revolutionaries," included posts that described Egyptian protesters in glowing terms. Specifically, these posts described protesters as brave, patriotic, and peaceful.

Revolution Frame. A week prior to the start of protests, on January 28, 2011, Ikhwanweb.com published a post titled "Tunis in Transition." The post wrote favorably about Tunisia's uprising and implied that Egypt would benefit from similar political upheaval. On the same day, another post put forth "five demands" that Ikhwanweb.com suggested could save Egypt from a crisis and put it on a proper democratic path. Importantly, the demands were consistent with Tunisia's revolution and included abolishing the state of emergency, dissolving Egypt's current government and parliament, revising constitutional articles related to the Egyptian presidency, and running new presidential elections. Collectively, the demands seem to constitute a call for regime change in Egypt.

A January 19, 2011, post presented a type of warning to the Mubarak government and implied that Egyptian desperation could lead to a national uprising. The post said, "This is a message that should reach all officials who should begin with immediate reforms to alleviate the state of anger to [prevent] the country from going through [a] reformist revolution." The post also featured a quote from senior Brotherhood leader Sobhi Saleh, who argued that Mohamed Bu Azizi (the Tunisian man who started Tunisia's uprising by setting himself on fire) "will be a symbol for all the oppressed who lost faith in their governments to bring about any reform or change."

Other January 19, 2011, posts were more explicit about the MB's apparent expectations for Egypt's protests. One post referred to protests scheduled for January 25 as an "uprising" and indicated that many Egyptians would partake. The post also remarked, "Egypt is no less than Tunisia," an apparent suggestion that Egypt may follow Tunisia's example. Another post relied on a quote from the president of the European Commission, Romano Prodi, to make the case for an Egyptian revolution. Prodi said, "Egypt may be vulnerable to an uprising similar to Tunisia." The post included commentary from the MB's web editor, who said that the Mubarak government was guilty of "miscalculation" about "the scale of popular outrage" in Egypt. Another January 19, 2011, post, titled "Arab Democracy Now!," spoke favorably about Tunisia's revolution, cited other global democratic revolutions (including in Eastern Europe and South Africa), and lamented that democratic revolution had not yet overtaken the entire Arab region.

A January 20, 2011, post included more warnings for the Egyptian government from the Brotherhood, as well as a warning from Mohamed El-Baradei, a prominent Egyptian and former head of the United Nations' International Atomic Energy Agency. The post paraphrased El-Baradei: "the self-immolation and widespread demonstrations planned for this week are only the beginning." Another January 20, 2011, post warned of "an uprising like that which took place in Tunisia," while another January 20, 2011, post indicated that the Mubarak government would have to engage in "immediate reform" in order to prevent a Tunisia scenario. The post continued, offering up perhaps the most concise summary of Ikhwanweb.com's view of the Egyptian protests: "We believe that the reasons and motives that led to this uprising in Tunisia are exactly the same in many countries in the region in which you live, in particular in our country Egypt."

On January 21, 2011, Ikhwanweb.com included a quote from a senior Brotherhood leader: "Like the people of Tunisia, the Egyptian masses will one day say enough is enough." On January 22, 2011, a post referred to scheduled protests as a "Day of Rage" and indicated that "45,000 members of the Khaled Saeed [Facebook] group" would participate in protests, along with many other Egyptians.

A January 22, 2011, post featured a message from Badie, who indicated that Egyptian Muslims should be "prepared to sacrifice a little today for a brighter future." The post also said that Badie "highlighted that a price has to be paid and that freedom of speech will not be attained unless the people learn to fight for what is rightfully theirs."

Two days prior to the start of protests, on January 23, 2011, Ikhwanweb .com featured a statement from Badie confirming that the Brotherhood would participate in protests "in solidarity with the other political [factions]" and in spite of "threats" from the government. This statement marked a shift in the Brotherhood's official position on participation in the protests—through January 22, 2011, the group had supported the idea of the protests, but remained ambivalent about its own participation. Another January 23, 2011, post indicated that Brotherhood youth members would participate in protests—this post seemed to leave the door open for well-known Brotherhood leaders to avoid direct participation (and possible arrest) themselves.

On the morning of January 25, 2011, the official start of protests, Ikhwanweb.com published a post titled "Egypt's Day of Rage a Day of Revolution." The post indicated that Brotherhood members had "been threatened" by the government, but that the group would "refuse to be threatened" and had "encouraged their members to participate" in protests. A separate January 25, 2011, post announced that Brotherhood members active on social media had established Facebook pages titled "I'm an MB member who will demonstrate on January 25." A Brotherhood activist is quoted later in the post: "The time has come to play a leading role and join hands with the people." Another January 25, 2011, post featured a blunt title: "Egypt's Revolution—In the Shadow of Tunisia." The post said that Tunisian army officials had "persuaded" former Tunisia President Zain El-Abidine Ben Ali to step down and that Egyptian army officials may be persuaded to do "something similar" with Mubarak. This statement was hitherto the Brotherhood's most explicit call for an overthrow of the Mubarak government.

Once protests started, Ihwwanweb.com became more passionate in its support for the protests. On January 26, 2011, a post read, "Egyptians have finally decided to discard their apathy and call for change." The post said Egyptians possess "the seed for a true revolution" and have "realized the extent of their burden, and cannot be shaken and will not run away." Another January 26, 2011, post provided a minute-by-minute update of events from January 25, including documentation of specific protest sites, clashes between police and protesters, police abuses, and arrests of activists.

A January 27, 2011, post was clear that Egyptian protesters were seeking regime change. The post said, "Egyptians have taken to the streets demanding an end to the 30-year rule of President Hosni Mubarak." The same post called Mubarak a "coward" and argued that he was "surely surprised at the extent and intensity of the demonstrations." The post said Egyptian protesters demanded Mubarak's removal and declared "their hatred for his son, Gamal."

Ikhwanweb.com didn't publish any reports from January 28, 2011, to February 1, 2011. When the site resumed on February 2, 2011, it continued to frame protests as a national revolution, but also pointed to the likelihood of a Mubarak government collapse. Discussion of the likely collapse of the Mubarak regime represents the development and progression of the Revolution frame. For example, a post published on February 3, 2011, speculated that Mubarak had "left Egypt." The post went on to question Mubarak's presidential legitimacy. Another February 3, 2011, post argued that the regime had lost control over the country's vital state institutions, including the security apparatus. The post read, "Police stations became deserted leaving detectives and soldiers without any command and then they were given orders to release the prisoners. Jail breaks occurred simultaneously, ushering in a sweep of violence, theft and murder around Cairo as well as other towns and villages around Egypt. This led to panic and intimidation because of the absence of security forces. The government hoped that by experiencing the harsh realities of anarchy the people would prefer Mubarak to no stability at all. However, despite the plotting, the streets of Egypt remain filled with peaceful, determined protesters calling for Mubarak and his regime to step down."

A post on February 4, 2011, said that a "massive popular democratic revolution" with support from "virtually every sector of [the] Egyptian society" was ongoing. A celebratory post that followed Mubarak's resignation on February 11, 2011, referred to the protest movement as "the Egyptian Revolution" and said Egyptians had shown the world a "method of procuring peaceful change in countries where change is badly needed."

Despite early ambivalence about whether it would officially participate in protests, Ikhwanweb.com ultimately argued that the Brotherhood constituted an integral part of the uprising. A pair of January 27, 2011, posts made it clear that the Brotherhood wanted to be seen as part of the protest movement. One post said, "The MB ... is participating" in the protest movement, while another indicated that the MB was determined to participate in a large protest planned for January 28, 2011, which, the post said, would represent a "massive demonstration of [Egyptian] solidarity." A February 9, 2011, post said that the "Brotherhood has been with those protesters from the very start." On February 10, 2011, Ikhwanweb.com cited a senior Brotherhood official, saying, "We in the Muslim Brotherhood are taking part in the popular uprising," and a February 11, 2011, post said that the "Muslim Brotherhood speaks as part of the people."

The Egyptian Revolution frame was accompanied by many posts praising Egyptian protesters as "revolutionaries."

Praise the Revolutionaries Frame. Ikhwanweb.com regularly referred to the bravery, peacefulness, patriotism, and dignified nature of Egyptian protesters. Some posts also referred to protesters killed by the Mubarak government as "martyrs."

For example, a January 27, 2011, post said protesters carried "banners denouncing Mubarak [and] sang the national anthem, expressing their loyalty to their country." A February 2, 2011, post was extensive in its praise for Egyptian protesters: "Has Mubarak not seen the faces of the fearless young people that are braving the guns of security officers? ... My great people of Egypt, you have shown the whole world that the Egyptian people are strong can can overcome their oppressors. Egyptians have endured hardships long enough. ... Power lies with the people of Egypt; this movement is a people's movement for change and reform."

A February 3, 2011, post said that Egyptians were engaged in "peaceful protests," and posts on February 6, 2011, and February 7, 2011, both referred to fallen Egyptian protesters as "martyrs." A February 9, 2011, post said that Egyptians had "broken the barrier of fear" and were "determined to achieve their demands, regardless of the sacrifices." Another February 9, 2011, post said that Egyptians had "proven that they are not passive [and] that they deserve respect." That post also praised the "dignified manner" of protesters, who, the post said, have earned "a great deal of international sympathy and respect." A February 11, 2011, post referred to protesters as "groups of brave, sincere Egyptians."

Blame the United States Frame

Many Ikhwanweb.com posts published during Egypt's revolutionary period seemed to speak to or about the United States, striking an accusatory tone and suggesting that America was at fault for problems in Egypt and the Muslim-majority world. Posts blamed the United States for being hypocritical on the issue of democracy in the Muslim-majority world. Posts accused the U.S. government of supporting repressive, authoritarian dictators, interfering in internal foreign affairs, and not supporting democratic movements and moments in the Muslim-majority world. Importantly, some of the posts were editorials originally published elsewhere and written by political scientists or Middle East analysts.

On January 19, 2011, Ikhwanweb.com published an article by analyst Yvonne Ridley that blamed the West, including the United States, for hypocrisy, propping up dictators, and suppressing democratic movements in the Arab world. The article, which was originally published in *CounterPunch*, blames British media for ignoring the Tunisian uprising and focusing narrowly on inconveniences to British tourists.

A separate January 19, 2011, post, written by Ikhwanweb.com's web editor, blames the United States for "supporting its traditionally authoritarian allies in the region" and suppressing democracy whenever it brings Islamists to office. For example, the post said that the United States "supported a boycott of Hamas after its victory in the 2006 Palestinian elections" and supported the repression of "Islamist oppositions to avoid both the Hamas and Algeria scenarios." The article also noted that "[t]he United States has remained largely aloof during Tunisia's Jasmine Revolution" and argued that the United States prefers "'stability' over democratic change." The article also quoted a *Foreign Policy in Focus* blogger, Rob Prince, who accused the West of "hypocrisy when it comes to supporting human rights in the Middle East countries." The post also cited Professor Stephen Zunes, who argued that the United States helped create "economic chaos that precipitated the protest." Zunes also said, "Tunisia—more than almost any country in the region—has followed the dictates of Washington and the International Monetary Fund in instituting 'structural adjustment programs' in privatizing much of its economy and allowing for an unprecedented level of 'free trade.'"

On January 23, 2011, Ikhwanweb.com published an article by Middle East analyst Emad Mekay. The article, which was originally published by the Inter Press Service news agency, referred to "flawed Middle East policy in Washington." On January 26, 2011, the Brotherhood published an editorial by political scientist Shadi Hamid, originally published in *The Atlantic*. The article, titled "After Tunisia: Obama's Impossible Dilemma in Egypt," blamed the United States for inconsistency in the Middle East. Hamid noted that although the United States has long said it wanted to "liberalize" the Middle East, it has, instead, supported reactionary autocrats for the sake of preserving its interests in the region. Despite the inconsistency, Hamid acknowledged that the American government faced a dilemma regarding its position toward its long-backed Arab dictators and the rising popular dissatisfaction with those dictators' policies. Hamid said, "In the growing battle between Arab autocrats and popular oppositions, the U.S. is finding itself torn between the reliable allies it needs and the democratic reformers it wants." According to Hamid, "nowhere is the U.S. dilemma more urgent than in Egypt," which is "the largest recipient of U.S. assistance," and where thousands of people were expected to participate in massive street demonstrations calling for an end to the rule of President Hosni Mubarak, a longtime U.S. ally. Hamid argued that if the Egyptian army "decides to shoot into a crowd of unarmed protesters, it will be shooting with hardware provided by the United States."

A January 26, 2011, article critiqued the Obama administration's early reaction to the anti-Mubarak protests in Egypt. The article was written by the *Washington Post* editorial board and originally published in the *Washington Post*. The editorial board claimed that U.S. Secretary of State Hillary Clinton acted "foolishly" when she decided to throw her "weight behind the 82-year old Mr. Mubarak." The article continued, noting that the United States is "dangerously behind the pace of events in the Middle East" and that the Obama administration "failed to anticipate Tunisia's revolution." The article also said that "blind U.S. backing for Mr. Mubarak makes a political disaster in Egypt more rather than less likely. Instead of stressing the government's stability, Ms. Clinton and Mr. Obama need to begin talking about how it must change."

During the heart of anti-Mubarak protests, Ikhwanweb.com posts focused on America's alleged blind support for Arab dictators, including military funding, and buying into a program of fearmongering that could serve to increase, rather than decrease, the threat of Muslim-perpetrated terrorism.

For example, a January 27, 2011, post suggested that the United States is "not aware of the state of affairs in Egypt" and may be "determined to support the Mubarak regime regardless of its tyrannical legacy," and a February 8, 2011, post blamed the United States for adopting a hypocritical stance toward Egypt. The February 8 post argued that the United States continued "to speak about democracy" while at "the same time [favoring] Mubarak and his tyrannical police state" and accused the American administration of supporting Arab dictators "who will do anything to stay in power." The post also accused the United States of buying into anti-Islamist fearmongering, noting that "the U.S.'s obsession with the Muslim Brotherhood" could drive "its focus away from the real issues" of authoritarianism and repression and ultimately "serve to increase terrorism." A February 10, 2011, article specifically blamed the United States for sending military aid to Egypt. The post cited fifty international organizations calling on "Washington to halt aid to Cairo" and stop providing aid "to anyone who violates basic human rights." Another February 10, 2011, post accused the United States of unfairly lumping together all Islamist organizations, regardless of their individual positions on violence and terrorism, something that the post argued leads to "policies" that undermine the "moderate approach of the MB and [its] efforts to help Egyptians gain their democratic rights." The post also accused the United States of being "unsure [about] whether to support its espoused principle of democracy or manipulate the political situation to protect its own interests."

A February 12, 2011, post that followed Mubarak's resignation asked why the United States had "remained silent about [the] corruption, and the terrible violations of human rights in Egypt and the region." The post also accused the United States and other Western governments of "turning a blind eye to the torture and killing" of civilians. The post argued that "the West now bears a moral responsibility to make up for its apathy throughout the last three decades when Egyptians suffered under the U.S.-supported Mubarak regime."

Despair and Hope Frames

Despair and hope frames emerged from our close reading of Ikhwanweb .com's coverage of the 2011 Egyptian uprising. In the lead-up to planned protests, Ikhwanweb.com explained the protest movement as the product of extreme despair on the part of Egyptians. According to the website, Mubarak regime repression, corruption, and acute poverty were the root causes of Egyptian despair and frustration. Once protests took root, however, the website suggested that the nationalist uprising was a sign of hope for Egyptians.

In the lead-up to protests, Ikhwanweb.com described various self-immolation attempts by Egyptians and referenced Bu Azizi's self-immolation in Tunisia. The MB suggested that extreme despair drove all the suicide attempts. For example, a January 19, 2011, post described "continued attempts" at self-immolation by several Egyptian citizens. A senior Brotherhood official was quoted as saying, "One would only burn himself after reaching a state of despair." Another Brotherhood official, Sobhi Saleh, said that the self-immolation attempts "are simple responses by the citizens and an expression of the despair of the people."

On January 21, 2011, Ikhwanweb.com published a report describing "over 100,000 suicide attempts in 2010 by desperate [Egyptian] citizens." The report, based on a study by Egypt's Cabinet Information Centre, said that two-thirds of the attempts "were by youngsters aged between 15 and 25." The report quotes a statement by the Brotherhood, which said it "believed the immolation attempts were a desperate message against … tyranny." A January 25, 2011, post implied that despair may be the cause of a forthcoming revolution in Egypt. An MB leader was quoted in that post: "[R]evolutions are only made when there is a state of frustration, blocking freedom and stopping all attempts to achieve peaceful political reform."

As scheduled protests drew closer, Ikhwanweb.com struck a more positive tone, implying that Egypt had entered a new stage of hope. On January 25, 2011, a post said that Egyptian activists had "hope" that the protests would be "the start of significant change." Another January 25, 2011, post said that "spirts run high in Egypt as the Day of Rage wears on." The same post said that the protests represented "the beginning of a new page in Egypt's history." On January 26, 2011, a post said that "the results might be small, [but] they are promising and are leading in the right direction." On January 27, 2011, Ikhwanweb.com wrote that "the time of apathetic subservience is over and a new page in Egypt's history has been opened." The same post also said that "Tuesday's huge [protest] turnout has changed the rules of the political game in Egypt, setting the Arab world on the next step towards democracy." After Mubarak stepped down, Ikhwanweb.com wrote on February 11, 2011, that Egyptians had achieved a "reward" for their "perseverance" and, in the process, showed "the world how struggle can be translated from the hearts of Muslims, onto social media and finally, overcoming apathy and fear, taking to the streets." A February 12, 2011, post included an official statement from the Brotherhood, which "cheered each and every Egyptian, including men, women, children, Muslims and Christians describing the joyful news as a new dawn for all Egyptians free from tyranny and oppression of Mubarak and his regime."

The MB as Saviors and a Superior Alternative to Mubarak

Unsurprisingly, Ikhwanweb.com framed the Brotherhood positively, particularly when the website compared the group with the Mubarak government. Like it did in its coverage of the 2010 parliamentary elections, Ikhwanweb.com framed the MB as a Savior, and also as a superior alternative to the Mubarak regime. In particular, posts highlighted the Brotherhood's popularity and social service programs.

For instance, a January 21, 2011, post drew attention to the Brotherhood's popularity, calling it "one of the largest banned political opposition groups" in Egypt. The post also said that the MB works for "equal opportunities, justice, political participation and reform" and to "eliminate hunger, disease, and unemployment" in Egypt. On January 25, 2011, a post quoted an MB member, who said that the group would take part in scheduled January 25 protests "in order to assure the whole world that the Muslim Brotherhood is the largest political faction and will eliminate corruption."

A February 2, 2011, article highlighted the MB's social service programs and compared the group favorably to Mubarak: "A community center near the Brotherhood's headquarters provided social services beyond the capability of the corrupt Mubarak government. In some neighborhoods, the Brotherhood operated an alternative government." The post also said that the MB "became the one viable organization where those dissatisfied with the regime could take a stand." A February 6, 2011, post maintained that the Muslim Brotherhood is "keenly interested to salvage Egypt's stability," and a February 9, 2011, post argued that "[w]here the [Mubarak government] has failed Egyptians, the [MB] has helped prop up peoples' lives." The post referred specifically to the MB's growing "popularity" among Egyptians and its "network of medical, legal, social and charitable services." A separate February 9, 2011, post claimed that the "Brotherhood has been carrying out the Mubarak government's role of providing food, clothing and shelter to Egypt's impoverished masses for decades."

MB Victimization

As it had in its coverage of the 2010 parliamentary elections, Ikhwanweb .com adopted an MB Victimization frame in its coverage of the 2011 Egyptian uprising. Specifically, posts described acts of alleged anti-Brotherhood and anti-Islamist harassment and oppression carried out by the Mubarak government (and other governments) before and during the uprising.

A January 19, 2011, article provided examples of how Islamists across the Arab region—including in Egypt, Tunisia, Algeria, Jordan, and the Palestinian Territories—have faced abuses. The post documents government attempts to keep Islamists out of office, including attempts to overthrow democratically elected Islamist governments.

A January 21, 2011, post claimed that Brotherhood members had been "subjected to harassment, imprisonment, and torture" by Egypt's Mubarak government. On January 23, 2011, a post described attempts by the Mubarak government to scapegoat the MB and blame them for scheduled January 25 protests. The post noted that Brotherhood "administrative leaders have been summoned by security personnel in a failed attempt by the ruling regime to intimidate political opposition forces."

Several January 25, 2011, posts implied that the Mubarak government was harassing the Brotherhood and attempting to scapegoat its members in the lead-up to planned protests. For instance, one January 25, 2011, post implied that the Mubarak government would attempt to blame the MB for a church bombing carried out in early January 2011—the post suggested that the government had, in fact, repeatedly fabricated evidence to implicate Brotherhood members in crimes they didn't commit. The post read, "Unfortunately, we became used to seeing such things being done as [the government has] formerly fabricated charges against [Brotherhood leaders] Khairat Al-Shater, Hassan Al-Malek and the MB leaders in the last military trial." Another January 25, 2011, post cited an Amnesty International report that documented "reports of police threats to opposition members," including the Brotherhood. The post also explained that MB members had "been summoned and threatened with arrest and detention if they go ahead with plans to protest against unemployment, police abuses and corruption." A third January 25, 2011, post wrote that "leaders of the [Brotherhood's] administrative office have been summoned and warned by security officials that members of their group will be arrested if they choose to take to the streets [to protest against Mubarak]."

Some posts documented alleged historical abuses carried out against the MB. A January 27, 2011, post claimed that Mubarak had used "the Emergency Law to hound the MB members," and also that the government had "never allowed a free election, fearing the MB would win too many seats." The post also noted that "[h]uman rights activists allege that the police regularly use torture, including waterboarding, to suppress the Brotherhood." A February 7, 2011, post said the MB endured a "harsh wave of repression … [following the MB's] strong showing in the 2005 parliamentary elections." A February 9, 2011, post also decried alleged election rigging in 2005, while a separate February 9, 2011, post—an article written by a senior Brotherhood official—said the group had been "constantly targeted by some of the most brutal government measures."

During the heart of the protest movement, one post described specific acts of anti-Brotherhood repression apparently designed to quell protests. The post, published on February 4, 2011, said that "[s]ecurity forces broke into the headquarters of the Muslim Brotherhood's news website and arrested 12 journalists inside."

The MB Is a Part of the Egyptian Fabric

Ikhwanweb.com posts published during the Egyptian uprising period regularly described the Egyptian nature of the Brotherhood, framing them as an integral part of the Egyptian fabric. This frame seemed to address both Western audiences and local Egyptian audiences. On the one hand, the MB may have wanted to send a message to Western governments that they are part and parcel of the Egyptian society and would have to be accounted for in any future political relationship. On the other hand, the MB may have been attempting to allay fears inside of Egypt that the group had designs on establishing a global Islamic caliphate. The group may have desired to send a message that they, too, are Egyptian patriots, sharing the same interests and goals as the Egyptian society at large.

A February 4, 2011, post summarized a statement by Badie, noting that he stressed that the MB "welcomed dialogue with all political opposition [groups]" and that "all groups have agreed on uniting in the call for peaceful political reform that would serve Egyptians as a whole." Badie also asserted that the Egyptian uprising was "not an Islamic revolution, but [rather] an Egyptian people's revolution that included Egyptians from all sects, religions and political trends." Another February 4, 2011, post was even more explicit. The post said that the MB is an "integral part of Egyptian society and if democracy is to flourish in Egypt, the Brotherhood must be given a voice."

On February 7, 2011, Ikhwanweb.com published a post documenting an official MB statement, which asserted that group members "have not and will not withdraw any of the people's demands which are equivalent to the group's demands and [are] in the best interest of Egypt and its people." Another February 7, 2011, post summarized a separate MB statement, which said the MB "are a part of this great nation of Egypt." The post also said that "[w]e cannot separate ourselves from it and will never cease caring about it and taking responsibility for it. We have the duty to be loyal to the nation during times of prosperity, hardship, sacrifice, and redemption." The statement went on to say, "We adhere to the demands of the people and the final world will be for the people." A February 8, 2011, post included the title "We Are Part of the People Working with Them and for Them."

Several February 9, 2011, posts make the claim that the MB is a uniquely Egyptian group, and not interested in dominating politics. For example, a February 9, 2011, post went out of its way to suggest that the MB was not interested in monopolizing the Egyptian protest movement. The post again argued that the Egyptian uprising was nationalist, not Islamic. A Brotherhood member was paraphrased: "Hamza confirmed that the current revolution in Egypt is the 'People's revolution' not an Islamic one, and includes all sects, trends and religions. Egyptian men, women, children, Muslims and Christians have unified in their call for freedom and democracy, and the MB group has participated as part of the people." Another February 9, 2011, post, an op-ed written by Mohammed Khan and originally published in *Al-Jazeera*, said that "[t]he Muslim Brotherhood—whether Mubarak's regime and his backers like it or not—is part and parcel of Egyptian society." Another February 9, 2011, post was titled "This Is Egypt's Revolution, Not Ours." The post also noted that "[t]he Muslim Brotherhood ... is at the heart of Egyptian society." Later, the post said, "[W]e see ourselves as part of the fabric of Egyptian social and political life." A fourth February 9, 2011, post said that the "MB are part of the people working with them and for them."

2011 CONSTITUTIONAL REFERENDUM

Ikhwanweb.com prominently covered the March 19, 2011, Egyptian constitutional referendum. In all, a total of sixty-four posts directly addressed the referendum during our sample period—March 12, 2011, through March 26, 2011. Posts focused primarily on the remnants of the Mubarak government, the Muslim Brotherhood itself, and Egypt's democratic roadmap, including the referendum. The MB's referendum-related posts tended to reflect their basic position about Egyptian politics. Collectively, posts tended to legitimate the MB's newfound political prominence, delegitimate the ousted Mubarak government, and propagate for the Brotherhood's position on the referendum.

A total of seven frames emerged from our close reading of the posts. While two of the frames reflected new patterns of writing, most of the frames represented a continuation of patterns emerging from our analysis of the 2010 parliamentary elections and the 2011 Egyptian Revolution. The seven frames are Mubarak Is Evil, the MB Is Tolerant/Inclusive, Do Not Fear the Brotherhood, the MB Is Peaceful and Democratic, Vote Yes on the Referendum, the MB Is a Popular Savior, and Embracing the Military Roadmap. The Mubarak Is Evil frame included two subframes: Mubarak Is Corrupt and Mubarak Is Brutal.

Mubarak Is Evil Frame

Interestingly, Ikhwanweb.com remained highly interested in ousted Egyptian President Hosni Mubarak during the referendum period and continued its earlier pattern of framing the ousted president as evil, corrupt, and brutal. The attention allotted to Mubarak regime performance and specific remnants of the Mubarak government in Egyptian politics suggests that the Brotherhood remained concerned about the possibility of a political setback that could derail the revolution. All the mentions of the Mubarak government were negative, and many attempted to blame the Mubarak government for many of Egypt's problems. Two specific subframes characterized Ikhwanweb .com's discussions of Mubarak and his government: Mubarak Is Corrupt and Mubarak Is Evil.

Mubarak Is Corrupt Subframe. Numerous posts described alleged corruption by Mubarak regime officials, ultimately serving to frame the Mubarak regime as a corrupt one. For example, a March 13, 2011, post summarized an announcement by the new National Democratic Party (NDP) secretary detailing efforts to lead the party through a "cleansing." The post listed twenty allegedly corrupt members of the NDP. Another March 13, 2011, post blamed "remnants of the ousted regime" for efforts to instigate both a "counterrevolution and "sectarian strife" between Egyptian Muslims and Christians. A separate March 13, 2011, post discussed public funds allegedly stolen directly by Mubarak; posts on March 15, 2011, and March 22, 2011, both described efforts by Egypt's Prosecutor General to persuade the government of the United Kingdom to freeze the assets of the Mubarak family and members of the ousted National Democratic Party.

A March 19, 2011, post wrote that "[d]ozens of former ministers, corrupt businessmen, and highly ranked security officers have been arrested and indicted." A separate March 22, 2011, post was more specific, documenting alleged crimes of Mubarak era ministers. The post said that the politicians carried out acts of "profiteering and squandering $70 million of public funds." A March 23, 2011, post documented an opinion by the Arab Network for Human Rights that is the prerogative of Egyptians to either accept or deny "deals" offered by wealthy Mubarak era businessmen looking to "escape trial" (by paying large sums of money). The article framed the businessmen in a highly negative manner—the post described the men as "a long list of opportunists who robbed the Egyptian people." A post published on March 25, 2011, called for the "dissolution of the former ruling National Democratic Party," arguing for "the liquidation and return of all of its assets to the state." The post also argued that "the NDP was behind the corruption of political life, the deterioration of democracy, and the poor state of the economy."

Mubarak Is Brutal Subframe. Ikhwanweb.com posts about the 2011 referendum also described the Mubarak regime as brutal. On March 12, 2011, the website published an article alleging criminal behavior on the part of Mubarak era state security officers. The article noted that the former head of state security, Hassan Abdel Rahman, admitted to destroying files, while other officers were accused of "murdering peaceful protesters." The article said that "[a]ccording to Human Rights records, close to 700 Egyptians were killed [by Mubarak's State Security] in the protests." A March 14, 2011, post referenced the "thuggery of [Mubarak era] state security" and called former officers "thugs."

A March 15, 2011, post referred to investigations carried out by the High State Security Prosecutor into the event that later came to be known as the "Battle of the Camel." The post said that investigations pointed toward the Mubarak regime's involvement in orchestrating the event and claimed that Mubarak regime members were guilty "of planning and financing [the] attacks on protesters." A March 20, 2011, post also discussed alleged Mubarak government violence against peaceful protesters. The post noted that Mubarak era interior minister Habib Al-Adly "was remanded in custody on Thursday for 15 days, pending investigations into charges of ordering security forces to open fire on peaceful protesters." A March 22, 2011, post described a lawsuit against Mubarak that accused him "of being responsible for the killing of two members of the MB" and "torturing a number of MB members."

A separate March 22, 2011, post described alleged crimes committed by Mubarak era police officers, who were "accused of killing demonstrators." The post said that "Officer Wael Komy was accused of killing 37 protesters, and Motaz Askalany and Mohamed Safaan were accused of killing tens during the People's January 25 Revolution." A March 24, 2011, post documented the brutality of former Interior Minister Habib Al-Adly, accused of "aiding the murder and the attempted murder of hundreds of protesters."

The MB Is Tolerant/Inclusive Frame

During the referendum period, Ikhwanweb.com wrote extensively about the Muslim Brotherhood organization and the group's positions on Egyptian politics and society. In so doing, the website framed the MB as a tolerant and inclusive organization. This represents a consistency with Ikhwanweb.com's earlier framing of the 2011 Uprising, when Ikhwanweb.com employed a "Do Not Fear the Brotherhood" frame, which included an "MB Is Inclusive" subframe.

Specifically, referendum period posts claimed that the Brotherhood was tolerant of Christians, non-Brotherhood Egyptians, Shiite Muslims, and political opponents, including those who held different views than the MB on the referendum. Some posts mentioned that the Brotherhood's new political party would be open to non-Muslims and females. Also, and importantly, a handful of posts went beyond the Brotherhood, framing Islam and Muslims as tolerant and inclusive. Many of these posts seemed to directly address Western audiences.

On March 13, 2011, an article that was originally published in the *Christian Science Monitor* was posted to Ikhwanweb.com. The article, written by David Faris and Stacey Philbrick Yadav, claimed that Brotherhood members "were among the many Muslims who protected Christians" during the Tahrir Square protests. The post also spoke directly to the U.S. government, suggesting that the Obama administration deal directly with the Brotherhood, which was described by the authors as popular.

A separate March 13, 2011, post paraphrased Badie, who said that "Egypt belongs to all its citizens," and "the MB promotes the principles of Islam, which advocates peace, tolerance and unity regardless of religion, color, sex and creed." Another March 13, 2011, post quoted prominent Coptic Christian activist George Isaac, who "told Ikhwanweb that the revolution eased the tensions between Egypt's Muslims and the Coptic Christian minority."

Posts published on March 14, 2011, and March 15, 2011, spoke to the Brotherhood's intent to include Christians, non-Brotherhood Egyptians, and women in its new political party, the Freedom and Justice Party. The March 14 post quoted an MB leader, who said, "Non-Brothers and Copts are expected to assume leadership positions in the party." The March 15 post posited that the new Freedom and Justice Party would "not discriminate in its membership between Muslims, Christians, males and females."

A March 19, 2011, post was more subtle in its meaning. The post described an attack against liberal political leader Mohamed El-Baradei, who was pelted with stones as he attempted to vote in the referendum. Importantly, El-Baradei, whose view on the referendum opposed the Brotherhood's view, had emerged in the weeks following the revolution as a prominent rival of the MB. The March 19 post described the attack on El-Baradei, condemning it in strong language. Specifically, the attack was described as "uncivilized and disgraceful." The dedication of a post condemning an attack on a Brotherhood opponent may be seen as an attempt by the group to demonstrate their tolerance and respect for their political opposition. Another March 19, 2011, post mentioned the group's respect for opposing viewpoints. The post said that the Brotherhood "respected differing opinions" regarding the referendum and Egypt's political transition.

Several posts were dedicated to describing attempts by the Brotherhood to reach out to members of the Coptic Christian minority in Egypt. For example, a March 21, 2011, post described a friendly exchange between Badie and the Coptic Pope, noting that Badie had sent the Pope "warm wishes" and that

that the Pope responded with thanks. A March 22, 2011, post was similar—it described an MB initiative to engage with Coptic youth. A Coptic intellectual cited in the post noted that the MB had "demonstrated willingness to provide assurances to the Coptics and remove any misgivings which came about by pressure exerted by the deposed Mubarak." The same post claimed that Badie had "enjoyed a good relationship with Bishops from Beni Suef, where he grew up." On March 23, 2011, a post described an initiative proposed by Badie to meet with Christian youth groups "to clarify MB position on various issues, and [allay] ... fears of Egyptian Christians."

On March 21, 2011, Ikhwanweb.com published an extended interview with Badie, originally published in Egypt's state-run daily, *Al-Ahram*. In the interview, Badie spoke directly to both the diversity of Freedom and Justice Party membership and the larger issue of Coptic Christian minority rights in Egypt. On membership, Badie said that the "Freedom and Justice Party will be independent and its membership will be open to all Egyptians." In response to a question about whether party membership would be open to Copts, Badie said, "Party membership will be open to all and they are [all] welcome, like [prominent Christian] Rafik Habib, who [already] announced his willingness to join the party." In response to a question about the Coptic right to building churches, Badie offered a particularly emphatic response. He said, "These issues were provoked by Mubarak's regime to sow seeds of discord among people. ... Christians have equal rights like Muslims and a law must be drafted to build places of worship for all." A post published on the next day, March 22, 2011, made a similar point, noting that the MB "calls for guarantees that all Egyptians will enjoy equal rights and full citizenship."

A March 26, 2011, post included comments made by prominent Islamic thinker and Brotherhood sympathizer Mohamed Selim El-Awa. He said that he "attended four masses ... held by Egyptian Coptic Christians ... showing solidarity and national unity and did not see anyone who is tempted to look down on religion or harm national unity." El-Awa also expressed his opposition to the concept of a religious state: "We do not want such a state in our country, but we call for the establishment of a civil state in which the nation is the ultimate source of authority with equal rights and duties." It is meaningful that the Brotherhood chose to publish these comments by El-Awa, particularly because he is a prominent Islamic thinker and noted for his relatively liberal position. Importantly, the post is also significant because publishing comments made by a noted MB sympathizer suggests that the Brotherhood desired to give the impression that they were in agreement with his views.

Interestingly, one post suggested a counter-frame, that the Brotherhood is not inclusive enough toward women. An article originally published in *Egypt Independent* was posted to Ikhwanweb.com on March 19, 2011. The article focused on female members of the Brotherhood, suggesting that women members did not stand on equal footing with men. The article relied exclusively on female Brotherhood sources, all of whom were critical of the organization. The article said that "[d]espite their dedication to the group, women remain excluded from the organization's two main decision-making structures: the Shura Council ... and the Guidance Bureau." One female Brotherhood member, Shorouk al-Shawwaf, said, "I always wondered why the Guidance Bureau did not have any women." She went on to say, "A woman inside the Guidance Bureau can better understand and represent the ideas of Muslim sisters." She also noted, "Things are changing in Egypt, and I expect a change within the group so that women can be represented within the organizational structure of the Muslim Brotherhood." Inclusion of these relatively critical comments suggests that Ikhwanweb.com editors wanted to provide the impression that the MB is both open to critique and willing to highlight organizational imperfections.

One post framed the MB as tolerant of Shiite Muslims. The post, published on March 14, 2011, addressed the relationship between the Brotherhood, the Palestinian faction Hamas, and Iranian Shiite Muslims. Ikhwanweb.com wrote, "With a history of being controlled and influenced by colonialist rule and the West's dedication to divide and rule the Muslim world, the Muslim Brotherhood has sought to combat sectarianism, put the Shiite-Sunni conflict aside, and create a unified Muslim front." The post also noted that "the Muslim Brotherhood denounces sectarian differences among Muslims, arguing that unity is necessary for the Muslims to become autonomous, democratic, and free societies." The post continued, "it is necessary that there be contact between Muslim Brotherhood and Iranian clerics in order to fulfill the main purpose of Islam's mission to converge the Islamic sects as much as possible."

Do Not Fear the Brotherhood Frame

Just as it did in its framing of the 2011 Egyptian uprising, Ikhwanweb.com employed a "Do Not Fear the Brotherhood" frame in its coverage of the 2011 referendum. This frame was quite pervasive and cut through more than a dozen referendum period posts. It is likely that Ikhwanweb.com editors thought it important to attempt to assuage fears about the Brotherhood, especially given its newfound influence in Egypt's post-Mubarak society.

For example, on March 13, 2011, Ikhwanweb.com published an article that appeared originally in the *Christian Science Monitor*. The article's Western authors argued that the Brotherhood is not an extremist group and that it would not "hijack" Egypt's uprising. The MB's use of Western analysts represented a strategic attempt to legitimate the Brotherhood's perspective using outside, expert sources.

Specifically, the authors posited that "the MB "is not the bloodthirsty threat to liberty its enemies would have us believe," and that it was "unlikely" that the Brotherhood will "dominate Egypt's future." In a later section of the article, the authors attempted to further calm Western fears about the MB. They wrote, "So why do American policymakers and media analysts continue to be governed by a politics of fear? As the bogeyman of Egyptian politics, the Muslim Brotherhood has been labeled a terrorist organization, murderer of Anwar Sadat, ally of Al Qaeda, and the social equivalent of the Taliban. … The reality is that the Brotherhood renounced violence decades ago, but the party's leadership and rank-and-file alike have continued to pay the cost of this now mistaken association, so carefully perpetuated by the Mubarak regime."

A separate March 13, 2011, post built on the same theme established in the earlier March 13 article. The post claimed that "Mubarak had spread myths" about the Brotherhood, but that the revolution succeeded in eliminating "distrust" between the MB and its revolutionary allies.

A March 14, 2011, post seemed to speak directly to Western governments afraid that the MB would seek to abandon the Egypt's peace treaty with Israel. The post said, "Choosing to empathize and support the Palestinian cause does not necessarily make an individual or group a threat to the West or Western interests. The Muslim Brotherhood is clear in its position of support for Palestine but has also reiterated its committed to the treaties made by the ousted Egyptian regime regarding the peace treaty with Israel."

A March 15, 2011, post spoke to the Brotherhood's conception of the Egyptian state, suggesting that the group does not believe in a strictly religious society. The post said that "the MB does not call for a religious state but rather urges that Egypt be run as a civil state which ensures equality for all regardless of religion, sex, ideological differences and creed."

On March 15, 2011, the Brotherhood again relied on a Western expert to make a pro-Brotherhood case. The post, a long article about the Brotherhood originally published in *Foreign Affairs*, described the Brotherhood's founding, early history, historical evolution, and current structure. The article's author, Professor Carrie Wickham, argued that the MB is essentially a nonviolent, democratic organization, and that the U.S. government should seek to reach out and work with the group. Wickham wrote, portraying the Brotherhood as eager and able to seize power and impose its version of shariah on an unwilling citizenry is a caricature that exaggerates certain features of the Brotherhood while ignoring others, and underestimates the extent to which the group has changed over time."

A March 16, 2011, post addressed negative comments made about the MB by the U.S. deputy assistant secretary of state. The MB's response to the negative statement argued that using the MB as a "scarecrow" was a tactic employed by the ousted Mubarak government that the strategy would no longer work. The response suggested that the United States should abandon such an approach and, instead, embrace the MB's involvement in Egyptian politics. The post said, "Islamists in Egyptian society are diverse and ... the Brothers are ... moderate Islamists."

A pair of March 18, 2011, posts described the MB as moderates. One post said that the group is a "school of moderation" and posited that the MB "will not be hostile to the West." The other post argued that "using the Muslim Brotherhood as a scarecrow" will no longer be effective. In the March 21, 2011, post that documented an interview with Badie, the MB's general guide said, "Internally, some claimed that when the MB achieve a majority we will exclude other opposition parties." Badie argued that those adopting this approach to thinking about the Brotherhood "are ... wrongly echoing [a] fear originally concocted by Mubarak to keep his grip on power." A March 23, 2011, post noted that American secretary of state John Kerry "is not afraid of the MB's growing power in Egypt."

MB Is Peaceful and Democratic Frame

Consistent with its framing of earlier events, Ikhwanweb.com's coverage of the 2011 constitutional referendum framed the Muslim Brotherhood as a peaceful and democratic group.

On March 14, 2011, a post said that the "Brotherhood continues to commit itself to peaceful democratic change in Egypt." A March 19, 2011, post noted that the group's leadership would not force its members to vote in accordance with the official Brotherhood line. "Although the group has pushed for Yes, no pressure has been put on its members to vote in favor of the amendments," the post read.

Another March 19, 2011, post described the MB's decision to join forces with members of its opposition. The post said that the Brotherhood "agreed in principle to run a joint list with other parties in the upcoming parliamentary elections." This strategy was described as both pragmatic and as a democratic strategy for competing in elections and pushing the country forward on broad-based principles.

On March 20, 2011, Ikhwanweb.com post stressed the Brotherhood's respect for the referendum process, regardless of outcome. The post also alluded to the democratic notion of the people's will. The post said that "the [Brotherhood] was committed to respect the referendum's results, regardless of its outcome," and that the group understood that "Egyptians are the ones who have the authority to choose and no one can force the free people of Egypt to do anything."

A March 21, 2011, post made extensive references to the claimed democratic nature of the MB. The post quoted Badie as saying, "We will respect the results of the referendum and those voting no." Badie was also quoted as saying, "The Brotherhood has always stressed that they do not seek a majority and are keen on the participation of others in order to ensure real reform." The post also included a long Badie quote about the Brotherhood's vision for Egypt's presidency. Badie grounded the vision on notions of democratic rule. He said, "Egypt is full of talent, and when the politicians lay the foundation for a new political organization through which the president becomes the people's servant, with safeguards to prevent the emergence of new tyrants, he must be held accountable by the people, who have the right to choose their representatives, as the president is elected from the people and must be committed to freedom and justice, preserve their rights and care for all citizens without discrimination on the basis of race, color, gender, language, or religion."

The March 26, 2011, post that cited El Awa also alluded to basic democratic norms. El Awa was quoted as saying, "[V]oters at the ballot boxes alone will determine who is the winner in the coming period and it will not be according to party affiliation or membership in a group or a political entity." Here, again, the Brotherhood's inclusion of this sentiment on their official English language website suggests their agreement with it.

Vote Yes Frame

Ikhwanweb.com's coverage of the 2011 constitutional referendum reflected the Brotherhood's political position on the vote. Many posts framed the Brotherhood's "vote yes" position favorably, often suggesting that voting yes was a necessary and positive step in Egypt's transition to democracy.

For example, a March 14, 2011, post that included extensive comments by MB leader Essam El-Erian implied that a yes vote represented the best "way to make a transformation to democracy." Al-Arian explained the consequences of both "yes" and "no" scenarios, indicating that the yes vote's emphasis on holding parliamentary elections prior to presidential elections would prove beneficial to the nation's future. El-Arian also questioned the opposition's "vote no" position by claiming that their fears about a counter-revolution were unwarranted. El-Arian said "there is no need to worry" about such a possibility.

Another March 14, 2011, post described the voting process, painting the proposed constitutional amendments—which would be implemented in the event of a "yes" victory—favorably. In particular, the post highlighted the fact the proposed amendments would facilitate political competition and allow for the easy formation of new parties. A March 16, 2011, post documented efforts by online activists to encourage their social media followers to vote yes. The post provided a litany of reasons why voting yes would prove beneficial. The post argued that a yes vote would "safeguard Egypt from turmoil and political instability" and "challenge attempts to counter the revolution's gains."

On March 17, 2011, Ikhwanweb.com published a post that stressed the importance of voting yes in the referendum, noting that a yes vote would allow Egypt "to restart political life and hand over power to civilian rule." Another March 17, 2011, post documented an effort by students at Alexandria University to encourage people to vote "yes" on the referendum. "The MB students held numerous seminars ... with professors, teachers and students in an effort to explain the referendum and encourage [people] to participate and vote for the amendments." Another March 17, 2011, post seemed to urge Egyptians to vote yes and support the amendments to the constitution. The post read, "The Muslim Brotherhood supports the amendments, hoping for a move from a transitional period to one of stability, and their stances are being supported by more and more Egyptians." A March 18, 2011, post warned Egyptians of the consequences of voting no, which, the post claimed, "would drag citizens toward the unknown" and argued that doubts "raised about the proposed constitutional amendments ... are unjustified."

A pair of posts provided more balance, laying out pros and cons of both voting scenarios, and seemingly offering the possibility that a no vote was viable. However, both posts ultimately framed the vote yes scenario more favorably, noting that that was the MB's voting stance. One of the posts, published on March 18, 2011, provided significant balance as it laid out the pros and cons, but then alluded to the Brotherhood position and indicated that it would facilitate "a transition to power ... in the new democratic era of Egypt." The other post, published on the day of the referendum, March 19, 2011, was written in a straight-news style, providing details about the event and the voting alternatives. The post closed with a note about the MB's position and a list of some apparently positive proposals included in the amendments.

The March 21, 2011, post that detailed Badie's lengthy Al-Ahram inter-view included comments on the vote. Badie said, "[W]e will vote yes." He also made the case for holding parliamentary elections ahead of presidential elections: "Holding elections for Egypt's lower and upper houses of parlia-ment before the presidential elections [will] guarantee that the new president will not have unlimited powers."

The MB Is a Popular Savior Frame

Continuing a pattern established earlier, Ikhwanweb.com framed the MB as a popular savior for Egypt. In covering the referendum, however,

Ikhwanweb.com further developed this frame to include the suggestion—made in several posts—that the Brotherhood is a political van guard, a leader of all of Egypt's political factions.

The March 13, 2011, article by Faris and Yadav, originally published in the *Christian Science Monitor*, said that the MB "is probably better known and respected for its charitable work, which includes running hospitals, fundraising, and other activities that are vital to many in Egypt." The article also claimed that "[t]he Brotherhood probably commands the loyalty of more Egyptians than any other organized social or political force."

Another March 13, 2011, post called the Brotherhood "the most popular opposition group in Egypt," while still another March 13, 2011, post—an article by Eric Walberg and originally published in *Dissident Voice*—referred to the MB's goals to "end corruption and improve social services." That article also said that "MB support of the revolution was key to its success." A separate March 13, 2011, post detailed a proposal put forth by the MB and other actors focusing on "restoring security and stability in the Egyptian street."

A March 14, 2011, post said the MB is taking steps to "ease the burden of Egypt's unemployed" and also "the families of those who lost loved ones during the revolution." The post also quoted an MB leader as saying that the group intended to help "build the damaged infrastructure of the state's institutions." In the March 21, 2011, post that documented Badie's *Al-Ahram* interview, he implied that the Brotherhood is popular among the Egyptian electorate. He said, "We [had] the ability to compete for 448 seats [in the 2005 parliamentary elections]. If we [were] able to do this at a time of distress, it is not difficult for us to do it now." A March 23, 2011, post said, "the Muslim Brotherhood is growing in popularity as its policy of transparency renews people's confidence in their work."

A handful of posts suggested that the Brotherhood is a political van guard. These posts witnessed Brotherhood leaders attempt to take on larger leadership roles inside Egypt, sometimes providing guidance and advice for the Egyptian nation at large. For example, a March 17, 2011, post documented an initiative by the MB to unite "all opposition groups" on the basis of broad-based principles. A March 18, 2011, post, meanwhile, revolved around announcements made by Badie, who warned Egyptians that the revolution was still ongoing, noting that all necessary measures should be taken to protect and defend the uprising and its causes. Badie argued that "for the revolution to reach its full potential ... [there should be a] renewed awareness of the core values behind the revolution." Another March 18, 2011, post included statements by MB leader Khairat Al-Shater, who stressed the Brotherhood's interest in "seek[ing] consensus among the opposition forces and the country in order to bring a cultural renaissance to the nation."

Embracing the Military Roadmap Frame

Ikhwanweb.com's coverage of the 2011 constitutional referendum tended to embrace the post-uprising transition. Coverage tended to speak favorably about the military-led roadmap, suggest that revolutionary demands were being met, stand opposed to protests, and imply that the referendum itself represented a democratic step forward. This is a meaningful coverage pattern, particularly because, during this period, some revolutionary actors were more critical of the military-led transition and continued to hold small protests at Tahrir Square.

On March 13, 2011, Ikhwanweb.com published a report that quoted Coptic Christian activist George Isaac, who said, "[S]ectarianism is completely rejected now, as [are] further protests ... particularly, labor strikes will harm national security and I urge the protests to stop."

A March 15, 2011, post suggested that revolutionary demands were being met. The post alluded to the dismantling of the State Security Investigation Service, something that had been demanded during the uprising against Mubarak.

A March 19, 2011, post defended the referendum as a democratic move in line with the revolution's demands. The post cited a statement made by the Norway-based Arab-European Center for Human Rights and International Law (ESME), which was officially authorized to monitor the referendum. The statement said that allowing international organizations such as ECME to monitor the referendum "represents an unprecedented change towards democracy in Egypt's political arena."

A March 19, 2011, article written by Esam Al-Amin and originally published in *CounterPunch* argued that it was "remarkable" how much had changed in Egypt in just a few short weeks. The article hailed the "victory of the popular revolutions in Tunisia and Egypt," and claimed that "many of the demands pressed by the pro-democracy forces have been met." The post also said that Egypt's state security apparatus "has been totally dismantled and many of its officers have been arrested or investigated."

On March 23, 2011, a post was published documenting a new, repressive law ushered in by Egypt's military government. Although the post struck a mostly neutral tone, the fact that it didn't critique the law can be taken as subtle evidence of the Brotherhood's tacit agreement with it (and, by extension, the military). A March 24, 2011, post noted that Mubarak's former interior minister Habib Al Adly was charged with murder, suggesting that this represented a positive, revolutionary move. The post said, "The charges, which are a welcome change, are the first move by Egypt's military-appointed provisional government to hold former officials accountable for the killings of over 300 demonstrators." Another March 24, 2011, post spoke glowingly about the scheduled parliamentary elections, suggesting that the roadmap was on track and in line with revolutionary demands. The post read, "According to MB leader Mohsen Rady the group is keeping in mind the demands of the revolutionaries." Still another March 24, 2011, post referred to meetings between the ruling military and members of the committee to amend the constitution. The tone of the article suggested that things were on a democratic track. In particular, the post highlighted expected elections for both the upper and lower houses of parliament and presidential elections. The post said that all of these elections "will be held before the end of this year." The post also noted that, "following parliamentary and presidential elections and giving power to an elected and civil president of the state, the elected government will have to draft a new constitution within a specified period of time."

Although Ikhwanweb.com struck a favorable tone about the military roadmap, one post from March 25, 2011, was quite critical of both the roadmap and the ruling military. The post described "mass protests"—participated in by Brotherhood leaders—against a newly proposed protest law. The post suggested that the military transition was jeopardizing the revolution. The post read, "The protesters objected to the intervention by the military, stressing that the Egyptian people have sacrificed much to get rid of the Dictator Mubarak and his repressive regime, adding they are prepared again to sacrifice if their freedom is taken away from them once more."

Chapter 5

The Post-Uprising Era

Between Clashes and Parliamentary Elections

The fifth chapter textually analyzes Ikhwanweb.com coverage of four events occurring in 2011 and 2012—the 2011 Maspero Massacre, the Mohamed Mahmoud protests, the 2011 parliamentary elections, and the 2012 Port Said Massacre. The chapter analyzes coverage of the events in the order in which they occurred.

THE 2011 MASPERO MASSACRE

Ikhwanweb.com covered the 2011 Maspero Massacre sparsely. In the one week that followed the October 9–10, 2011, massacre, only eight Ikhwanweb.com posts were devoted primarily to discussing it. Interestingly, the Brotherhood's framing of the event changed only two days following the initial violence. Early coverage pinned blame on Coptic Christian protesters, while later coverage tended to attack and blame the military government, albeit cautiously. The frame change may have been the result of new information provided to Brotherhood leaders and Ikhwanweb.com web editors. Some of the website's coverage of Maspero deviated from the massacre itself, focusing instead on future Egyptian elections. Three frames emerged from our analysis of the Ikhwanweb.com coverage of the Maspero Massacre: Blaming the Protesters frame; Blaming the Military Government frame; and Elections Will Solve Egypt's Problems frame.

Blaming the Protesters Frame

Ikhwanweb.com posts published on October 9 and 10, 2011, generally blamed Coptic Christian protesters for clashes with the military. Although posts expressed sympathy with Christian victims, ultimate blame was placed on the demonstrators. The military government was defended and painted as a victim of protester aggression.

For example, an October 9, 2011, post—which reproduced a translation of a Freedom and Justice Party (FJP) official statement on the Maspero violence—sent "deep condolences" to the family members of victims. The post referred to the dead as "martyrs" and called for "urgent investigations" into the violence. Despite this apparently sympathetic tone, the post was overwhelmingly critical of protesters.

The post suggested that the protests may have been violent, and also that the transition to democracy required more patience and less protest. For example, the post said that while peaceful protests are a right for all Egyptians, protests "must be exercised within the framework of non-aggression on others and not endangering the safety and security of the homeland, citizens or institutions." The post also said that "[d]emands should be expressed in the context of the commitment to peaceful action," and that it would be wrong to "turn this right to peaceful demonstration into violent clashes and shootings." These words seem to put the onus on the protesters, not the military, and are consistent with the statements of Brotherhood figures interviewed on television in the days following the Maspero Massacre. Ikhwanweb.com's characterization is also significant in light of the fact that widely available video evidence clearly showed aggression on the part of the Egyptian military, which both opened fire on unarmed Coptic Christians and also ran over protesters with tanks.

A long October 10, 2011, post—an "appeal by the Muslim Brotherhood to all Egyptians"—similarly blamed protesters for violence. The statement was highly critical of demonstrators, noting that "this is not the right time to claim [rights via protest]." Also, the statement suggested that the Maspero protests were guided by "domestic and foreign hands endeavoring to abort the revolution and disrupt the march towards freedom, justice and democracy, even if that leads to civil war." Here, the onus was placed on the protesters, with no mention of state injustice.

The statement also defended the transitional military government, the Supreme Council of the Armed Forces (SCAF). The post read, "It is not right, nor is it the right time to seek retribution and vent anger now at this critical period in Egypt's history, not on the current transitional government which is not responsible for whatever happened in the past."

Later, the post also implied that the Muslim Brotherhood had suffered more than Egypt's Coptic Christians and would have thus been more justified in protesting. The post said that injustices were "committed [against all Egyptians] by a corrupt despot who did not respect religion and betrayed the trust of the people. ... It is no secret that the Muslim Brotherhood were subjected to many times the suffering and injustice inflicted upon others."

The tone here suggested that the Copts were wrong, in the first place, to take to the streets.

There was one notable exception to the Brotherhood's early opposition to Coptic Christian protesters and sympathy with the Egyptian military government. An October 9, 2011, post was written not about the Maspero events, but, rather, about the detention of Maikel Nabil, a prominent atheist blogger from a Coptic Christian background. The post documented the view of Brotherhood leader Mohamed Al-Biltagy, who said that he stood "in solidarity with Maikel Nabil and the thousands of civilians who have been tried and jailed by military courts." The post is significant because of its timing—it was published on the first day of the Maspero Massacre. Additionally, the post is important because it represents contentiousness and disagreement inside the Brotherhood. It was well known that Al-Biltagi adopted views that were both more critical of the ruling military and consistent with non-Islamist Egyptian revolutionaries.

Blaming the Military Government Frame

Ikhwanweb.com framing of the Maspero events changed starting on October 11, 2011. Several posts tended to blame the military government, but, importantly, Ikhwanweb.com wording was cautious. Posts avoided mentioning the military directly and bluntly pointing fingers, instead speaking vaguely about the "current government" or "remnants" of the Mubarak regime that had allegedly penetrated the Egyptian power structure. The cautious approach likely reflected the Brotherhood's desire to critique the current political environment without instigating a complete falling out with the Egyptian military.

One October 11, 2011, post was highly critical of Egyptian State Television, which had been very supportive of the Egyptian military and overwhelmingly critical of Coptic Christian protesters, whom it blamed explicitly for the violence. A Senior Member of the Freedom and Justice Party, Mohsen Rady, was quoted: "Strangely, the Maspero events unfolded directly in front of the Egyptian Television building, and all around it. Nevertheless, they never gave us the full clear picture! If these unfortunate events happened in front of any free media network, things would have been totally different, and everyone would have seen the truth." The statement seemed to express a Brotherhood frustration about being misled as the massacre and its aftermath unfolded. Rady was also reported to have said that "it is time to abolish the Ministry of Information and transform Egyptian TV into free television, away from the control of the state."

Another October 11, 2011, post—another official statement by the Freedom and Justice Party—was more explicit in placing blame on the transitional military government. The post extended "its sincere condolences to the families of all martyrs" and explained the need to allow Egyptian Christians to build churches. Importantly, the initial Maspero demonstration was held over the failure of the Egyptian government to grant church building licenses to the Coptic Christian minority. This post's emphasis on church building rights represented a shift from Ikhwanweb.com's October 9 and 10, 2011, coverage, which claimed that the time period was not appropriate for protesting or seeking individual or group rights. The Freedom and Justice Party statement read, in part, "The party emphasizes the need to remove the current tension caused by the lack of codification of unlicensed churches status, a problem planted by the previous regime. ... The FJP believes that the current and future governments need to create a timeframe for licensing these churches to prevent any further disputes and troubles. ... The FJP also believes that the right to worship is linked to every citizen's right to free thought and belief, and that it is necessary to remove all the obstacles set by authoritarian regimes in the way of implementing this human and religious right." This sympathy with Christians was also reflected in an October 16, 2011, post that documented an FJP leader's visit to a church in the governorate of Suez. That post said the FJP leader offered "condolences to the victims of the Maspero events" and "emphasized that Suez is but one family."

An October 12, 2011, post seemed to entirely exonerate Coptic Christian protesters and place direct blame for the Maspero violence on the military. The post documented the view of Dr. Rafiq Habib, a prominent Coptic Christian intellectual and noted Brotherhood sympathizer. Habib said, "Certain parties tried to take advantage of the Copts' dignified anger, causing the situation to [turn] violent the way it did. ... These parties may well be the remnants of the former regime. ... We should not underestimate those factions, which disintegrated from the large network of interests into small networks with funds and information that facilitate their interference with the stability of the country, with the help of thugs and bullies who are very much like an armed militia." He also said, "But I would rule out the possibility that the Copts have just practiced brinkmanship or tried to push matters to this sticky point to force the military to respond to their demands. It is just not their way of doing things." Although Habib referred to "remnants of the former regime" and "thugs," the implication that the military bore blame was clear, particularly given that the acts of violence—by that time broadcast widely on Egyptian satellite television—were perpetrated by uniformed members of the Egyptian military.

An October 13, 2011, post blamed the military government for setting back the Egyptian revolution and further exonerated the Coptic Christian protesters at Maspero. Specifically, the post defended the demonstrations, noting "[e]very peaceful demonstration has become vulnerable to penetration by those disaffected remnants and supporters of the former regime." The post also said, "It has now become clear to all that there are certain parties and powers betting on a scenario of total chaos" and blamed the "current government" for lacking "political will." The post also offered advice to SCAF, calling on them to stop "referring civilians to military [courts]" and to avoid turning "on its promise to lift the emergency law, because such exceptional measures are not the way to resolve the current situation."

An October 16, 2011, post—about an FJP leader visiting a church to offer condolences for the Maspero victims—featured a subtle dig at the military government. The FJP leader, Ahmad Mahmoud, "stressed that the solution to the current problem lies in establishing the 'State of Justice' in which everyone is subject to the rule of law." Given that a week had passed since the massacre and that it had become widely known that military officers committed acts of aggression, this statement's reference to "everyone" can be seen as an indirect suggestion that even military officers should be "subject to the rule of law."

Elections Will Solve Egypt's Problems Frame

Some Ikhwanweb.com posts about Maspero deviated from the primary event and delved instead into the issue of Egypt's forthcoming parliamentary elections, which had been scheduled for November 2011. The website used the Maspero tragedy as an opportunity to convince readers of the Brotherhood's vision for a complete transition to democracy, something that was represented most clearly by elections for parliament. Importantly, this framing was consistent with the Brotherhood's late 2011 political modus operandi—the group aggressively pushed for parliamentary elections, which it was expected to dominate, despite calls for a postponement by some non-Islamist political factions.

An October 10, 2011, post said that "wisdom dictates patience and prudence" and suggested that Egyptians should wait for upcoming elections and allow the democratic process to play out. The post read, "The current government is only transitional, and the general conditions of our country are uniquely chaotic and confused." It continued, "wait for a government elected by the people, which derives its legitimacy from the public, is loyal to the masses, and endeavors to meet their fair and legitimate demands." The post went on to mention voting multiple times, noting that the country was at "the eve of free elections." The post also called "upon the armed forces and the security forces to spare no effort in protecting the electoral process."

An October 11, 2011, post seemed to attempt to convince readers of the need for elections, and specifically encouraged Coptic Christians to get involved in the electoral process. The post advised Copts and other Egyptians "to form a parliament and an elected government able to provide and develop radical solutions that should over time solve the problems of the whole country, and which will shoulder the full responsibility for the construction of an independent, free and democratic country for all of its citizens."

The October 12, 2011, post documenting the views of Habib noted that he believed that elections would help solve Egypt's problems, and an October 13, 2011, post both implied that the military government was to blame for the current crisis and that democratic elections would help solve it. That post read, "This confirms that the current government is suffering from lack of political will, which requires speedy transfer of power through free elections." The post also said that "it is time to ... solve all the problems suffered by all Egyptians at the hands of the former regime. However, the solution will not come from any specific party. ... It will come when we shoulder our collective responsibility, and when all parties play their roles in society effectively [via the democratic process]."

MOHAMED MAHMOUD PROTESTS

The events of Mohamed Mahmoud, which took place from November 19 to November 21, 2011, were shorter in duration and intensity than other events addressed in this study. Ikhwanweb.com, however, devoted a total of fourteen posts to the events between November 20, 2011, and November 27, 2011.

In all, five frames emerged from our analysis of Mohamed Mahmoud–related posts: Stop Protesting frame; Elections Are the Solution frame; Condemning the Police frame; Condemning the Military Government frame; and Sympathy with the Protesters frame. The Elections Are the Solution frame is similar to the earlier "Vote Yes" frame that Ikhwanweb. com employed in its coverage of the 2011 constitutional referendum. In this case, however, the focus was only on convincing readers of the importance of holding elections, not voting in a particular direction. Also, the "Stop Protesting" frame employed in Ikhwanweb.com coverage of the Mohamed Mahmoud incidents is similar to the website's initial coverage of Maspero protests, which was characterized by a "Blame the Protesters" frame. Finally, the Condemning the Military Government frame is similar to the "Blaming the Military Government" frame employed in coverage of Maspero. Here, however, the frame represented an escalation—rather than simply blame the military government, Ikhwanweb.com issued blunt condemnations of the military government, threats that another revolution could remove them from power, implications that officials may have been guilty of murder, and suggestions that officials should be legally held to account.

Importantly, framing of the Mohamed Mahmoud events shifted early on. Early posts tended to place relatively equal blame on police and protesters, but, interestingly, later posts were much more critical of the police and military and suggested a fundamental shift in the Brotherhood's position on the Mohamed Mahmoud incidents.

Stop Protesting Frame

The Muslim Brotherhood did not participate in the Mohamed Mahmoud protests. Their English-language website's initial reaction to reports of violence was cautious. Posts tended to both blame police officers for the use of force and imply that it was wrong to protest in the first place. This framing was not very prominent—the Stop Protesting frame was only adopted in three posts, and, importantly, all three of these posts were published relatively early on.

A November 20, 2011, post described a statement by Saad El-Katatni, secretary general of the Brotherhood's Freedom and Justice Party. In the statement, Katatny condemned violence, but avoided pinning direct blame on either police or protesters. The post said that Katatny "condemned the violence witnessed in Tahrir on Saturday night stressing the people's right of expression and peacefully protesting so long as it adhered to the laws and did not obstruct public life." The second part of the statement implies that some protesters may have been guilty of either committing crimes or obstructing public life, or both. This could be seen as a subtle justification for police force. However, the statement goes on to quote Katatny offering an admonition to police: "I call on police officials to demonstrate restraint and not to follow the same measures used [by] the former regime."

Another post published on the same day—perhaps after more information was released about the events—condemned "brutal violence used by riot police," but also seemed to blame protesters, or, at least, suggest that it was wrong to protest at this time. Katatny was again quoted: "Peaceful expression of opinion is the right of one and all so long as it conforms to the law," he said, implying that some of the Mohamed Mahmoud protesters may have broken the law. The post also said that Katatny opposed "long-term occupation of the Square, describing it as 'paralyzing the city.'"

A November 21, 2011, post was highly critical of the police, but also seemed to criticize the act of protesting. The post said that the FJP calls "on all protesters who ignited the January revolution after decades of oppression to demonstrate restraint and tolerance, [and] protect public entities."

Elections Are the Solution Frame

Ikhwanweb.com used the events of Mohamed Mahmoud as an opportunity to argue the Brotherhood's position that elections and a full democratic turn could solve many of Egypt's political problems, particularly those related to police and military excesses. As we noted earlier, critics of the Brotherhood have argued that the MB's preference for elections during the transition period had more to do with the group's belief that they would win elections and be able to exert influence over Egyptian politics than it did with solving Egypt's problems.

On November 20, 2011, an Ikhwanweb.com post condemned Tahrir Square violence, but went on to emphasize the importance of holding upcoming parliamentary elections on time. The post said, "There is no reason to delay the elections and the current security situation can be controlled."

A long post published on November 21, 2011, was more explicit about the Brotherhood's vision for Egypt's transition. The post said, "We [the Freedom and Justice Party] call on all political factions and national forces to protect the revolution and its achievements ... and to work toward the upcoming parliamentary elections which will pave the way towards a civil rule, stability and the handing over of power to a [civilian] elected authority."

Several November 22, 2011, posts emphasized the importance of holding the upcoming parliamentary elections on time. One post again quoted Katatny, who said that "there is no solution to [ending] the current crisis except by adopting the just demands of [the] protesters, and [moving] ahead with parliamentary elections on time." Another post seemed to imply that the military government or figures associated with the former Mubarak regime were out to disrupt the revolution. The post said that there are "desperate attempts to disrupt or delay the handover of power to the people through parliamentary elections." A third November 22, 2011, post said that it was imperative to complete the "handover of power to [an] elected civilian authority no later than the first of July 2012" and also begin preparations for "a draft law to regulate the procedures for presidential elections." A fourth November 22, 2011, post—an article by political scientist Shadi Hamid and originally published by the Brookings Institute—made the same point. Hamid said, "All the major political forces have more or less concluded that a transfer of power to civilian leadership is necessary and urgent. ... What I do know is that delaying elections—particularly so soon before the date—would be fraught with dangers that could make the last few days look tame by comparison." A fifth November 22, 2011, post also stressed the importance of holding elections on time.

On November 24, 2011, Ikhwanweb.com published a statement by the FJP, which, again, highlighted the importance of carrying out elections at the scheduled time. The post also described the relationship between elections and the democratic process more generally.

Condemning the Police Frame

Ikhwanweb.com posts tended to place significant blame on both Egyptian police and the military. However, discussions of the police and military diverged considerably, thus warranting two separate media frames. The Condemning the Police frame was quite prominent. Posts seemed to blame police officers for excessive use of force at the Mohamed Mahmoud protest site.

For example, a November 20, 2011, post summarized a statement by Badie. The post was titled "Badie Slams Police Violence," and it explained Badie's views opposition to "the forceful ending of the peaceful protests in Tahrir and escalated assaults on individuals." Another November 20, 2011, post was perhaps even more forceful. The post, titled "FJP Condemns Brutal Violence Used by Riot Police Against Protesters," documented alleged police abuses by "thousands of riot police" who "streamed into Tahrir Square" and initiated clashes "with protesters."

A long November 21, 2011, post documenting an official statement by the FJP included strong condemnations of Egyptian police. The post alleged that "police officers and security personnel" had "abused their power while dispersing protesters ... using excessive rubber bullets and tear gas resulting in several fatalities and over 1,000 injuries."

Another November 21, 2011, post offered more blunt criticism and more detailed description of alleged police transgressions. The post was a summary of a long official statement by the MB, and included a photo of the group's general guide, Badie. The post said that "Central Security Forces brutally attacked young demonstrators occupying Tahrir Square, including wounded victims of the January 25 Revolution. ... Following those unfortunate events, we were shocked ... by an even more brutal and ferocious attack, in which Central Security Forces were joined by Military Police Forces in killing over twenty people and injuring hundreds. The so-called security forces attacked the field hospital in Tahrir and swept across the square systematically burning the tents and personal property of young people in horrendous scenes of horror witnessed and watched by the Egyptian public on TV screens, with security elements dragging the bodies of martyrs on the streets and dropping them over piles of garbage."

The post also described the use of violence against protesters as a "heinous crime," and included what amounted to one of the strongest condemnations of violence from an Islamic perspective. The post used a well-known verse from the fifth chapter of the Qur'an that suggests that killing one person is akin to killing all of humanity. Use of this verse in this context implies that the Brotherhood viewed Mohamed Mahmoud violence as tantamount to mass murder (committed by police against civilian protesters). Later in the post, the

MB quoted another Qur'anic verse that condemns unjustifiable killings. That verse read, "But whoever kills a believer—his recompense is Hell, wherein he will abide eternally, and Allah has become angry with him and has cursed him and has prepared for him a great punishment."

A November 22, 2011, post summarized another FJP statement regarding the events of Mohamed Mahmoud. In the post, Ikhwanweb.com said that the nation's "strife" had been "sparked by the Interior Minister," leaving "lawlessness [to] prevail in many governorates, while striking demonstrations with an iron fist."

Condemning the Military Government Frame

The Condemning the Military Government frame was the most prominent of all the frames identified in Ikhwanweb.com's coverage of the Mohamed Mahmoud incidents. The frame was complex and included several subframes. Overall, this frame served to rebuke Egypt's Supreme Council of the Armed Forces (SCAF) and cast doubts about their political legitimacy. It is important to note, however, that Ikhwanweb.com's framing of the military was relatively cautious. Although the military government (SCAF) was called out directly in a number of instances, most posts fell short of doing that. Most posts offered only indirect criticism of the military, and, instead, focused on other areas of the Egyptian government. This may have been part of a Brotherhood strategy to avoid escalating the already-present rift between them and the military. The Brotherhood's relatively cautious approach, however, can be criticized as a type of subtle acquiescence to the status quo. Indeed, this is what many of Egypt's liberal revolutionaries accused the Brotherhood of. It is also important to note that the Brotherhood failed to participate in the Mohamed Mahmoud protests. From the perspective of many of the liberal protest participants, the Brotherhood's unwillingness to participate or help on the ground equated to a type of revolutionary betrayal.

In all, the Condemning the Military Government frame included three subframes: the Denouncing Military Governance subframe; the Counterrevolution subframe; and the Hold Authorities to Account subframe.

The Denouncing Military Governance Subframe. Ikhwanweb.com blamed the military government for mismanaging the country during the transition. A November 21, 2011, post blamed police for violence against protesters, but also placed ultimate responsibility on the military government. The post said, "The government must issue an apology to the Egyptian people in general and the protesters in particular." Another November 21, 2011, post called out the military government for its continued use of military trials for civilians. The post said, "It is without a doubt that these military trials trigger angry responses from the people."

Another November 21, 2011, post placed ultimate blame for violence on the military government. The post's title read "MB Holds SCAF Responsible for Violence." The post went on to say that the Brotherhood "holds [the military] responsible for all that happened and calls upon it to stop the killing and the aggression against the demonstrators everywhere immediately, without delays and withdraw all troops, vehicles and equipment."

A November 24, 2011, post seemed to directly address Egypt's military government. The post implied that the military rulers should soon hand over power to elected civilians and seemed to blame it for intentionally sowing strife in Egypt. The post was titled "FJP Calls for Speedy Handover of Power to Elected Civilians." The post accused state authorities of using excessive violence as a matter of policy and said that the government had knowledge that violence was carried out against protesters by "other unknown parties undisclosed by SCAF," which, the post said, had allowed "third parties to add fuel to the strife [in Egypt]." A November 27, 2011, post included a statement by Badie and seemed to echo similar sentiments. Badie was quoted as saying, "There are hidden hands that spark the fires and ignite the violence. ... Those are known by the Military Council (SCAF)." The post also implied that the military government was ultimately "responsible for plotting the murderous events of Tahrir Square, Imbaba and Maspero in Cairo, so Egypt would not reap the fruits of its revolution." The post also said that Badie had "advised the military to close Mohamed Mahmoud Street. However, SCAF's 'too little, too late' action inflamed the situation even more. With harrowing wounds still bleeding, people started killing each other, although we did warn against extreme actions and against dealing with protests with excessive force." Badie also said critiqued the military government's performance more generally and said that "the people's confidence is running out."

The Counterrevolution Subframe. As time elapsed after the initial Mohamed Mahmoud clashes, Ikhwanweb.com expressed increasing frustration with the military government. Several posts suggested that the military government was not on board with Egypt's democratic uprising and that it was, rather, staging a counterrevolution. Some of these posts compared the tactics of the military government with those of the ousted Mubarak government.

A November 20, 2011, post said that government methods were "reminding people of methods used during [the] ousted Mubarak's reign." A November 21, 2011, post said government force was "reminiscent of the former regime's methods." The same post said that Egyptians should "be aware [of] those who aim at countering the revolution and its achievements."

Another November 21, 2011, post alluded to a press release issued by a "movement" of Brotherhood-affiliated professors calling themselves "Academics for Reform." The group called on Egyptian authorities to end military trials against civilians and compared the suffering of Egyptians during the military-led transition to their suffering "during the reign of the former regime." The group of academics also expressed its opposition to "the continuation of [patterns of injustice and oppression] which were present during the [time of the] former regime. These measures are repressive, inhumane and unjustified, and are a complete violation of the constitution. ... The movement emphasized the need to respect the rights and freedoms of citizens within the framework of peaceful means." The movement also called on the military "to respond to the people and respect their will."

A November 22, 2011, post implied that elements within the military government were attempting to delay the transfer of power to civilians, and also to "spread chaos throughout the homeland, and to distort the great Egyptian revolution." Later, the post appeared to cautiously implicate the ruling government in a conspiracy to undermine Egypt's democratic move forward. Although not mentioning the military directly, Ikhwanweb.com referenced the "security services," which included the military, and which were under the direct control of the military government. The post said, "Many keenly interested parties have conspired to derail the revolution and block the Egyptian people's march towards its objectives to build a sound democratic regime. Those include the remnants of the former regime, the security services, as well as domestic, regional and international stakeholders, who do not want ... independence, freedom or democracy [for Egypt]."

Another November 22, 2011, post described "a plot to cause chaos and use it as an excuse to deprive the people of the benefits of democracy and further delay the handover of power from the military to an elected civilian authority." On November 27, 2011, Ikhwanweb.com published a post summarizing the views of Badie. The post was titled, in part, "Sovereignty Is of the Egyptian People." Badie's remarks can be seen as being addressed to Egypt's military rulers. He was quoted in the post: "[T]he bullying, violence, arson, banditry and other events are intended to disrupt and derail the democratic movement in Egypt, so it would never reach its destination or achieve its goal of restoring the right to the Egyptian people to freedom and dignity. ... The fate of those who plot against Egypt and its people is that their endeavors will badly backfire, true to the meaning: 'Evil scheming falls upon those who scheme it' (see Quranic Chapter 25)."

While suggesting that a counterrevolution was being attempted in Egypt, Ikhwanweb.com also included threats to those parties involved in the alleged counterrevolution. For instance, a November 21, 2011, post was titled "MB Holds SCAF Responsible for Violence, Threatens People Can Revolt Again." The post can be seen as an apparent threat to the military government that there could be another revolution in Egypt if state violence doesn't end. Another November 21, 2011, post was titled, in part, "MB Warns Arab

Dictators: People Always Prevail." The post, which represented another official statement by the MB, included a veiled message to all Arab governments, including the Egypt's ruling military government, that the people's will would eventually prevail in all circumstances. The statement warned Arab rulers that the consequences of their corruption would haunt them. "History has proven that the people's will has always and will always prevail and justice will definitely be served," the post read.

The Hold Authorities to Account Subframe. Several Ikhwanweb. com posts published during the Mohamed Mahmoud period suggested that Egyptian authorities responsible for crimes should be held to account. The military government was implicated by the fact that they were running the country at the time, something that was made clear in more than one post.

A November 20, 2011, post said that Badie called for "an immediate and just investigation" into state-perpetrated violence against protesters. A November 21, 2011, post clearly indicted the military government, although it did not explicitly place primary blame for violence on the military. It read, "SCAF is governing the country, and therefore responsible for investigating the crimes committed against protesters and bringing perpetrators to justice." The post also said that the FJP called on "all responsible" for violations to be referred "to court immediately."

A post published on November 22, 2011, included an official statement by the MB's secretary general Saad Katatni, who called for the "withdrawal of forces arrayed against the protesters and immediate trials for all those who caused death of demonstrators." Another November 22, 2011, post was similar in tone. It noted that "certain parties are intent on igniting the situation in Egypt's Tahrir Square by attacking the demonstrators for three days running, with dozens dead and thousands inured. We therefore call for the rapid persecution of all those who caused the heinous crimes that took place and were reported to the Attorney General." A third November 22, 2011, post alluded to a meeting held between the FJP chairman, Mohamed Morsi, and the army chief of staff, Sami Annan, after which a joint statement was issued "announcing the start of the investigation with all those accused or suspected of killing martyrs, paying compensation to the families of martyrs and the injured, and the release of those arrested in the recent Tahrir Square events."

A fourth November 22, 2011, post documented an official statement put out by the Muslim Brotherhood. The statement included several MB demands, some of which directly implicated the government of Prime Minister Essam Sharaf, who was appointed directly by the military. Specifically, demands included "[a]cceptance of the resignation of Essam Sharaf's government … fast-tracking trials of all those officers and officials suspected of ordering or carrying out the killing and wounding of citizens … ridding the Ministry of Interior of officers who hate and deride the great Egyptian people … rapid compensation for the families of the martyrs and the injured and ensur[ing] their treatment at the expense of the state ... immediate unequivocal apology to the Egyptian people for the crimes committed and the violation of their rights, and for the tens of thousands of fallen martyrs and wounded during the past three days."

A November 24, 2011, post also called for prosecutions for officers guilty of crimes. The post urged the "riot police to withdraw their forces immediately to avoid further casualties ... [and] the immediate prosecution of all involved in the killing incidents, and compensation paid to families of martyrs killed and treatment for those injured ... at the expense of the state."

Sympathy with the Protesters Frame

As noted earlier, Ikhwanweb.com's initial reporting about the Mohamed Mahmoud events was relatively critical of the protesters, placing blame on them for protesting in the first place. However, as time elapsed, and, perhaps, as new information became available to the Muslim Brotherhood, Ikhwanweb.com reporting became more sympathetic to the protesters, thus warranting a "Sympathy with the Protesters" frame. Posts referred to the protesters as "peaceful" and to those who lost their lives as "martyrs." Posts also suggested that the protesters' cause was just.

A November 21, 2011, post referred to the "bodies of the martyrs." Meanwhile, a November 22, 2011, post said, "the blood of the martyrs will not be lost—but will continue to be a curse on the heads of those who contributed to the bloody events." Another November 22, 2011, post expressed sympathy with the cause and struggle of the Mohamed Mahmoud protesters. That post read, "The young people who have been incensed by scenes of brutal attacks by security and military police forces on the protesters and rushed to Tahrir Square to support and join the demonstrators, are purely patriotic youths and sincere citizens." A November 24, 2011, post called Mohamed Mahmoud demonstrators "peaceful protesters" and again referred to those who had been killed as "martyrs."

2011 PARLIAMENTARY ELECTIONS

Our research examined two weeks of Ikhwanweb.com coverage of Egypt's 2011 parliamentary elections, which were carried out over multiple rounds and approximately six weeks in total (from November 28, 2011, through January 11, 2012). Specifically, we analyzed the one-week lead-up to the elections (from November 22, 2011, through November 28, 2011) and the one-week period immediately following the elections (from January 11,

2012, through January 17, 2012). A total of twenty-eight posts about the 2011 parliamentary elections were found and studied.

During the two weeks in question, the Brotherhood's English-language website allotted significant coverage of the parliamentary elections and their consequences for Egypt. Overall, the MB's coverage seemed to attempt to grant democratic and revolutionary legitimacy to the electoral process, paint the Brotherhood as an inclusive sociopolitical movement, and warn Egyptians about a possible counterrevolution. All of these emphases warranted frames, which we will return to after describing other less-prominent aspects of Ikhwanweb.com's coverage of the elections.

Some of the less-prominent, but nonetheless important, aspects of Ikhwanweb.com's coverage of the parliamentary elections focused on the Egyptian military. The website didn't take a clear position vis-à-vis Egypt's armed forces—some posts praised the military for carrying out the elections and overseeing what was described as a "free and fair" electoral process, but other posts discussed alleged military violations and seemed to warn Egyptians of the consequences of prolonged military rule. For example, several posts explicitly stated that the military should stay out of Egyptian politics and return to its barracks.

Additionally, some Ikhwanweb.com posts published during the parliamentary election period were devoted to defending the Brotherhood against allegations leveled against them in Egyptian media. Several different posts criticized Egyptian media outlets for their alleged lack of professionalism, inaccuracies, and anti-Brotherhood bias. Interestingly, several Ikhwanweb .com posts published during the election period praised and glorified the "martyrs" of the revolution, with Brotherhood leaders often quoted as desiring to both honor and avenge their deaths and compensate their families. This is interesting, and arguably dovetails with the Brotherhood's attempt to paint the electoral process as legitimate and consistent with Egypt's revolutionary objectives.

Three dominant frames emerged from our analysis of Ikhwanweb.com coverage of the 2011 parliamentary elections: The Elections Represent a Democratic Solution; the MB Is Inclusive; and Beware of a Possible Counterrevolution.

These framing patterns are significant, particularly in light of criticisms from the April 6 Movement, Mohamed El-Baradei, and other Egyptian non-Islamists that the parliamentary elections were ill-timed, politically counterproductive, and inconsistent with Egypt's revolutionary objectives and trajectory. The framing patterns are also important because the Brotherhood had been repeatedly accused of being an exclusive clique and attempting to monopolize Egypt's political scene.

In late 2011 and early 2012, El-Baradei, the April 6 Movement, and other mainstream Egyptian political forces accused the Brotherhood of propping up the parliamentary election process simply as a means to acquire political power—the MB was widely viewed as the most organized political group in Egypt, and, thus, the most likely to directly benefit from the holding of elections. Importantly, El-Baradei and others believed that writing a new Egyptian constitution should have taken precedence over holding parliamentary elections. Given this larger context—which includes the Brotherhood's basic position that holding elections was necessary, and that a constitution should only be written after the election of a civilian government—it is perhaps unsurprising that Ikhwanweb.com went to some lengths to legitimate the elections, the Freedom and Justice Party (FJP)'s overwhelming victory, and the MB's position in Egyptian society.

The Elections Represent a Democratic Solution Frame

An Elections Represent a Democratic Solution frame emerged from our analysis of Ikhwanweb.com coverage of the 2011 parliamentary elections. The frame was highly prominent and featured a wide array of subframes: Go Vote; Elections Are a Solution to Egypt's Problems; The Elections Are Legitimate; The Elections Ensure that the Egyptian People Will Be the Source of Political Power; and the MB Are Legitimate Representatives of the Egyptian People.

The Go Vote Subframe. In the lead-up to the elections, Ikhwanweb.com featured posts that appeared to attempt to encourage Egyptians to show up in large numbers at the polls. Given the political contestation that existed about whether or not the elections were the best course for Egypt's revolutionary moment, these posts are significant. Posts did not attempt to encourage Egyptians to vote in a particular direction, but regular updates about FJP candidates made it clear that Ikhwanweb.com desired Egyptians to vote for FJP candidates.

Several posts published on November 26, 2011, encouraged Egyptians to vote in the elections. For example, one post documented a statement by Badie encouraging Egyptians to vote. The post said that Badie "called on all Egyptians to take to the polls and practice their constitutional right in freely and safely choosing their representative in parliament. Badie explicitly related the voting process to Egypt's uprising. He was quoted as saying, "Protect the revolution and its achievements. ... Everyone must go and take part and choose with integrity their representative in parliament."

Another November 26, 2011, post featured a statement by Katatni, who urged "the Egyptian people to participate effectively in parliamentary elections." He "emphasized the importance of each vote" and indicated that the elections would have ramifications for "Egypt's future." A third

November 26, 2011, post included a statement from Morsi, who, at that time, was serving as the FJP chairman. The post said that Morsi "called on all Egyptians to take to the polls and cast their votes in the upcoming historic parliamentary elections." On the first day of voting, November 28, 2011, Ikhwanweb.com published a post that again encouraged Egyptians to vote. The post said that Egypt's democratic process required "the Egyptian public, with all its constituents, sectors and political currents to partake in this new experience, watched closely by the whole world."

Elections Are a Solution to Egypt's Problems Subframe. Another subframe suggested that the elections, in and of themselves, would ensure that at least some of Egypt's problems would be solved. Some posts implied that the elections would help bring about a democratic polity and that democracy would serve Egypt well.

For example, a November 28, 2011, post said that "the electoral process is going smoothly, which ensures the restoration of a civil state based on democracy." Another November 28, 2011, post quoted Katatni: "We regard these elections as a blessed portal through which Egypt shall cross safely to democracy." Another November 28, 2011, post quoted Morsi describing the elections as a "tremendous democratic entitlement."

This subframe continued after the elections. On January 12, 2012, a post was published that suggested that Egypt's "elected representatives" would help build "Egypt's future under the umbrella of democracy on the basis of parliamentary legitimacy and national consensus." A January 14, 2012, post argued that the election results would affect "democratic change and [help Egypt] achieve stability, security and rejuvenation ... [and] that this change should be a role model for all countries of the region." On January 16, 2012, a profile of Katatny, the FJP's nominee for parliament chairman, was published. The post stated, "Under the new parliament, FJP MPs hope that Egypt's glory will be restored and it will once again rise and be a leading nation in the region and the world."

The Elections Are Legitimate Subframe. Immediately following the elections, in January 2012, Ikhwanweb.com featured a number of posts alluding to the legitimacy of the elections. This subframe may be seen as a response to those Egyptian political factions that opposed the elections and complained that they were characterized by serious violations. The Brotherhood's emphasis on the alleged democratic legitimacy of the elections is significant, particularly in light of the fact that their Freedom and Justice Party dominated the elections. In effect, this subframe amounts to an argument that the newly elected FJP members of parliament are legitimate representatives of the Egyptian people.

Several January 12, 2012, posts framed the elections as legitimate. One post used an American authority figure—Assistant Secretary of State William

Burns—to confirm that the Egyptian parliamentary elections were "clearly free and fair" and that the FJP, having secured many votes in the elections, were rightful representatives of the Egyptian people. The post said that Burns indicated that the United States "welcomes the outcome and respects the choice of the Egyptian people." Another January 12, 2012, post was matter-of-fact in its characterization of the elections as "free and fair." The post applied this description in two separate places. A third January 12, 2012, post documented a meeting between Morsi and former American president Jimmy Carter, who described the elections as democratic. The post indicated that the Carter International Foundation "monitored and analyzed the electoral processes in eighty-seven different parts of the world, and that it can therefore whole-heartedly confirm the integrity of the electoral process in Egypt and its compliance with international standards of transparency and fairness."

A January 15, 2012, post pointed to the FJP's "celebration of its first electoral experience that is truly free from interventions and fraud, with tremendous, effective and positive participation in the election re-runs and runoffs." A January 16, 2012, post quoted Morsi: "There is no doubt that the parliamentary election results were expressive of all Egyptians and their free will."

People Are the Source of Power Subframe. Another subframe, "People Are the Source of Power," suggested that the elections were ultimately democratic because they would ensure that political power would be handed over to the Egyptian people.

A November 22, 2011, post alluded to the Egyptian peoples' "[receiving] of power," while a November 26, 2011, post said that the elections would ensure that Egyptians would become the "source of legitimate power." This phrase may be seen as implying that undemocratic leaders are illegitimate, and it may also be seen as a message to both the previous Mubarak government and SCAF.

A November 28, 2011, post quoted Katatni, who praised "the transfer of power to the Egyptian people," while a separate post published on the same day quoted Morsi, who referred to "the democratic handover of power to an elected civilian authority that expresses the Egyptian people as a whole."

This framing trend continued into the period immediately following the elections, in January 2012. A January 11, 2012, post praised Egyptians for turning out to vote in large numbers, and indicated that the turnout was a confirmation of the Egyptian peoples' "determination to contribute in the making and shaping of their future." A January 14, 2012, post highlighted a meeting between Badie and Carter. The post said that Badie indicated that the elections "reaffirmed that this is the era of Popular Sovereignty ... and expressed hope that foreign countries, especially the United States, shall respect the will of the people."

A January 16, 2012, post spoke of both the parliamentary elections and Egypt's upcoming constitution-writing process as two important components of Egypt's new democracy, and that, like the elections, the constitution would reflect the fact that Egyptian citizens are the ultimate source of Egypt's political power. The post said that Morsi said that the upcoming constitution "should be reflective of the desire, the choice and the will of all the Egyptian people."

The MB Are Legitimate Representatives of Egyptians. The final subframe in the "The Elections Represent a Democratic Solution" frame represented the most explicit attempt to describe the Brotherhood as Egypt's new political leaders and to directly frame them as key players in the unfolding democratic process.

For example, on January 12, 2012, a post included an official press release by the MB in which the group expressed its "appreciation of [the] trust given by the Egyptian people to FJP candidates." In the press release, the group "extend[ed] [its] sincere thanks and gratitude to the Egyptian people, and … [its] commitment … to build together the future of modern Egypt which aspires to freedom, justice, dignity, democracy and stability."

A pair of posts relied on meetings with Carter, an external authority figure, to declare the Muslim Brotherhood's legitimacy. A January 12, 2012, post—the one that described the meeting between Morsi and Carter—highlighted the FJP's new position of leadership. The post said that Carter congratulated Morsi on "the FJP's leading position in [the parliamentary elections'] race … and on the results achieved by the party, pointing out that there is international consensus to respect these results which reflect the Egyptian people's desires and choices." The January 14, 2012, post that described a meeting between Carter and Badie included the headline, "Former U.S. President Jimmy Carter … 'I recognize Egyptian People's Love for the Muslim Brotherhood." The body of the post said that "Carter congratulated the Muslim Brotherhood on the legislative elections results, stressing that he's come to recognize the love of the Egyptian people for the Muslim Brotherhood as a result of their sacrifices and their interaction with all people in society."

A January 17, 2012, post said that the British ambassador to Cairo, James Watt, "congratulated the FJP on its lead in the parliamentary elections, highlighting that the British government was working on sustaining bi-lateral relations through reinforcing Egypt's economic sector."

The MB Is Inclusive Frame

In a continuation of a pattern established in its earlier coverage of other events, Ikhwanweb.com described the Muslim Brotherhood as an inclusive and tolerant group that is open to political collaboration with other Egyptian political and religious factions. Interestingly, November 2011 posts did not employ an "MB Is Inclusive" frame—all evidence of this frame came from posts published in January, immediately following the elections. Given the timing, then, in one sense, evidence of this frame can be seen as an attempt by Ikhwanweb.com to allay Egyptian fears about a possible Brotherhood take-over of Egyptian politics. Many of the posts relied on statements by Morsi, the FJP chairman, to drive home messages of inclusiveness.

A January 12, 2012, post documented a meeting between Badie and Coptic Christian Pope Shenouda III. The meeting was described as "warm" and "cordial" and having been "infused with patriotic spirit and determination to safeguard Egypt's future." The post also suggested the MB was committed to "[n]ational consensus to serve and nurture all components of this nation, without dominance, hegemony, exclusion, discrimination or bias."

Another January 12, 2012, post cited Morsi as saying "the FJP believes that leadership of Egypt during this stage cannot be undertaken by any single faction, political party or stakeholder along, and that consensus between all political parties, stakeholders and civil society organizations is essential for Egypt to cross the current transitional phase." Morsi was also reported to have alluded to the importance of involving "people from across the entire spectrum ... in drafting the next constitution, which is an agreement between the people and the government, and therefore it must be based on definite consensus and solid agreement."

On January 15, 2012, a post again cited Morsi, who stressed "the import-ance of cooperation among all segments of society." A January 16, 2012, post again sourced Morsi, who said that the FJP would "work with all political parties, forces and stakeholders represented in Parliament in order to unify efforts to safely take Egypt across this critical transitional phase."

On January 16, 2012, Ikhwanweb.com published a post documenting a meeting between Morsi and the German assistant minister of foreign affairs. The post went to some lengths to describe the FJP's claimed inclusiveness. The post said that, in the meeting, Morsi "stressed that cooperation, con-sensus and coordination between the parties during the transitional period will undoubtedly be more effective than focusing on differences." The post also said that Morsi highlighted the significance of cooperation among "spectrums in the community [that will] be represented in [the] Constituent Assembly." The post also said that Morsi argued that his party "is keen that all of Egypt's differing sectors will be involved in this process, including both parliamentarians and non-parliamentarians, and will include members from the judiciary, army, police, in addition to workers and farmers ... Muslims, Christians, trade union members, youths, university professors, and men and women will all be represented so that the new constitution be reflective of the people's equal interests."

A January 16, 2012, post was headlined, in part, by the phrase, "New Parliament Formation Will Be All-Inclusive." The post quoted Morsi as saying, "We have agreed to translate the clear will of the people in the composition of Parliament without exempting anyone or excluding any party." A January 17, 2012, post again quoted Morsi: "It is important all political parties coordinate in order to get through this crucial period and end the transition smoothly."

A separate January 17, 2012, post documented a statement released by a number of political parties, including the FJP. The post said that "[t]he statement highlighted the importance of coordination among all parties represented in the PA for formation of committee offices."

Beware of Electoral Fraud / Counterrevolution Frame

Ikhwanweb.com quite obviously viewed the FJP as the favorite to sweep the parliamentary elections. Perhaps unsurprisingly, especially given Egypt's history of electoral fraud, the website seemed to warn Egyptians of possible transgressions. The website also subtly warned against a possible counterrevolution that would reverse the gains made by Egyptians in the post-Mubarak era.

For example, a November 26, 2011, post cited Katatni and seemed to direct a message to Egypt's security forces. The post called on the security forces to safeguard voting stations and thereby "contribute to healthy democratic elections that reflect the will of the Egyptian people." This post seemed to reflect a fear that the elections could somehow be tampered with. On November 28, 2011, a post said that Katatni called on Egyptians to "defend their right to peaceful transition of power by participating in the elections positively and effectively, to protect ballot boxes." Another November 28, 2011, post cited Morsi, who was said to have "pointed out that popular control and high attendance at polling stations are the best guarantees for the integrity of the electoral process ... and that full judicial supervision also helps, and so does follow-up by civil society organizations and the media."

Dovetailing with warnings against possible electoral fraud were warnings against a possible counterrevolution. A November 22, 2011, post seemed to be directed at Egypt's armed forces. After clearly stating that SCAF should "hand over power to civilian representatives" and "return to their barracks" the post warned of a possible counterrevolution. The post said that "the FJP expects more than SCAF apologies and consolations: immediate action to reveal all the facts about invisible hands ... followed by trials for the crimes they committed, especially in the recent events, and compensation to be paid quickly to the injured and the families of the martyrs." The use of the phrase "invisible hands" and references to crimes committed against protesters suggests a counterrevolution frame, and it can be argued that this represented a subtle accusation against SCAF itself.

On November 28, 2011, Ikhwanweb.com seemed to implicate some Egyptian media outlets (and their owners) in a possible counterrevolution. The post read, "Some TV channels still launch campaigns directed against the candidate lists of the Democratic Alliance and Freedom and Justice Party, which violates the norms and honor of the press and the whole profession. Some even went farther, mocking the overwhelming turnout by citizens for the most important elections in the history of the Egyptian people. But we believe this is not surprising, especially as these channels are owned by businessmen who have a 'special' position regarding this homeland's democratic transformation."

This theme continued briefly following the completion of voting. On January 12, 2012, Badie was cited as stressing "the need to achieve the full objectives of the revolution and not allow any parties, stakeholders or forces to divide the Egyptian people."

THE PORT SAID MASSACRE

Unlike other events studied here, the Port Said Massacre, which took place on February 1, 2012, was short and did not stretch over multiple days or weeks. In the days that followed the massacre, the Brotherhood's English-language website covered the event regularly. Our study of the one week following the massacre yielded a total of thirteen Ikwhanweb.com posts about the event. The Brotherhood's web editors showed sympathy with those killed in the massacre and blamed police and the military. In all, five frames emerged from our analysis of coverage: Massacre frame; Blame frame; Accountability frame; Counterrevolution frame; and Sympathy with the Martyrs frame.

Massacre Frame

Ikhwanweb.com did not leave much doubt as to its position on the Port Said Massacre. The website repeatedly condemned the violence and the perpetrators and referred to the killings as "massacres." The choice of the word "massacre" both indicated that Ikhwanweb.com viewed the violence that was carried out as criminal and viewed the victims sympathetically.

On February 2, 2012, in the first post published about the events at Port Said, MB leader Mahmoud Hussein was quoted as saying that "what happened Wednesday night in [the] Al-Ahly/Al-Masry football match was nothing less than a massacre." A second post published on February 2, 2012, referred in the title to the "Port Said Massacre" and said that "the Muslim

Brotherhood is shocked, saddened and dismayed at news of the massacre that took place in Port Said Stadium after Al-Ahly vs. Al-Masry match, and claimed the lives of more than seventy martyrs." The post also referred to the events as "vicious aggression" and to a "hidden plot behind the massacre." The title of a post published on February 6, 2012, also described the events as a "massacre."

Blame Frame

At the core of Ikhwanweb.com's coverage of the Port Said Massacre was an intimation that the Egyptian police and military were to blame for the killings. We identified two subframes: Blame the Police and Blame the Military.

Blame the Police Subframe. The Brotherhood blamed Egyptian police for failing to protect fans at Port Said Stadium. For example, a February 2, 2012, post said that the government should "investigate the involvement of the police force, who, plainly, could have prevented this disaster, but [instead] contented themselves with being spectators, which makes them fully liable ... for the violent crimes Egypt has been witnessing." Another February 2, 2012, post went further, suggesting that the police had intentionally sabotaged match spectators. It described the "failure of the police to protect citizens" and argued that their actions "cannot be simply described as neglect." The post said that "we fear that some police officers aim to punish the Egyptian people for the revolution, for banishing their tyranny over the people, and cutting down their privileges."

A third February 2, 2012, post implicated the heads of Egypt's Interior Ministry. The post cited Brotherhood leader Essam El-Erian, who said that the "survival of the Interior Ministry's senior leadership" is unacceptable, given that "they are complicit with the gang now detained in Tora prison." The post also said that "Dr. El-Erian accused the Interior Minister of negligence" and that he "presented to parliament a request for prosecution of the Interior Minister on charges of negligence."

Other Muslim Brotherhood leaders also appeared to blame police. On February 4, 2012, a post was published documenting the views of Badie, who said that "the police [are] reluctant to perform [their] role." When he cited a sacred Islamic tradition, Badie seemed to indirectly accuse police officers of murder. He said, "Indeed, the entire world is less important to Allah than the [unlawful] taking of a Believer's soul." Another MB leader, Mohamed Beltagy, was quoted in a separate February 4, 2012, post. He argued that there exists "a strong relationship between the security services, led by the Minister of Interior, and the thugs [guilty of violent crimes committed across Egypt]."

Blame the Military Subframe. In addition to blaming the police, Ikhwanweb.com blamed Egypt's military government, the Supreme Council of the Armed Forces (SCAF). For example, a February 2, 2012, post cited Hussein, who said that "SCAF's failure to hold accountable those who committed crimes against Egyptians and Egypt in the past months does encourage recurrence of such measures." The post's title said that "SCAF, Ministry of Interior Bear Football Massacre Responsibility." The post also referred to the "massacre for which the Supreme Council of the Armed Forces (SCAF) and the Ministry of Interior bear the ultimate responsibility."

On February 2, 2012, Ikhwanweb.com published an official statement from the Muslim Brotherhood regarding the Port Said Massacre. The Brotherhood's statement read, in part, "Certainly, the authorities covered up for those responsible for the disasters that occurred previously in Maspero, Mohamed Mahmoud Street, and the Cabinet area, blaming unknown persons for bloody crimes every time, allowing the real criminals intent on spreading death and destruction to come out and do their worst, completely safe from prosecution."

The February 4, 2012, post documenting Badie's views also pinned blame on the military. After indicating that SCAF was "responsible" for the massacre, Badie included a short prayer that the Prophet Muhammad had taught the early Muslims: "O Allah, cause distress to those who take charge over my people and cause them distress."

A February 6, 2012, post documented recommendations of a parliamentary committee, of which Freedom and Justice Party members were part. The committee, titled the Committee on Defense and National Security, suggested that "charges" be brought against "the Director of Military Police," among others. The post also said that the committee "held SCAF fully responsible for the latest violent events and their repercussions in the country, criticizing the government top officials for being preoccupied with protecting the country's former president and his corrupt cronies."

Accountability Frame

As discussed, Ikhwanweb.com blamed the police and military for the Port Said Massacre. The website, however, did not stop there. Editors also published numerous posts suggesting that military and police officials be held to account for crimes. This Accountability frame included two subframes: Hold the Police to Account and Hold the Military to Account.

Hold the Police to Account Subframe. On February 4, 2012, Ikhwanweb .com argued for "investigations and accountability of all negligent officials in the Ministry of Interior, which must be judiciously cleansed." The post also called for the "questioning [of] the Interior Minister." This call for accountability was immediately followed by a Qur'anic verse focusing on retribution: "There is life for you in retribution, O men of understanding, so that you may ward off (evil)."

Another February 4, 2012, post said that the parliament's Youth Committee "called for PA legislation to ensure a full judicious cleansing of the Interior Ministry." The post also said that "the Ministry's top officials" were "fully responsible for the events of Port Said." A third February 4, 2012, post "demanded that the Egyptian People's Assembly must issue legislation to ensure full and proper cleansing of the Interior Ministry." A February 5, 2012, post said that the "People's Assembly ... will not allow anyone to disgrace or dishonor Egypt or derail the revolution. And will not allow criminals to go unpunished," while a February 6, 2012, post said that the Parliament's Committee on Defense and National Security recommended "bringing charges against the Minister of Interior, and summoning top officials such as the President of Intelligence ... Director of National Security Service, and head of the Central Security Service, to attend before the Committee, to account for recent events."

Hold the Military to Account Subframe. The February 4, 2012, post citing Badie placed indirect blame on SCAF. Badie was quoted: "This event cannot pass without investigation, accountability and retribution. Egypt has recently witnessed many disasters, crimes and tragedies—in the transition period—but no one has been punished for any of them; no retribution for the martyrs, which enticed more thugs, criminals, plotters and saboteurs to do their worst." Badie also noted that "covering up for such murderous crimes cannot be accepted."

Another February 4, 2012, post went further, suggesting that members of the Egyptian military should be held to account for the Port Said crimes and other crimes committed prior to them. In that post, Beltagy alluded to "the need to summon representatives of the Egyptian general intelligence and military intelligence, who should be held accountable for all events beginning from 28 January to the tragic events the country is witnessing today."

Counterrevolution Frame

In addition to blaming the police and military, and suggesting that police and military officials be held to account, Ikhwanweb.com also implied that members of Egypt's key institutions were resentful of the nation's new democratic course and participating in a type of counterrevolution. These posts tended to blame officials for the Port Said Massacre and, in the same breath, imply that the orchestration of events was part of a larger counterrevolutionary attempt.

The February 2, 2012, post highlighting Hussein's views quoted him: "[E]veryone agrees that there is a total security breakdown in the whole country, and perhaps even complicity of certain characters determined to bring the country down into chaos and complete disorder." Another February 2, 2012, post called the incidents "horrific events" and referred to "attempts ... made to incite chaos and destroy the revolution's accomplishments."

A third February 2, 2012, post, an official statement by the FJP, included many references to an alleged counterrevolution. The post argued that "what happened in this game was ... an integral part of a deliberate scheme to ignite strife, originally aiming to push Egypt into a downward spiral of crises." The post also noted, "The FJP believes that what happened in Port Said cannot at all be separated from the overall scene emerging since a few days ago, with organized robberies of a number of banks, post offices and security vehicles, as well as a proliferation of cases of robbery and banditry. These acts have indeed emerged clearly after the completion of parliamentary elections, which was a major shift for the Egyptian revolution. This points to treacherous hands which are no longer hidden, intent on forcing Egypt into chaos and destruction."

The post also said that what is happening in Egypt is "aimed at derailing the process of peaceful democratic transition of power," and offered a lengthy description of the ways in which the alleged counterrevolution was being carried out: "These [crimes] are, evidently, the handiwork of domestic parties and dubious forces that still have strong ties with the former regime, which manages the sabotage scheme from the cells of Tora prison, taking advantage of a number of businessmen who were the pillars of the failed system and still enjoy freedom, despite the many crimes of corruption they are involved in, using their money and a number of print and broadcast media they own."

On February 4, 2012, Badie also indicated he believed that a counterrevolution was ongoing. He said, "It has now become evidently clear to everyone that there are individuals who are plotting for burning this homeland and demolition of its institutions. They are trained for this. They are known to the Supreme Council of the Armed Forces (SCAF) and the police, who are delaying bringing them to justice, which is totally unacceptable." Another February 4, 2012, post was even more explicit. An FJP member of parliament, Helmi Al-Gazzar, posited that "a number of officers involved in counterrevolution activities, in addition to remnants of the former regime, are still amongst the ranks of the security services."

Sympathy with the Martyrs Frame

Given Ikhwanweb.com's position on the Port Said Massacre, it is not surprising that the website expressed some sympathy with victims, who were often described as "martyrs."

On February 2, 2012, Ikhwanweb.com said that FJP Member of Parliament "[Osama] Yassin offered his condolences to the families of the victims killed." The February 2, 2012, post documenting the FJP's official Port Said statement said, "The FJP extends its sincere condolences to the families of the dead, prays to God for mercy and forgiveness for them, and wishes the injured a speedy recovery." The Muslim Brotherhood's official statement, also published on February 2, 2012, offered a similar sentiment: "In conclusion, we offer our most sincere condolences to the families of martyrs. Our hearts bleed for them as we pray to God to grant them His ultimate mercy."

Badie also expressed sympathy in the February 4, 2012, post discussed previously. He said, "I talk to the Egyptian people and my heart aches in pain for those who perished, martyrs in no real fight, without facing any real enemy." Another February 4, 2012, post suggested "that a delegation" from parliament be sent to Port Said to "offer their condolences for the martyrs of the Port Said tragedy." On February 7, 2012, a post was published documenting a People's Assembly effort (led by the FJP MPs) "to raise the value of martyr compensation from 30 to 100 thousand Egyptian pounds (approximately $16,667)."

Chapter 6

From the 2012 Presidential Election to the 2012 Constitutional Referendum

Chapter 6 is the last of three chapters presenting results of our analysis of Ikhwanweb.com. The chapter analyzes reportage of three major events—Morsi's June 2012 electoral victory, Morsi's November 2012 constitutional decree, and the 2012 referendum on the constitution.

THE 2012 PRESIDENTIAL ELECTION

Ikhwanweb.com prominently covered Egypt's 2012 presidential election. Our search of the website yielded a total of thirty-two posts about the election between June 17, 2011, the day after the second-round voting, and June 30, 2011, the day Morsi was sworn in as president. We studied all thirty-two posts. The level of prominence allotted to the election is perhaps unsurprising, especially given the Muslim Brotherhood's primary stake in the election, which took place in the summer of 2012. Much of the website's coverage was focused on obvious Brotherhood interests and concerns, including, importantly, the need to respect the outcome of the election, which the Muslim Brotherhood (MB) expected to be won by their veteran leader, Mohamed Morsi.

But during the summer of 2012, the Brotherhood was concerned about much more than the presidency. During the heart of the presidential election campaign season, the ruling military issued a declaration dissolving the recently elected parliament. The MB and Freedom and Justice Party (FJP) strongly opposed the decision. This disagreement with the Supreme Council of Armed Forces (SCAF) represented the culmination of several months of serious political disagreement, and, in some ways, brought the MB's relationship with the ruling military to a head. The issue became a prominent one for Ikhwanweb.com.

Ikhwanweb.com was clearly invested in both condemning SCAF and warning Egyptians about the need to protect the revolution from attempts (by SCAF) to sabotage it. Additionally, Ikhwanweb.com attempted to impress upon readers the importance of respecting the people's free will. The website also went to some lengths to defend both the Brotherhood and Morsi against what it deemed as media "fabrications."

In all, five dominant frames emerged from our analysis: People's Free Will Should Be Respected; Condemning SCAF; Protect the Revolution; Do Not Fear the Brotherhood; and Beware of Media Fabrications. The Do Not Fear the Brotherhood frame included two subframes: The MB Is Inclusive and the MB Is Democratic.

People's Free Will Should Be Respected

The Muslim Brotherhood nominated Morsi to run for president in 2012. Given their rising popularity and overwhelming victory at the parliamentary elections, the MB clearly expected Morsi to be victorious. So, apparently, did many other Egyptians, some of whom were scared of the prospects of a Morsi presidency. Ikhwanweb.com went to some effort to respond to implicit, and sometimes explicit, suggestions that the 2012 presidential elections should not be respected. Additionally, the Brotherhood was concerned about the dissolution of parliament, which the military announced on June 14, 2012, a few days before the second round of presidential elections was scheduled to begin. Ikhwanweb.com also positioned this as an attack on the free will of the Egyptian people. In the context of both the presidential election and the decision to dissolve parliament, Ikhwanweb.com prominently featured a People's Free Will Should Be Respected frame.

For example, after the start of the second round of presidential elections, on June 17, 2012, Ikhwanweb.com published a post calling on Egyptians to protect their revolution by protecting their free will, represented here by voting for president. The post repeatedly alluded to the importance of the Egyptian people's will in protecting the outcomes of the 2011 revolution and determining the country's future following the revolution. It also specifically highlighted the importance of voting in the presidential elections. The stressing of the importance of popular will was evident in the post's title, which called on people to "defend the revolution and [their] free will." The post also noted, "The increasing number of people turning out to the ballot box during the first day of the runoff presidential election is evidence of this great people's commitment and determination to defend the revolution, safeguard their free will and complete the march towards democracy." The post closed with an explicit call: "Now, we exhort you, all Egyptians, to defend your free will, come out en force and caste your votes."

Also, on June 17, 2012, Ikhwanweb.com published a post denouncing the decision to dissolve parliament, framing the decision as an attack on the Egyptian popular will. The post's title was instructive: "Brotherhood: Parliament Was Created by Popular Will; Can Only Be Dissolved by Popular Will." The post included an official MB statement that reminded the readers that the "parliament was elected by pure popular will ... [and] that the Constitutional Declaration does not confer on the Supreme Council of the Armed Forces (SCAF) the power to dissolve parliament." The post also said that the "parliament was created by popular will ... and it was SCAF itself that passed the law on which parliamentary elections were conducted."

A post published on June 18, 2012, said that "since the decision to dissolve parliament ... does not rely explicitly or implicitly on any text in the Constitutional Declaration currently governing the country, SCAF should have maintained the free will of the people that produced Parliament." The post also said that a Brotherhood leader "called upon SCAF to maintain the democratic accomplishments of the revolution, out of respect for popular will and to uphold the interests of the country." Another June 18, 2012, post expressed a similar sentiment: "It is the duty of the people to defend and impose their will. Referring matters to the people is a must in any case, because they are the makers of the revolution and they alone have the right to build the constitutional institutions and to choose their parliamentary representatives and the President."

On June 22, 2012, Ikhwanweb.com published a pair of posts that quoted Brotherhood leaders who spoke of Egyptian free will. In one post, Essam El-Erian said, "The parliament was elected by the will of the people, and the will of the people must be respected. On the other hand, the Constitutional Court ruling does not mean the dissolution of parliament." Another June 22, 2012, post quoted a different Brotherhood leader, Gamal Heshmat, who argued that "the will of the Egyptian people who toppled the tyrant Mubarak will continue to reject any military tactics, maneuvers or actions aiming to frustrate the hopes of the people in establishing a true civil modern state."

Following Morsi's electoral victory and subsequent informal inauguration speech at Tahrir Square, Ikhwanweb.com published a post on June 30, 2012, documenting some of what Morsi said about Egyptian popular will. Morsi said, "I believe that you are the source of power and legitimacy. There is no person, party, institution or authority over or above the will of the people. The nation is the source of all power; it grants and withdraws power. ... You are the owners of the will."

Condemning SCAF

As previous sections have discussed, by the summer of 2012, the Brotherhood's English-language website had, for some time, been critical of Egypt's ruling military. The critical tone stemmed largely from serious political disagreements the Brotherhood had with SCAF. The dispute came to a head in the summer of 2012, when SCAF decided to dissolve the elected parliament and appeared, at least in the eyes of the Brotherhood, to seek to strip Egypt's newly elected president of real political power. The Brotherhood's tone toward SCAF changed considerably, as evidenced by Ikhwanweb .com's framing of the events. In covering the 2012 presidential election, Ikhwanweb.com put forth its most critical coverage of SCAF to date, often implying that SCAF was explicitly plotting for a power grab against both the Egyptian popular will and the Egyptian revolution. Overall, the coverage warranted a "Condemning SCAF" frame.

On June 17, 2012, a post provided a direct accusation and condemnation of SCAF. "The constant threat to dissolve a parliament elected by the will of 30 million Egyptians confirms the Supreme Council of the Armed Forces (SCAF)'s desire for a total power grab, against the popular will, and its resolve to fake legitimacy never granted to it by the people, in a blatant attack on the great Egyptian revolution." The post also described SCAF's decision to dissolve parliament as "indefensible," noting that "SCAF does not have the authority to dissolve parliament, and neither the Constitutional Declaration nor the ruling of the Constitutional Court itself confer any such power on SCAF. Hence, any decision SCAF issues in this regard will be null and void."

A separate June 17, 2012, post said that "SCAF's recent rush to grab legislative power was illegitimate, indeed a coup against the democratic process as a whole, taking us back to square one." The post also alerted readers to "steps taken by SCAF to turn back the clock, through the issuance, by the Minister of Justice, of a decision to grant military intelligence officers broad state-of-emergency powers to arrest and detain civilians without judicial warrant—which effectively reproduces the climate of terror and oppression of bygone dark times, and obliterates the people's hope of democracy."

According to a June 18, 2012, post, FJP leader (and former Speaker of the People's Assembly) Saad El-Katatni "rejected a complementary constitutional declaration authored by SCAF ... [and] stressed that SCAF's decision to dissolve the parliament is null and void because it is not based on any constitutional legitimacy, principle or procedure, according to the existing Declaration." Another June 18, 2012, post included an official statement by the FJP that urged the Egyptian people "to see their will implemented positively, and to prevent the Supreme Council of the Armed Forces (SCAF) from grabbing the reins of power and mounting a coup against democracy." The post also said that "there is no justification for SCAF to try and maintain its hold on legislative powers" and "SCAF's decree is null and void, because SCAF does not have the power to dissolve the first democratically elected People's Assembly in the history of modern Egypt."

On June 19, 2012, Ikhwanweb.com published a long Muslim Brotherhood statement on SCAF's constitutional decree. The statement, which was lengthy, was used largely to condemn SCAF's alleged power grab. "After Egyptians rid themselves of the oppressive nightmare that weighed heavily over their lives on February 11, 2011, they hoped SCAF would honor its pledge to transfer power to the elected civilian authority. … However, after a transition period filled with confusion, uncertainty and anxiety, people were surprised by SCAF's issuing a so-called complementary constitutional declaration, when in fact SCAF does not have the right, power or authority to issue any constitutional article." The post reminded readers that "although the people were allowed to choose their representatives parliament in a complete and democratic electoral process, hurdles … were continually, purposely placed by [SCAF] in the way of lawmakers striving to do their duty … SCAF issued a decree to dissolve the People's Assembly. … The matter of fact is, SCAF does not have the constitutional authority for dissolving parliament. … We find that there is [an] encroachment on the popular will and a genuine desire not to relinquish power, but to circumvent this requirement and to frustrate people's hopes. There is a clear and deliberate attempt to grab legislative power, and to strip [the] president of many of his traditional powers."

Another June 19, 2012, post documented an alleged violation by SCAF. The post read, "Recently, SCAF prevented lawmakers from entering the Egyptian parliament building, after an SCC decision reported by the media in Egypt … [alluded to] the dissolution of parliament."

A June 21, 2012, post also condemned SCAF's decision to dissolve parliament. It read, "positive participation in the million-man marches and demonstrations on Tuesday June 19, 2012, rejecting the Supreme Council of the Armed Forces (SCAF)'s so-called constitutional supplement and its decision to dissolve the People's Assembly."

Brotherhood leader Mohamed Beltagy was quoted in a post published on June 22, 2012: "[A]ll revolutionary groups and movements have serious doubts regarding SCAF's departure from the agreed path of power handover, as evident in its declaration of a constitutional monopoly on all state power." Another June 22, 2012, post quoted Heshmat: "SCAF is repeating ousted Mubarak's old statements, talking about things that it does not apply or adhere to. SCAF hinders democratization by declaring such an unconstitutional declaration which is quite simply an impediment to the next president's work, and by restricting freedoms through emergency-law-like powers and procedures with which SCAF pits military police forces against the Egyptian people; not to mention SCAF's encroachment on and total disrespect for the people's will."

A June 23, 2012, post focused on a meeting between Morsi and a group of revolutionary youth representatives to deliberate over SCAF's "decision to grant low-ranking intelligence and military police officers sweeping powers to arrest and detain civilians without judicial warrant ... the dissolution of the recently elected parliament, the constitutional declaration addendum that curbs the powers of the President, and the delay in announcing presidential election results, which raise serious doubts about the handover of power in Egypt in a democratic manner."

In the June 30, 2012, post that documented Morsi's Tahrir Square speech, Morsi was quoted: "I will not tolerate any curbing of the powers of the President of the Republic. I have no right to give up presidential powers and functions on the basis of which you chose me. This is a contract between you and me. That is the concept of the modern state." This quote may be seen as an indirect condemnation of SCAF decisions and their view on democracy.

Protect the Revolution Frame

During the presidential election period, a significant portion of Ikwhanweb .com coverage was devoted to discussions of the 2011 uprising. The website's posts argued that both the parliamentary and presidential elections represented extensions of Egypt's revolutionary path, and that the revolution and both sets of elections were under attack by counterrevolutionary forces, namely SCAF and remnants of the Mubarak regime. Three subframes emerged from our analysis: The Revolution Is Not Over; Beware of the Counterrevolution; and Beware of Election Fraud.

The Revolution Is Not Over Subframe. In numerous reports, Ikhwanweb .com suggested that the 2011 Egyptian revolution wasn't over, and that, in fact, elections represented a continuation of the uprising. This is an important subframe because it represents an attempt by Ikhwanweb.com editors to link the Brotherhood and their electoral successes to the Egyptian revolution. This offers a type of protection against claims that the MB was an anti-democratic, counterrevolutionary force.

A June 21, 2012, post documented FJP "participation in all popular actions to achieve revolution goals" and specifically commented on a scheduled million-man march against the SCAF decree to dissolve parliament. The post said the FJP "affirms that it will join the Egyptian people and all political and revolutionary parties, groups and movements, in all public actions and events, until the demands of ... [the] million-man demonstration [are met] under the banner 'In liberty square, until parliament returns.'"

Three posts published on June 21, 2012, and June 22, 2012, relied on Brotherhood leadership authority to make points about the continuation of the revolution. A June 21, 2012, post cited Brotherhood leader Khairat Al-Shater, who "highlighted the need to continue protests in Tahrir Square until the people's demands are met, and also to support their president-elect until he gets in office and with full power to represent and serve all Egyptians." On June 22, 2012, Ikhwanweb.com published the views of Beltagy, who argued that "all stakeholders have agreed to continue to call for revolutionary action, until usurped legitimacy is restored where it belongs, and the Constituent Assembly is allowed to resume its work." Also, on June 22, 2012, a post citing El-Erian's views was published. He said, "We are in Liberty Square, until parliament returns."

A June 23, 2012, post attempted to link Morsi's incoming presidency to the continuation of the revolution. The post was titled "Morsi and National Accord Front Vow to Keep Revolution Peaceful; Maintain Freedom and Democracy." The post shed light on the participation of key political figures, including Morsi, in the rallies at Tahrir Square that were held "to protect the legitimacy of the peaceful Egyptian revolution." The post quoted Morsi, who said, "With the revolutionary spirit and vitality persisting positively [and] peacefully in Tahrir Square, we continue our discourse, seeking public good and national stability."

A June 27, 2012, post alluded to an official statement by Mahmoud Hussein, the MB secretary general and media spokesman. He said, "The Brotherhood will join the revolutionary groups and parties in the 'power handover' million-man marches and protests starting from Friday, June 29, 2012, in Tahrir Square—the symbol of the Egyptian revolution and the platform for its demands."

The June 30, 2012, post documenting Morsi's Tahrir Square speech quoted Morsi discussing his thoughts about how the presidential election related to the revolution. He said, "The revolution continues to achieve its objectives. It is reshaping to reflect the free will of the Egyptian people, with an elected president steering the ship home, leading this revolution, standing in front of patriotic revolutionaries, leading them on the path to full democracy, and doing all he can to achieve all the objectives of the great revolution." Later in the post, Morsi was quoted again: "I will always be the first supporter of the revolution; so it should continue everywhere in the farthest corners of the homeland. I want these voices to continue to be heard, announcing that we are always free, revolutionaries, and we are going to continue the march, [and] complete the journey." In some ways, Morsi's words can be seen as a message to SCAF that the incoming president wasn't intending to bow to their military authority.

The Beware of the Counterrevolution Subframe. Continuing a theme established earlier, Ikhwanweb.com warned readers against what it considered to be a growing counterrevolutionary movement in Egypt. Here, SCAF was clearly implicated, with posts often subtly implying that the ruling military governors were responsible for orchestrating counterrevolutionary efforts.

A June 17, 2012, post included a direct plea to the Egyptian people to safeguard the outcomes of the parliamentary elections. Specifically, the post encouraged Egyptians to "fight with determination, persistence and resolve against any attempts to lay to waste the gains you made in free and fair parliamentary elections." The post also urged Egyptians "to remember the blood of the martyrs and the pain of the maimed and wounded. And never, under any circumstances, allow the defunct former regime to reclaim power, with its loathsome repression and tyranny." Another June 17, 2012, post called on the Egyptian people "to be vigilant and positive and to come out en force to vote in the runoff presidential elections, to protect the democratic gains, to prevent all hidden hands from forging their will and replicating the despotic former regime."

Several Brotherhood figures, including Morsi, were also quoted warning against the alleged counterrevolution. The June 21, 2012, post that documenting Al-Shater's views quoted him warning against a counterrevolution in progress. He said, "[T]wo major forces [are] locked in conflict: The first is the Egyptian people, from across the entire spectrum, endeavoring to achieve the goals of the revolution honestly and faithfully. The second is a group of special interest parties trying desperately to reproduce the Mubarak regime, once again, albeit in a modified forum." Meanwhile, a June 22, 2012, post included remarks made by Ahmed Ashri, the FJP's Chairman of the Legal Committee, who criticized the authorities' delay in announcing the results of the presidential elections. Ashri said, "This dubious maneuver is totally unacceptable. … At the latest, results must be announced on Friday. But certain interested parties want to cause even more anxiety among the people and further confuse the political scene." On June 23, 2012, Morsi, the then president-elect, was quoted: "we … reject the supplementary constitutional declaration that was never referred to Egyptians in public referendum, which clearly shows that attempts are being made to restrict the powers of the next president."

The Beware of Election Fraud Subframe. As part of its Protect the Revolution frame, Ikhwanweb.com warned Egyptian readers against possible electoral fraud. The website suggested that counterrevolutionary forces were interested in forging the results, thereby delivering a blow to the revolution.

A June 17, 2012, post alluded to several incidents of alleged voting violations, including attempts to bribe the voters, burn the ballot boxes, and rig the elections. The post said that the Muslim Brotherhood called "upon the competent army and police security services to quickly investigate and apprehend these [violators] and bring them to trial."

A June 18, 2012, post alluded to the official complaint filed by Morsi's campaign "to Egypt's attorney general, accusing the government's printing presses of printing ballots with a candidate's name already selected, without inspecting the material being printed before packaging and delivery to the Supreme Presidential Elections Committee (SPEC)." The post included several incidents of violations at various voting sites across the country. For example, the post referenced "attempts ... made to prevent a number of ... [the MB] candidate's official delegates from staying overnight to make sure ballot-boxes are not tampered with. Meanwhile, a number of armed forces retirees, who participated in the first round of the presidential elections, were surprised to find that their names had been removed from the voter rolls, in flagrant violation of the law."

Another June 18, 2012, post attempted to advise SCAF on issues pertaining to voter fraud prevention. The post read, "Instead, SCAF must respect the will of the people and safeguard the remaining steps in the electoral process, preventing any voter fraud. It should also announce the results as counted in ballot boxes and in accordance with results signed by sorting judges."

On June 21, 2012, a post was published documenting a series of fraud-related complaints made by the Morsi campaign allegedly supporting Morsi's election rival, Ahmed Shafiq. The post pointed to a specific complaint submitted by Morsi's legal team to the Supreme Presidential Elections Committee (SPEC) "related to irregularities and violations that marred the electoral process." The post highlighted irregularities, including "voting by certain factions not allowed to do so by law (such as army recruits and some police and army officers); vote-rigging, multi-ballot registry papers; directing citizens to vote for the rival candidate; vote buying; mismatches between numbers of the cards inside the ballot boxes and the actual number of voters; [and] voting by polling stations' employees on behalf of citizens unable to use the ballots, against their choice (for Shafiq instead of Morsi)."

A June 24, 2012, post attempted to explain what the MB might do if fraud caused them to lose the election. The post documented a press conference held in Lebanon by Mahmoud Ghozlan, an MB official spokesman. He said, "The FJP will accept the result [of the presidential elections]. However, if it became clear that there is fraud, the Egyptian people will ... protect their free will and choice."

Do Not Fear the Brotherhood Frame

Continuing an earlier pattern, Ikhwanweb.com's coverage included a Do Not Fear the Brotherhood frame, which was characterized by two subframes: the

MB Is Inclusive and the MB Is Democratic. As noted earlier in this book, this framing is likely a calculated response to allegations that the MB is anti-democratic, exclusive, and sectarian. With the Morsi presidency approaching, Ikhwanweb.com editors likely sought out opportunities to assure readers. The website frequently cited MB leaders speaking to the group's claimed inclusivity and democratic nature.

The MB Is Inclusive Subframe. The Brotherhood's English-language website framed the group as inclusive, tolerant of all people, including, importantly, Christians. For instance, a June 18, 2012, post emphasized the unity of Egypt's Christian and Muslim populations. Morsi was quoted promising "the Egyptian people to be [a] servant of all [Egyptians] and to stand at the same distance from all Egyptians, Muslims and Christians, those who gave him their votes and those who did not." In a television interview summarized by Ikhwanweb.com on June 18, 2012, MB vice chairman Khairat Al-Shater made reassuring remarks about the MB's commitment to unity, inclusivity, and human rights. According to Al-Shater, the MB's main goal was to establish "a modern democratic political system, based on ... the rule of law and respect of human rights and the rights of citizenship, as well as rights of minorities." The MB, according to Al-Shater, is "keen to safeguard independence of the judiciary, and to provide security and safety for all Egyptians."

On June 22, 2012, Beltagy was cited affirming that the FJP "continues to consult with all Egyptian parties and stakeholders to achieve national harmony over a strong consensus initiative with positive participation of all political and revolutionary players, and in which all social factions and denominations will contribute to the shaping and development of key features."

A June 23, 2012, post described a meeting of the National Accord Front, of which the MB was part. Meeting attendees agreed on the need to strengthen "national accord and partnership in an all-inclusive national initiative which reflects the goals of the revolution and all sectors of Egyptian society, including women, Copts and young people." Another June 23, 2012, post included a promise from Morsi that "the presidential institution will include deputies, advisers and officials, will have Christians, youths, women and former presidential candidates."

A post published on June 24, 2012, highlighted a news conference held by MB spokesman Ghozlan. Ghozlan "assured Christians in Egypt [that they] would be given all their rights in full, pointing out that there has not been even one incident of violence between the Brotherhood and Christians." A June 25, 2012, post shed light on remarks made by Safwat Al-Bayadi, head of the Evangelical Church in Egypt, who said that "the success of Dr. Morsi is the first experience of democracy in Egypt's history." He added, "We have no sectarian demands. But we do want to see the goals of January 25 revolution achieved. ... These are the aspirations of all the people, men, women, Muslims and Christians. Egyptians are all equal. We cannot differentiate or discriminate between them on grounds of religion or sex."

As Morsi's inauguration approached, Ikhwanweb.com's focus on inclusivity emphasized his incoming presidency. For example, a June 25, 2012, post included feedback from public figures about Morsi's first televised speech after his election as president. In the post, the Wasat Party "confirmed its support for the conciliatory messages in the speech, both with state institutions including the army, police and the judiciary, and with all political actors and parties from across the Egyptian political and intellectual spectrum." The post quoted Mansour Hassan, former chairman of SCAF advisory board, as saying, "Dr. Mohamed Morsi ... was keen to extend his hand to all people, without exception, including our Coptic brothers and the police."

On June 27, 2012, a post was published that included remarks made by Yasser Ali, acting spokesman for the president-elect, who said that "when ... [Morsi] raised the slogan 'Our strength, in our unity' during his presidential campaign, he was fully mindful of the meaning of this slogan, that the Egyptian People must be one fabric again, and that all past incidents, under the defunct regime, were meant to cause division and strife between Egyptian Muslims and Christians." The June 30, 2012, post documenting Morsi's Tahrir Square speech quoted him: "I stand here with you ... those who elected me and those who did not—I am for all of you, at the same distance from all. I will never subtract from the rights of those who told me 'No,' nor will I add [to] the rights of those who said to me 'Yes.' This is democracy."

The MB Is Democratic Subframe. In a smaller handful of posts, Ikhwanweb.com com alluded to the Brotherhood's claimed democratic nature. For example, a June 28, 2012, post documented a meeting between El-Erian and James Watt, the British ambassador to Egypt. El-Erian "affirmed that the FJP seeks to build a sound democratic system to achieve security, stability, social justice and the independence of the judiciary, and to uphold the rule of law, so as to achieve the objectives of the January 25 revolution."

A June 29, 2012, post shed light on a meeting held between President-Elect Morsi and various Egyptian political party leaders. During the meeting, Morsi highlighted the need for "respecting freedom of speech for all, and political practice that begins from the grassroots and presence among the people." Morsi also affirmed "that the nation is the source of authority, and highlighted the importance of the principle of peaceful transfer and rotation of power and governance."

Beware of Media Fabrications Frame

During our analysis of Ikhwanweb.com's coverage of the 2011 parliamentary elections, we mentioned how the website included posts defending the Brotherhood against allegations leveled against the group by Egyptian media outlets and personalities. At that time, the relatively infrequent allusions didn't warrant a frame per se. However, during its coverage of the 2012 presidential elections, Ikhwanweb.com emphasized media fabrications to a much greater extent, warranting a new frame—Beware of Media Fabrications.

On June 17, 2012, Ikhwanweb.com published a post titled "Morsi Campaign Refutes Media Lies and Fabricated News." The post warned against alleged attempts by the news media, particularly *Al-Youm Al-Sabea* newspaper, to falsify news about Morsi's campaign. According to the post, the website published photos that it claimed were shot inside Morsi's operations room, but, according to Ikhwanweb.com, that was not the case. The post included a statement by the general coordinator of Morsi's campaign, who "urged all media outlets to refrain from fabricating false fables and 'news' about public figures and institutions."

Another June 17, 2012, post referred to various instances of allegedly false media reporting about the Morsi campaign. In particular, the reports, according to the post, falsely accused the campaign of "vote rigging." The post argued that these reports "are mere fables fabricated by certain interested parties tampering with the voting process, determined to accuse us of these illegal acts, although we evidently are the most committed to laws and regulations." The post also claimed that several news websites cited "unknown security sources ... claim[ing] that the Muslim Brotherhood is making preparations to break into voting centers. This is a completely unfounded lie. It certainly runs contrary to the policies and historic discourse of the Muslim Brotherhood."

A June 19, 2012, post included statements by El-Erian, who "rejected as fabricated fables [the] false news reported on Al-Youm Al-Sabea newspaper's website alleging that the FJP is holding consultations with political parties and a number of public figures on forming the next government." El-Erian "called on the media to investigate the accuracy of [the news] and commit to objectivity in what they publish, so they would not circulate false information and statements that have no basis."

On June 21, 2012, a post cited Al-Shater, who argued that the MB is "witnessing a very massive campaign of false reports and rumors—aimed at further confusing the political scene, depriving the Egyptian people of their natural right to rejoice at the victory of their first democratically elected President ... [by] airing vilifying fabricated fables."

A June 22, 2012, post announced that the Freedom and Justice Party was suing a prominent Egyptian daily, *Al-Dostour*, for "slanderous fabrications."

The post included remarks by El-Erian regarding the party's decision to commission its legal department "to file a libel and defamation complaint against the owner and board chairman and editor in chief of Al-Dostour newspaper because of fabricated falsehoods published by the paper." According to El-Erian, "Al-Dostour is adopting the same old approach favored by the corrupt former regime, which it applied through the state security apparatus against the Muslim Brotherhood and its honorable leaders in this country, making all sorts of vilifying claims against them, all of which have been proven fabricated fables and lies."

Ghozlan was cited in a June 24, 2012, post, which rejected a claim about an alleged deal between Morsi and SCAF. The post indicated that Ghozlan claimed "contrary to vilifying media claims ... there is absolutely no agreement of any kind between the Brotherhood and SCAF."

A June 27, 2012, post referred to remarks made by Farid Ismail, a member of FJP's executive office, who refuted reports in some media outlets that alleged "that the FJP has decided to increase its share in the next government from 30 percent to 50 percent." Ismail said: "I hope the media would commit to accuracy and objectivity in reports, information and statements they publish about FJP leadership."

MORSI'S 2012 CONSTITUTIONAL DECREE

Morsi's November 22, 2012, constitutional decree was deeply controversial. Perhaps unsurprisingly given its relationship to Morsi and the Brotherhood, Ikhwanweb.com defended the decree. Additionally, in the context of its coverage of the decree, the website defended Morsi's performance more generally and blamed problems in Egypt in the former Mubarak government. Our analysis of Ikhwanweb.com coverage of Morsi's 2012 constitutional decree focused on all twenty posts published by the website in the one week following the decree. Our examination revealed three dominant frames: Protect the Revolution; People's Free Will Should Be Respected; and Egypt Still Suffers from Mubarak's Corruption. Two of these frames— Protect the Revolution and People's Free Will Should Be Respected— represent continuations of patterns established in the website's coverage of the 2012 presidential elections.

The website also emphasized three other issues, although they didn't warrant frames per se. Coverage tended to blame the police for problems in Egypt, glorify "martyrs" killed by police during and after the revolutionary period, and claim that Morsi was the legitimate president of Egypt. The website's blaming of police and glorification of "martyrs" represent important dimensions of coverage, particularly because these issues have been consistent points of emphasis. Defending Morsi as a legitimate president is also significant, if not predictable. The website obviously felt it necessary to shield Morsi from allegations that his decree had caused him to lose his democratic authority.

Protect the Revolution Frame

During its coverage of Morsi's November 2012 constitutional decree, Ikhwanweb.com continued to emphasize the 2011 Egyptian uprising, with numerous posts indicating both that the revolution was ongoing and that Morsi's presidency represented a continuation of the revolutionary process. Posts also warned Egyptians of an alleged counterrevolution. The Protect the Revolution frame was characterized by three subframes: The Revolution Is Not Over; Morsi Is the Revolution's Protector; and Beware of the Counterrevolution.

The Revolution Is Not Over Subframe. Numerous posts suggested that Egypt's revolution was ongoing, and that Morsi's decree was, in fact, a part of the revolutionary moment. For example, a November 23, 2012, post included remarks made by Pakinam Al-Sharkawi, Morsi's assistant for political affairs. She was quoted saying that Morsi's decree was "appropriately timed to re-correct the path of the revolution which has been facing many challenges and persistent attempts to abort it."

On November 25, 2012, Ikhwanweb.com published an official statement by the Muslim Brotherhood about Morsi's decree and planned protests in response to it. The Brotherhood was quoted invoking Egypt's revolutionary movement: "We therefore call upon all national, revolutionary, Muslim and youth groups and movements to join protest marches in liberty squares across Egypt's provinces, after sunset prayers on Sunday to reaffirm their support for these Decrees." Another November 25, 2012, post included remarks by Mohamed Beltagy, the Freedom and Justice Party's secretary-general, who said that Morsi's decree was needed because "the revolution had to be put back on track."

FJP media adviser Murad Ali was quoted in a post published on November 26, 2012. Ali said, "[T]he new constitutional declaration aimed to achieve stability and security, and to help the January 25 revolution complete its course." Essam El-Erian, the FJP's vice chairman, expressed similar sentiments in a November 28, 2012, post that quoted him. He said, "We should move on with the revolution to the vital phase of laying the foundations of democracy and building state institutions."

A November 29, 2012, post summarized an official MB statement calling on Egyptians to participate in a million-man march "in order to achieve the demands of the glorious January 25 revolution, including retribution for martyrs and the wounded, cleansing the country of former regime cronies and senior officials, speeding up the completion of the constitution and rebuilding the state's legislative institutions."

Morsi Is the Revolution's Protector Subframe. In addition to suggesting that the January 25 revolution was still in progress, Ikhwanweb.com framed Morsi as the revolution's protector. Numerous posts linked Morsi's presidency with the continuation of the revolution, sometimes implying that a threat to Morsi's presidency represented a threat to the revolution.

For instance, a November 23, 2012, post focused on an Al-Jazeera Mubasher interview with a prominent Egyptian judge, Walid Sharabi, spokesman for the "Coalition of Judges for Egypt." According to Sharabi, "Mohamed Morsi is the President of revolutionary Egypt. Thus, his decisions, resolutions and decrees favor the revolution. Meanwhile, Abdel-Meguid Mahmoud, the Public Prosecutor, has long defended the toppled regime, sought to corrupt the judiciary and to create a justice system rotten to the core."

A November 23, 2012, post cited Mahmoud Ghozlan, a MB spokesman, who "affirmed that President Mohamed Morsi's decrees are revolutionary—a positive response to popular will." Ghozlan also said, "These decrees protect the original demands of the revolution, since its early days—the dismissal of the Public Prosecutor and real investigations and trials for those who murdered unarmed revolutionaries."

A November 24, 2012, post included comments made by prominent soccer player Mohamed Abu-Treika, who argued that "President Mohamed Morsi's Decrees, sacking Abdel-Meguid Mahmoud, the Public Prosecutor appointed by the former regime, and announcing a new constitutional declaration, are revolutionary decrees that echo the pulse of the Egyptian street and bring hope for the future." According to Abu-Treika, "These Decrees are a new beginning for national harmony that should help Egypt stand steadfast on its feet." Another November 24, 2012, post cited Yasser Ali, a spokesperson for the presidency, who said that Morsi's decree would constitute "a solution that restored to the revolution its rights, its thrust and momentum."

On November 25, 2012, a pair of posts were published highlighting official statements by the MB and FJP, respectively, about the public response to the decree. The MB statement noted that Morsi's decrees aim to "achieve security and protect the revolution and its gains." Meanwhile, the FJP statement said that the decree would "fulfill many revolutionary goals demanded by all political, social and popular groups that participated in the January 25 revolution—for freedom, dignity and social justice."

The November 25, 2012, post that cited Beltagy included a long quote from him that explained the decree as necessary for the revolution's survival. Beltagy said, "Did they want us to wait until the Constitutional Court restored the Military Council's Supplementary Constitutional Declaration and brought

back Field Marshall Tantawi and General Annan? Abdel-Meguid Mahmoud
is a former regime holdover; his dismissal is the real revolution."

A November 26, 2012, post was quite explicit in its support for the decree.
The post's title said that Morsi's decree "protects revolution," while the body
of the post cited a prominent Egyptian judge, Mohamed Awad, who argued
that the decree "achieves the goals of the Egyptian revolution."

Beware of the Counterrevolution Subframe. Ikhwanweb.com's coverage
of the decree also warned readers about an apparent counterrevolution in progress. Posts implied that the decree would help thwart the counterrevolution.

A November 24, 2012, post cited Tharwat Badawy, a professor and expert
on the Egyptian constitution. He spoke directly of the alleged counterrevolution. Badawy said, "The President's decision to make his Constitutional
Declarations immune from appeal and legal wrangling is due to the fact that
some individuals—supporters of the counterrevolution—still exert considerable influence within the judiciary, and also due to lack of confidence in
decisions of the Constitutional Court, which—by being openly politicized
and clearly going beyond its competence, has lost the impartiality essential
for the judiciary."

The November 25, 2012, post documenting an MB statement also
referenced the counterrevolution, albeit indirectly. The statement was quoted
at length and described how counterrevolutionary forces planned on reversing
the gains Egyptians had made during the revolution. The statement read,
"[M]any parties, forces and groups seek to prevent [the completion of the
revolution's goals] ... by demanding dissolution of the Constituent Assembly
and preventing the completing of the new Constitution. They therefore seek
to prevent parliamentary elections and deprive the homeland and the people
of the legislative and regulatory authority, so that the country remains in
a vacuum, in a state of chaos as a prelude to toppling the elected regime
and grabbing power." The statement continued: "Certain political leaders
condemned the Declaration, together with their supporters who did not
realize the seriousness of the situation for the Egyptian people's revolution,
having received a ... distorted image of that Declaration. Thus, they went out
in counter-demonstrations chanting insults. ... Joining them were groups of
thugs who went on the rampage, destroying and burning the headquarters of
the FJP in Alexandria and other cities. Others attacked police officers with
Molotov bombs and stones, setting public and private institutions on fire."

On November 25, 2012, a post alluded to tweets by Mohamed Mahsoub,
the Minister of State for Legal Affairs and Parliamentary Councils. Mahsoub
wrote on Twitter that "Hitler is created by those who delay drafting ... the
constitution for no reason other than their imaginary fears, whims and a desire
to take the country back to square one."

The November 29, 2012, post documenting the MB statement on protests also invoked the alleged counterrevolution. Specifically, the post referenced apparent attempts to undermine the constitution-building process and disrupt Egypt's post-revolution democratic transition. The statement read, "We had persistent attempts to hinder the work of the charter-writing constituent assembly creating on the basis of a popular referendum. ... This was clearly a plot to demolish all elected legislative institutions, disrupt the completion of the constitution and stop the march of the desired democratic transformation of our new Egypt after its glorious revolution." The statement also said, "We invite you all to ... stand together as one to confront all misinformation, agitation and subversion attempts witnessed by all, and endeavor to complete the process of democratic transformation."

People's Free Will Should Be Respected Frame

As it did in earlier coverage, Ikhwanweb.com also emphasized Egyptian popular will. Given the timing and circumstances, this is a significant frame. The website was writing in a context of opposition to Morsi's presidency, and invoked basic democratic norms—in this case, the ballot box—to defend the presidency as legitimate. By calling on Egyptians to respect the popular will, the website was implicitly calling on Morsi's opponents, who had been calling on him to resign, to stand down.

A November 23, 2012, post referred to Egypt's post-revolution parliament, noting that it was "elected ... by the Egyptian people's free will." In describing the decree, the post referred to Morsi as "Egypt's first democratically elected president." A November 26, 2012, post included a quote from the official Facebook page of Mohamed Badie, the MB chairman, who criticized the opposition's "escalation" against Morsi and referred to the fact that the president had been elected by a majority. He wrote, "We heard irresponsible calls for escalation, sabotage and strike actions to disable state facilities. All this is certainly neither wise nor patriotic. In fact, it ignores the higher interests of the country, the popular will and the majority that represents the principles of democracy, which all parties claim to respect."

The November 26, 2012, post that cited Mahsoub's Twitter page also raised the issue of the "popular will." Mahsoub wrote the following on Twitter: "[D]ictatorship exists in the heads of those who accept ignoring [the] popular will, desperately try to prevent completion of the Constitution for flimsy reasons, and fight for the goals of the revolution, but bet on its enemies."

On November 28, 2012, a post was published citing an Al-Jazeera interview with Mahmoud Ezzat, the MB's vice chairman, who argued that "the will of the people is above the judiciary, legislative and executive."

Egypt Still Suffers from Mubarak's Corruption Frame

Ikhwanweb.com featured an Egypt Still Suffers from Mubarak's Corruption frame in its coverage of the 2012 constitutional decree. The frame was highly prominent, and may have been employed either as an attempt to justify Morsi's decree or shield Morsi from potential criticism.

On November 23, 2012, the website published a report that quoted Sharabi, who complained that Mubarak's public prosecutor—whom Morsi dismissed as part of his decree—had "put to waste the pure blood of honorable martyrs, and declared innocent [the] killers of unarmed revolutionaries." Al-Sharkawi's remarks, cited in the November 23, 2012, post referenced previously, praised Morsi's decree as part of his presidency's "long overdue reform pathways to truly democratic transformation, shedding Mubarak era remnants, loyalist and cronies."

Numerous reports relied on sources to make the point about Mubarak. For example, a November 23, 2012, post quoted Ghozlan, who made a vague reference to Egypt's "deep state," which Mubarak was said to have presided over. He said, "Everyone knows how [the] 'deep state' is prevalent in all Egyptian state institutions." A November 24, 2012, post included remarks by Badawy, who argued that Morsi's decree effectively "put an end to a plot [by Mubarak loyalists] to totally destroy Egypt's peace and stability." In the November 24, 2012, post that sourced Abu-Treika, the soccer star said that Egypt "inherited a heavy legacy of corruption and trouble." On November 26, 2012, Ali was quoted saying, "The Public Prosecutor [whom Morsi dismissed as part of his decree] played a key role [in] supporting remnants of the Mubarak regime." Another November 26, 2012, post sourced Gamal Shoaib, assistant secretary-general for the FJP in Cairo, who said, "[M]indless attacks on FJP personnel, smashing up and torching the FJP's headquarters are all the work of thugs ... [and] former regime loyalists who feel they are facing a new State that will deprive them of what they usurped under the former regime." Also, on November 26, 2012, El-Erian was quoted at length discussing figures from the Mubarak government he argued were guilty of crimes. He said, "Those [Mubarak regime figures who are] fearful of accountability for theft and systematic plundering of the people's resources, the country's wealth, [and] those who failed to escape out of the country with smuggled treasures ... fear the new constitution, which has a whole chapter on independent oversight tools ... capable of exposing corruption and prosecuting all culprits in real trials—with real evidence—in the name of the people." Erian added, "Those fearful of their own files getting finally opened, exposing their collaboration with the Mubarak regime, politically and in the media ... are now afraid [that] all the secrets will be revealed." On November 28, 2012, Ezzat was quoted: "Everyone has the right to object to the President, but there is no justifying alliance with Mubarak-era remnants and thugs."

Official FJP and MB statements cited by Ikhwanweb.com also referenced acts of crime and corruption allegedly committed by Mubarak loyalists or remnants. The November 25, 2012, statement summarizing an FJP statement focused heavily on Mubarak regime remnants: "We faced together many obstacles during the tumultuous transitional period—obstacles [put in place] by former [Mubarak] regime loyalists in order to discredit the revolution and halt its progress … [and we witnessed] violent bullying and chaos on the streets meant to aggravate the economic crisis inherited from the toppled government." The November 29, 2012, MB statement said the following about Mubarak regime remnants: "Unfortunately, some agitators and former regime leftovers have exploited these political circumstances to mobilize numbers of thugs and criminals to disrupt peaceful demonstrations by organizing attacks on some Muslim Brotherhood and FJP headquarters."

THE 2012 CONSTITUTIONAL REFERENDUM

During the 2012 constitutional referendum period, Ikhwanweb.com allotted significant coverage to the vote. We searched sixteen days of the website's coverage—from December 10, 2012, through December 25, 2012. Our search yielded a total of fifteen posts, all of which were studied here. Unsurprisingly given the Brotherhood's stake in helping to draft the document, the website was supportive of both the constitution's text and the voting process. Posts tended to praise aspects of the draft constitution and link it to Egypt's larger democratic project. In all, two dominant frames emerged from our analysis: The Constitution Is in Egypt's Best Interests and Glorifying Egyptians.

The Constitution Is in Egypt's Best Interests Frame

Posts published on Ikhwanweb.com consistently argued that Egypt's 2012 draft constitution was in the best interests of the nation. The Constitution Is in Egypt's Best Interests frame featured several subframes: Praising the Constitution; Fulfillment of Democracy; The Constitution Will Unify Egyptians; The Constitution Is Based on National Consensus; and Defending the Constitution against Allegations.

Praising the Constitution Subframe. Ikhwanweb.com consistently praised the 2012 draft constitution. The website did not include any posts critical of the draft constitution.

On December 10, 2012, a post included remarks from Mahmoud Hussein, the MB secretary-general. Hussein said that "the draft constitution being put to public referendum is the best ever for Egypt, and will certainly achieve stability." A December 11, 2012, post featured comments by a high-ranking Egyptian judge and scholar of constitutional law, Tariq Bashri, who argued that the Constituent Assembly "made a tremendous effort and produced a great Constitution, worthy of all Egyptians." A December 12, 2012, post summarized an official MB statement about the referendum. The post quoted the statement: "Now is the time to make your decision, to approve a constitution that helps improve your life, and uphold your will and your dignity." The post also said that the constitution was "as perfect as humanly possible," and called it "the greatest draft constitution Egypt ever knew."

Fulfillment of Democracy Subframe. Ikhwanweb.com's coverage of the 2012 referendum suggested that both the vote and the text of the constitution represented positive steps toward Egypt's democratic aims.

On December 12, 2012, a post quoted Gamal Heshmat, an FJP leader, who said, "Voting yes for the constitution will help achieve the democratic transformation we all long for, and will certainly aid the building the state institutions and protect the rights of citizens at home and abroad." Another December 12, 2012, post drew attention to the fact that Constituent Assembly was democratically assembled. The post read, "The constitution was written by the Constituent Assembly elected indirectly by the Egyptian people. The Assembly made a great effort in drawing up this important document, and put it to the people for community dialogue six times over the past six months."

A December 14, 2012, post posited that the referendum would produce a democratic outcome. The post said, "[T]he vote on the constitution will surely end the instability that has prevailed throughout Egypt for two years, and will draw a clear road map, and then continue immediately to complete the rebuilding of democratic institutions." The same post also spoke to the text of the constitution, claiming that the text would create a democratic political framework for Egypt. The post specifically referenced presidential powers and the democratic notion of the separation of powers. The post said, "The vilifying campaign extends beyond reason and logic, claiming that the Constitution gives the President dictatorial powers, while the truth is that articles of the Constitution reduce the powers of the President, and stipulate that the government the President forms must win the confidence of Parliament, and that the President must resign if people reject the dissolution of parliament in a referendum."

A December 16, 2012, post wrote about the "massive crowds" at polling stations. Heshmat, who was again quoted, argued that the referendum represented a powerful democratic moment. He said, "The wheels of democracy in Egypt have started turning. No one can stop it after today. The Egyptian people have acquired a high degree of political awareness."

Following the completion of voting, some posts defended the referendum by drawing attention to its allegedly democratic features, including high voter turnout and independent monitoring. For example, a December 20, 2012, post highlighted "strong voter turnout" and "judicial supervision," arguing that these features "ensured the integrity of the referendum, and made fraud impossible." The post also mentioned the presence of "independent observers" and "millions [of voters] that stretched in incredibly long lines." Brotherhood leader Helmy Gazzar was quoted in the post. He mentioned "positive participation by millions" and "close monitoring by Egyptian and international observers." He also called the voting process "transparent." Gazzar also defended the referendum against accusations. The post said, "Gazzar stressed that all these safeguards guarantee the integrity of the referendum and significantly reduce the credibility of those who are trying to throw accusations of fraud or forgery." A December 23, 2012, post also drew attention to high voter turnout. The post noted that "millions of citizens in seventeen provinces turned out to vote on the draft constitution." The post continued, "For the second time in one week, the world saw those millions of Egyptians patiently standing in line for long hours, determined to express their opinion and announce their decision." The post also cited FJP monitors, who were said to have ascertained "that voting and counting were completed under full judicial supervision and monitoring of human rights organizations, with full local and international media coverage." The monitors indicated that while "some irregularities were reported, they were so few and limited [that] they had no effect on the integrity of the referendum." A December 24, 2012, post cited FJP leader Katatni, who said, "For the first time in Egyptian history, the people chose their Constitution of their own free will and after a long debate." Meanwhile, a December 25, 2012, post cited reports from domestic judicial bodies and representatives of international human rights organizations, all of which pointed to the "integrity of Egypt's recent referendum." According to Egyptian Judge Ashraf Zahran, who was quoted in the post, "the referendum was successful and fair, conducted under full judicial supervision, and ... all allegations of violations were merely attempts by certain parties to question a major celebration of democracy in which the whole nation positively participated." The post also cited Observers to Protect the Revolution (OPR), who argued that "all violations and irregularities witnessed did not affect the integrity of the draft referendum process."

On December 20, 2012, a leading Egyptian judge, Tariq Bashri, was cited. He argued that the constitution would lead to "political cooperation between different political currents, and better representation in the new parliament." He also said that "[a]pproval [of the constitution] would also help accelerate the formation and rebuilding of state institutions and the distribution of powers in peaceful and appropriate ways. Thus, the House of Representatives will take away the legislative power now in the hands of the President." Bashri also said that approving the constitution would lead to opening "up new avenues for dialogue and cooperation between the various parties, groups and movements in political decision-making" and "a stronger mechanism for government monitoring."

The Constitution Will Unify Egyptians Subframe. Ikhwanweb.com posts framed the referendum as a unifying event, implying that both the voting process and the draft constitution would bring Egyptians from diverse backgrounds together.

For example, a December 23, 2012, post argued that the "new constitution would be an historic opportunity to reunite national forces on the basis of mutual respect and sincere dialogue." The title of a December 24, 2012, post—"Constitution approval opportunity for dialogue and unity"—also spoke to the theme of unification. The post also included a quote from Katatni: "Once again, we extend our hands to all political parties and all national and patriotic groups and movements to set together features of the future of our homeland. I do hope we can all turn a new page." In the same post, Murad Ali, the FJP's media adviser, "expressed the hope that the adoption of the new Constitution would represent a chance to reunite national forces on the basis of mutual respect." According to Ali, "We hope that the approval of the country's basic law would be a historic opportunity for all patriotic political forces to close ranks and unite on the basis of mutual respect and genuine dialogue in order to achieve stability and complete rebuilding Egypt's constitutional institutions."

On December 25, 2012, MB chairman Mohamed Badie was quoted offering his "heartfelt congratulations" to Egyptians for adopting a new constitution. Badie was quoted speaking specifically to possible opportunities for Egyptian unity. He said, "Let's start—all together—the building of renaissance Egypt of our free will, with sincere intention and strong determination, men and women, Muslims and Christians alike."

The Constitution Is Based on National Consensus Subframe. Given allegations that the Brotherhood played an unfairly heavy role in writing the 2012 constitution, it is unsurprising, perhaps, that Ikhwanweb.com went to some lengths to suggest that the constitution was based on national consensus, and not the product of a narrow Islamist vision.

For instance, a December 14, 2012, post said that the text was written by "members elected from the full spectrum of Egyptian society for the first time in the history of constitution-making in Egypt." Later, the post said, "The irrefutable truth is that the full spectrum of Egyptian society did take part in drafting at all stages of the preparation and writing of the Constitution." A December 23, 2012, post published following results made it clear that the referendum would pass highlighted the lopsided nature of the vote. The post read, "This indicates that the majority of the Egyptian people (about 64% of those who voted) have made their decision to accept the draft constitution." A post published on December 24, 2012, made a similar point. That post included the arguably hyperbolic remarks of FJP leader Essam El-Erian, who argued that the "approval of Egypt's new Constitution, by 63.8 percent, is one of the world's highest rates, adding that this means Egyptians have broken world records for national charter approval."

Defending the Constitution against Allegations Subframe. Egypt's 2012 constitutional referendum was held amid widespread debates about both the text and the way in which the document was drafted. Some Egyptian political parties argued that the Brotherhood exerted inordinate influence over both the text and the writing process. Some facetiously called the new constitution "The Muslim Brotherhood Constitution" (or "Dustoor Al-Ikhwaan" in Arabic). Given this context, it is predictable that several Ikhwanweb.com posts about the referendum were dedicated to defending the draft against allegations. Some defenses focused on the text and others focused on the voting process. A handful of posts, meanwhile, focused on defending against the allegation that the constitution was a narrow Muslim Brotherhood project rather than a comprehensive national one.

A December 10, 2012, post included remarks by Hussein, who deflected claims that the constitution was the product of the Muslim Brotherhood. He said, "The constitution was approved by members of the Constituent Assembly (tasked with writing the new constitution), at a time when there was no Islamist majority at all. The most basic principle of democracy is that everyone has the right to say yes or no." A December 23, 2012, post seemed to make a similar point when it argued that the passing of the constitution represented the "decision" of "millions of Egyptians."

A December 19, 2012, post was dedicated to defending the draft constitution against allegations put forth by the National Salvation Front, a large anti-Brotherhood political movement consisting of several political parties. "In a press conference, Tuesday, Justice Mahmoud Abu-Shusha, spokesman for the Supreme Elections Committee (SEC), refuted allegations by the National Salvation Front of vote rigging in the first round of the constitutional referendum," the post read. Abu-Shusha was also quoted: " 'There is a hostile campaign against the referendum and its supervising judges. In fact, judges overseeing the vote are certainly above any doubt. This talk about fraud and violations is completely void, impossible to happen. There is an absurd and irrational campaign waged against the judges." The post continued, "For his part, Dr. Mohamed Eliwa, member of the Muslim Brotherhood's Shura Council, said in a statement: 'National Salvation Front members, with their allegations as refuted by SEC, have lost all credibility. They have proved that they run a secret campaign against the referendum after their utter disappointment at the results of the first phase.'" A December 14, 2012, post defended the draft constitution against what it calls "false allegations about the text."

Glorifying Egyptians Frame

Similar to a pattern established in coverage of other events, Ikhwanweb .com glorified and praised Egyptians in its coverage of the 2012 constitutional referendum. On December 15, 2012, a post was published citing Brotherhood leader Karem Radwan. The post said, "Radwan pointed [out] that the Egyptian people are still making history, with the highest rates of progress and awareness of the real situation in their homeland, and that they still strive for the advancement of their homeland without further delay." The post continued, "The Brotherhood leader also denounced opposition statements describing the Egyptian people as illiterate and ignorant. He stressed that 'the people of Egypt have always been makers of civilizations, and that no one ... is entitled to insult or underrate our people.'" A December 16, 2012, post quoted Heshmat, who indicated that "the constitutional referendum is the most powerful proof yet of the Egyptian people's political maturity and awareness of their rights and higher interests." Heshmat was also quoted: "The long queues seen in the media and the Supreme Elections Committee having to consider extending the vote period by another day due to heavy turnout, are a resounding response refuting elite accusations charging that the Egyptian people are illiterate, ignorant and have no perception of their own higher interests."

A December 23, 2012, post summarizing a statement issued by the FJP also praised Egyptians. The post read, "It is a true measure of this enlightened nation's civilized nature that no violent incidents were reported during voting, despite all the sharp political differences. This indicates that the great Egyptian people are embracing the democratic process." The December 25, 2012, post that cited Badie also included a quote praising Egyptians: "My heartfelt congratulations to all honorable Egyptian people on the endorsement of modern Egypt's first Constitution. ... I thank all Egyptian people, who have just proved that they still have a lot to teach the world, as they did in the past and will again do in the future."

Chapter 7

Discussion

This study used framing theory to examine about two years of content from the Egyptian Muslim Brotherhood's English-language website, Ikhwanweb .com. Our analysis focused on 375 posts centered on ten separate events related to Egypt's 2011 uprising and its immediate aftermath. The study was carried out in order to shed light on Muslim Brotherhood positions on foundational political events in Egypt, and, importantly, how the Muslim Brotherhood (MB) wanted to be seen by English-speaking audiences. There are two underlying assumptions of our study: first, that Ikhwanweb.com is an important carrier of MB values and positions; and second, that the website reflects the Brotherhood's desired image in key English-speaking publics. Overall, and unsurprisingly, Ikhwanweb.com content reflected a coherent, consistent message of sympathy for the Brotherhood's political cause and national ambitions.

The framing analyses carried out here uncovered many dominant frames, and also a series of important subframes. Overall, the Brotherhood tended to frame the Egyptian uprising as something positive, their political project as a force for good in Egyptian society, and their political rivals as corrupt, evil, unpopular, or some combination of these traits.

In all, the analysis of posts about the ten events studied here uncovered a total of fifty-one dominant frames and thirty-three subframes. As would be expected, more frames were identified in coverage of events that were allotted heavy coverage by Ikhwanweb.com, and fewer frames were uncovered in reportage of events that garnered comparatively little attention. For instance, the website devoted 116 posts to the 2011 Egyptian uprising, and our analysis of that event revealed a total of ten dominant frames and ten additional subframes. At another end of the spectrum, the 2012 constitutional referendum was addressed in only fifteen posts, yielding only two dominant frames and five subframes. Certainly, and as one might anticipate, Ikhwanweb.com proved to be much more a public relations tool for the Brotherhood than any sort of independent, detached journalistic enterprise. Results from this study underscore that the website functions more as an MB media relations tool than a traditional news outlet, a point to which we will return in the below subsection titled "Ikhwanweb.com as Social Capital."

FRAMING THE BROTHERHOOD, MILITARY, MUBARAK REGIME, AND SPECIFIC EVENTS

Three groups seemed to garner most of Ikhwanweb.com's attention—the Brotherhood, the Egyptian military, and the Mubarak government. Indeed, most of the fifty-one frames and thirty-three subframes uncovered as part of the analysis focused on these three factions. Importantly, though, coverage of these groups was largely dictated by how the MB and Ikhwanweb.com approached specific events. Ikhwanweb.com's focus—and also its tendency to employ highly specific framing—seemed to be more or less dictated by how political events unfolded on the ground and, importantly, also by the Brotherhood's policy agenda and positions vis-à-vis these specific entities and events.

Overall, the revolution and democratic transition were celebrated by Ikhwanweb.com as historic, extraordinary moments for Egypt, and the website went to some lengths to frame the Brotherhood positively and associate it with the revolution and the more redeeming qualities of its aftermath. In this context, Ikhwanweb.com described the Brotherhood as a civilized, modern, nonviolent, and revolutionary political movement. The Mubarak government and Egyptian military, meanwhile, were, for the most part, covered critically—minor exceptions notwithstanding, both of these entities were frequently described in negative terms and blamed for Egypt's problems.

Framing the Brotherhood. Much of the positive framing of the Brotherhood came in the context of elections. Around elections, Ikhwanweb.com seemed to go out of its way to try and demonstrate that people—Egyptians, Americans, Christians, and others—should not fear the Egyptian Muslim Brotherhood. During its coverage of the 2010 parliamentary elections, the 2011 constitutional referendum, and the 2012 presidential election, dozens of Ikhwanweb.com posts framed the MB as peaceful, democratic, tolerant, and inclusive, all while suggesting that the group is a popular and legitimate representative of the Egyptian people. It was during coverage of these events that variations of the Do Not Fear the Brotherhood, The MB Is Tolerant/Inclusive, The MB Is Peaceful and Democratic, and The MB Is a Popular Savior frames dominated coverage.

Framing the Military. Framing of the Egyptian military was also determined, to a meaningful extent, by specific political circumstances and the nature of the Brotherhood's dynamic relationship with the military. Significantly, framing of the military changed over time, and in ways that seemed to reflect both the Brotherhood's complicated relationship with the Egyptian armed forces and the MB's policy agenda. For instance, in its coverage of the March 2011 constitutional referendum, which occurred fairly early on in Egypt's democratic transition, Ikhwanweb.com offered up relatively positive framing of the Egyptian military. In particular, our analysis uncovered an Embracing the Military Roadmap frame, which tended to afford legitimacy to Egypt's military governors and show the Brotherhood's support for the armed forces' plan for the country.

Soon after the referendum, however, Ikhwanweb.com's coverage of the military changed to become more negative. This change was most likely a reflection of the Brotherhood's evolving, and worsening, relationship with the armed forces. For example, Ikhwanweb.com placed blame squarely on Egypt's military government (including Egyptian police) for the Maspero Massacre, Mohamed Mahmoud protest violence, and Port Said Massacre, respectively. In its coverage of these three violent events, variations of the Massacre, Blaming the Military Government, Condemning the Police, and Condemning the Military Government frames tended to dominate coverage. It should be noted, however, that Ikhwanweb.com did display at least some ambivalence about the Maspero and Mohamed Mahmoud events—although the military government was framed negatively and blamed for violence, framing patterns showed at least some critical coverage of protesters, who were painted as unwise for initiating protests at inopportune times. Importantly, the Brotherhood didn't officially endorse or participate in either the Maspero or Mohamed Mahmoud protests—coverage, then, again more or less reflected the official Brotherhood line.

By the time of the 2012 presidential election, the Brotherhood's falling out with the military was complete, something that seemed to drive critical framing of the military during Ikhwanweb.com's coverage of the election. The military did not figure prominently into the website's coverage of the final two events studied here—Mohamed Morsi's 2012 constitutional decree, and the 2012 constitutional referendum—but the site's focus on a "counter-revolution" seemed to imply the involvement of Egypt's deep state, which included at least some elements of Egypt's military.

Framing Mubarak. Ikhwanweb.com's coverage of the Mubarak regime also seemed to change based on political circumstances in Egypt. Specifically, the Mubarak government figured prominently into the website's coverage of the first three events studied here—the 2010 parliamentary elections, the 2011 Egyptian uprising, and the 2011 constitutional referendum. During all three of these events, the Mubarak regime was covered in a highly critical manner, with posts suggesting that Mubarak and his most important officials were fundamentally evil, corrupt, brutal, authoritarian, and treasonous. The Mubarak government was talked about in such a way as to suggest a certain kind of treatment from Egyptians (and, by extension, the Brotherhood). Following Mubarak's ouster, and in particular after the 2011 constitutional referendum, the Mubarak government was seemingly forgotten by Ikhwanweb.com. Interestingly, though, Mubarak reappeared in posts related to the second-to-last event examined in this study, Morsi's 2012 constitutional decree, which was issued nearly two years after Mubarak's fall. The website justified Morsi's decree by arguing that it was a legitimate and necessary response to the continued effects of Mubarak era corruption.

IKHWANWEB.COM, THE BROTHERHOOD, AND RATIONAL CHOICE

Assuming that Ikhwanweb.com can provide at least some indication of the Brotherhood's political positions, this frame changing underscores the fact that MB positions cannot be oversimplified into one-size-fits-all formulas. For example, during Egypt's revolution and democratic transition, the Brotherhood was neither absolutely pro-military nor absolutely anti-military. Rather, and importantly, the MB behaved as a self-interested political actor, making decisions about support based on its unique political objectives. While the Brotherhood likely made decisions to either support or oppose certain groups, events, and policies based on what the group deemed to be in the best interests of Egypt as a whole, the MB, like all political factions, also undoubtedly made decisions based on calculations of self-interest.

One way to understand the Brotherhood's support and/or opposition to individual entities and particular policy positions—as represented here by the directionality of its English-language website reportage—is through reference to rational choice theory, a large umbrella notion for understanding individual human behavior and collective social action by seeing both as the natural byproduct of rational assessment and ordering of preferred outcomes (see Geddes, 1996; Ostrom, 1998; Scott, 2000; and many others). A large body of evidence from rational choice research in sociology and political science suggests that "humans [are] self-interested, short-term maximizers" (Ostrom, 1998, p. 2).

Although there is significant scholarly debate around the precise definition of rational choice and the limits of its application to studies of human behavior, there is a near, if imperfect, scholarly consensus about the purposive nature of both individual and collective behavior (Huber & Dion,

2002). Evidence from rational choice research in political science is clear on the ramifications for political outcomes—in particular, evidence suggests that both individual politicians and political factions seek to maximize personal (or group) benefit by actively rank-ordering choice options, and ultimately basing decisions on the most likely positive outcomes (Scott, 2000).

Rational choice scholars distinguish between "thin" rationality and "thick" rationality. Thin rationality refers to the general, basic human search for attainable preferences, while thick rationality refers more specifically to politicians' interest in the "preservation or augmentation of power" (Huber & Dion, 2002, p. 3).

The Brotherhood, then, like all other Egyptian political factions, made policy decisions—and choices about editorial positions—not only on determinations of broad national interest, but also on the basis of calculations of self-interest. This reality helps to explain how the MB supported the military's roadmap in the spring of 2011, but came to fiercely oppose the military at later junctions of the transition. Importantly, rational choice also helps explain Ikhwanweb.com's framing of specific protests and acts of violence. At the heart of all MB decisions—including editorial ones—was a basic calculation of what might best serve the group's goals.

IKHWANWEB.COM'S FRAMING MECHANISMS

As we discussed in an earlier section of this book dealing with framing theory, media scholars have drawn attention to the ways in which reports can be framed, or the framing mechanisms through which reports are given meaning. Frames can be cemented by keywords, associations, visual imagery, and sourcing. The Brotherhood's English-language website relied most heavily on two important framing mechanisms: keywords and sourcing.

The website's use of both keywords and sourcing demonstrated some sophistication. The website homed in on important keywords that can drive narratives—terms such as democracy, inclusivity, peace, revolution, authoritarianism, and brutality, among many others, were employed frequently, ostensibly to highlight certain realities and suppress others. With respect to sourcing, Ikhwanweb.com relied on authority figures, including scholars and experts, to make larger points about Egyptian politics, and, importantly, to support dominant MB narratives. Stephen Zunes, Shadi Hamid, Michele Dunne, Amy Hamzawy, Rob Prince, the Carnegie Endowment, the *Huffington Post*, and a host of other expert sources, were frequently employed, always to confirm Brotherhood positions. It is important to note that, out of the 375 posts studied here, no anti-Brotherhood sources were drawn from, and no sources overtly contradicted basic Brotherhood positions on events in Egypt.

Significantly, the Brotherhood's framing of events suggests an acute awareness of anti-Brotherhood discourses. Many of the frames that drove Ikhwanweb.com coverage seemed to be direct responses to what the group likely sees as unfair stereotyping. For example, the Do Not Fear the Brotherhood frame and its variants—The Brotherhood Is Peaceful, The Brotherhood Is Democratic, The Brotherhood Is Inclusive, and The Brotherhood Is Tolerant—seem to be a direct response to allegations that the MB is a terrorist group along the lines of Al-Qaeda or ISIS. Interestingly, Ikhwanweb.com features numerous points censuring Al-Qaeda and its former leader, Osama Bin Laden, and explaining how the Brotherhood is different. Also, Ikhwanweb.com's repeated emphasis on freedom and democratic norms and ideals—as represented in frames and subframes such as Elections Are the Solution, Elections Represent a Democratic Solution, Go-Vote, People Are the Source of Power, and People's Free Will Should Be Respected—suggests that the MB was aware of criticisms suggesting that the group's Islamist agenda conflicted with basic democratic principles.

IKHWANWEB.COM AS SOCIAL CAPITAL

French sociologist Pierre Bourdieu defined social capital as "the aggregate of the actual or potential resources which are linked to possession of a durable network of more or less institutionalized relationships of mutual acquaintance and recognition—or in other words, to membership in a group—which provides each of its members with the backing of the collectivity-owned capital, a 'credential' which entitles them to credit, in the various senses of the word" (Bourdieu, 1986, 249).

Putnam (1996) argued that social capital entails "features of social life—networks, norms, and trust—that enable participants to act together more effectively to pursue shared objectives." The two pillars of social capital are trust and social connectedness. "When people are tightly bound to an association, their trust of their fellow members usually grows, and the aggregate social capital increases. As a result, people are more likely to participate in civic or political activities" (Zhang & Chia, 2006, p. 282).

The internet can play a critical role in enhancing, or at least facilitating, participants' access to social capital. Virtual communities serve as a venue through which contributors with shared interests can engage in a collective pursuit of common good for themselves or for the group(s) to which they belong (Wellman et al., 2001).

In one important sense, Ikhwanweb.com represents for the Muslim Brotherhood an important tool of social capital. At one level, the website is an online manifestation of the group's sociopolitical and religious network. At another, more important level, the site is a tool through which the group communicates with the outside, English-speaking world, and, importantly, a "credential" with which the MB demonstrates its political skill and professionalism.

In several places in our analysis, we made clear that Ikhwanweb.com denotes an attempt by the Brotherhood to communicate directly to the United States. Many of the coverage patterns—and specific frames—uncovered in this study speak to how the MB likely *wanted to be seen* in 2011 and 2012 by key Western power brokers. The website seemed to speak the language of the West, and respond specifically to Western governmental concerns about political Islam in general and the Muslim Brotherhood in particular. The site's editors are obviously aware of the accusations leveled against the MB—that they are extremists, anti-democratic, prone to violence, anti-women, and anti-Christian, among other allegations—and use the site as a platform to respond to these concerns. The website is sophisticated both in its deployment of the English language and its capacity to cast the Brotherhood in terms agreeable to Western governments, including, significantly, the American government. For example, as our analysis noted, posts spoke explicitly to anti-extremism, democracy, tolerance, and inclusivity. Also, and as we've noted elsewhere, posts played up the importance of "the will of all the Egyptian people" (Ikhwanweb.com, January 16, 2012) and the Brotherhood's basic democratic commitment.

Some posts seemed to emphasize democracy through references to the United States and American political figures. For instance, and as we noted in our analysis of Ikhwanweb.com coverage of the 2011 parliamentary elections, the website extensively quoted both the American assistant secretary of state William Burns and former U.S. president Jimmy Carter. Both Burns and Carter were quoted attesting to the democratic nature of the Egyptian elections. After extensively sourcing Burns and Carter, the post quoted an FJP leader, who said, "There is no doubt that the parliamentary election results were expressive of all Egyptians and their free will." The juxtaposition of the quotes suggests that Ikhwanweb.com's sourcing decisions were meant to serve as a means of placing onus on the United States to respect basic principles it claims to represent. The placement of the quotes further serves to reinforce—through association—the Brotherhood's respect for democracy and its similarity to American politicians. Another post covering the same event was even more explicit in this regard—it said Brotherhood Chairman Mohamed Badie expressed "hope that foreign countries, especially the United States, shall respect the will of the people." The website was often crude, and largely devoid of basic journalistic principles, but, insofar as it was a public relations tool for the Brotherhood, it demonstrated that the group knew exactly who their primary audiences were, that its editors understood the value of this form of social capital to the Brotherhood's cause.

FUTURE RESEARCH

Although we hope this analysis of Ikhwanweb.com can be used to shed light on some of the Brotherhood's policy positions vis-à-vis the 2011 Egyptian revolution, this book should be seen primarily as a media study and not as a political science study of policy positions. It was beyond the purview of this book to determine whether Brotherhood claims about itself, the Mubarak government, and the Egyptian army were fair, accurate, and grounded in some political reality, or simply a type of fantastical thinking. Future political research should attempt to assess the Brotherhood's policy positions, and outline more clearly the group's relationship to the 2011 Egyptian revolution.

Our foray into Ikhwanweb.com paints a relatively complicated picture of the MB's relationship to the 2011 uprising. The Brotherhood was cautious about the revolution at the start, perhaps because they were fearful of arrest, and didn't lend the uprising its initial impetus. But the group formally joined the uprising relatively early on—on day four of eighteen—and offered important contributions. Questions will likely remain for some time about whether the Brotherhood's role in the post-revolution democratic transition was positive or deleterious. As we've noted here, the Brotherhood, like all political groups, sought power and influence. But one should be careful not to dismiss the Brotherhood's competitive politics as an entirely selfish foray devoid of any broader interest in the well-being of Egypt and the Egyptian general public. If research into Islamism has taught us anything, it is that Islamist groups deserve to have an opportunity to play politics alongside other groups in the Muslim-majority world, speak for themselves, and have their policy positions and written and spoken claims both counted as part of legitimate public discourse and scrutinized alongside all other forms of discourse.

Future research should also assess the extent to which the Brotherhood's English-language website is consistent or inconsistent with the group's Arabic-language site and various social media accounts. Given the different audiences to which these sites speak, some differences in tone and emphasis might be expected. But basic principles and positions should hold consistent across language. To date, and in spite of considerable discussion about alleged inconsistencies, little empirical work exists in this regard.

Importantly, future research should also employ in-depth interviews with Brotherhood content contributors—web editors, writers, and decision makers—to examine the kinds of meanings they assign to Brotherhood-produced content and also to determine how MB media content is planned, produced, and constructed.

References

Abdelhadi, M. (2012, June 24). Muslim Brotherhood's Mursi declared Egypt president. *BBC*. Retrieved from http://www.bbc.com/news/world-18571580

Abdo, G. (2000). *No God but God: Egypt and the triumph of Islam*. London: Oxford University Press.

Aboelezz, M. (2014). The geosemiotics of Tahrir Square: A study of the relationship between discourse and space. *Journal of Language and Politics, 13*(4), 599–622.

Abou Bakr, S. (2012, November 22). Morsy issues new constitutional declaration. *Daily News Egypt*. Retrieved from https://dailynewsegypt.com/2012/11/22/morsy-makes-new-constitutional-declaration/

Al-Anani, K. (2016). *Inside the Muslim Brotherhood*. London: Oxford University Press.

Al-Arian, A. (2014). *Answering the call: Popular Islamic activism in Sadat's Egypt*. London: Oxford University Press.

Al-Awadi, H. (2004). *In pursuit of legitimacy: The Muslim Brothers and Mubarak: 1982-2000*. London: Tauris Academic Studies.

Al-Awadi, H. (2013). Islamists in power: The case of the Muslim Brotherhood in Egypt. *Contemporary Arab Affairs, 6*(4), 539–551.

Albrecht, H. (2012) Authoritarian transformation or transition from authoritarianism? Insights on regime change in Egypt. In *Arab Spring in Egypt: Revolution and beyond*. B. Korany & R. El-Mahdi (Eds.), pp. 251–270. Cairo, Egypt: The American University in Cairo Press.

Allagui, I., & Najjar, A. (2011). Framing political Islam in popular Egyptian cinema. *Middle East Journal of Culture and Communication, 4*(2011), 203–224.

Amin, G. (2013). *Whatever happened to the Egyptian revolution?* Cairo, Egypt: The American University in Cairo Press.

Ashour, O. (2012, December 3). Egypt's Democracy Dictator? *The Brookings Institution*. Retrieved from https://www.brookings.edu/opinions/egypts-democratic-dictator/

Baker, R. W. (2003). *Islam without fear: Egypt and the new Islamists*. Cambridge, MA: Harvard University Press.

Bardhan, S. (2014). Egypt, Islamists, and the internet: The case of the Muslim Brotherhood and its rhetoric of dialectics in Ikhwanweb. *Digest of Middle East Studies, 23*(2), 235–261.

Bassiouni, M. C. (2017). *Chronicles of the Egyptian revolution and its aftermath: 2011-2016.* London: Cambridge University Press.

Bayat, A. (2007). *Making Islam democratic: Social movements and the post-Islamist turn.* California: Stanford University Press.

Beattie, K. J. (2000). *Egypt during the Sadat years.* New York: Palgrave.

Blommaert, J., & Bulcaen, C. (2000). Critical discourse analysis. *Annual Review of Anthropology, 29*, 447–466.

Bourdieu, P. (1986). The forms of capital. In *Handbook of theory and research for the sociology of education,* J. Richardson (Ed.), pp. 241–258, New York: Greenwood Press.

Bradley, M. (2012, February 2). World news: Dozens killed at Egypt soccer match – Post-game riots involving armed "Ultra" fans underscore country's persistent security problems and popular rage. *The Wall Street Journal.* Retrieved from https://www.wsj.com/articles/SB10001424052970204652904577197233516122226

Brotherhood to run in Egypt polls: Main opposition group announces plan to contest November's legislative vote, despite calls for some for a boycott. (2010, October 9). *Al-Jazeera.* Retrieved from http://www.aljazeera.com/news/middleeast/2010/10/201010911379428759.html

Carpenter, S. (2007). U.S. elite and non-elite newspapers' portrayal of the Iraq ear: A comparison of frames and source use. *Journalism & Mass Communication Quarterly, 84*(4), 761–776.

Carvalho, A. (2016, March 31). Mediated discourse and society. *Journalism Studies, 9*(2), 161–177.

Celebration in Egypt as Morsi declared winner: Muslim Brotherhood candidate and president-elect in victory speech vows to unite the country and stand up for democracy. (2012, 24 June). *Al-Jazeera.* Retrieved from http://www.aljazeera.com/news/middleeast/2012/06/201262412445190400.html

Chong, D., & Druckman, J. N. (2007). Framing theory. *Annual Review of Political Science, 10*, 103–126.

Chouliaraki, L., & Fairclough, N. (2005). *Discourse in late modernity: Rethinking critical discourse analysis.* Edinburgh: Edinburgh University Press.

Chyi, H. I., & McCombs, M. (2004). Media salience and the process of framing: Coverage of the Columbine school shootings. *Journalism & Mass Communication Quarterly, 81*(1), 22–35.

Dabbous-Sensenig, D. (2006). To veil or not to veil: Gender and religion on Al-Jazeera's Islamic Law and Life. *Westminster Papers in Communication and Culture, 3*(2), 60–85.

de Vreese, C. H. (2005). News framing: Theory and typology. *Information Design Journal + Document Design, 13*(1), 51–62.

Duboc, M. (2015). Reluctant revolutionaries? The dynamics of labor protests in Egypt, 2006-13. In R. Abou-El-Fadl (Ed.), *Revolutionary Egypt: Connecting domestic and international struggles*, pp. 27–42. London: Routledge.

Echchaibi, N. (2008). Hyper-Islamism? Mediating Islam from the halal website to the Islamic talk show. *Journal of Arab & Muslim Media Research, 1*(3), 199–214.

Egypt braces for nationwide protests. (2011, January 26). *The Daily Star*. Retrieved from http://www.thedailystar.net/news-detail-171577

Egypt Copts mark massacre anniversary: March staged to commemorate dozens of Coptic Christians killed in Cairo last October by security forces. (2012, October 9). *Al-Jazeera*. Retrieved from http://www.aljazeera.com/news/middlee ast/2012/10/201210916741376710.html

"Egypt: Don't cover up military killing of Copt protesters." (2011, October 25). Retrieved from the Human Rights Watch Website: https://www.hrw.org/news/2011/10/25/egypt-dont-cover-up-military-killing-copt-protesters

Egypt elections set for November 28: Government clamps down on opposition as Hosni Mubarak, the president, announces date for parliamentary elections. (2010, October 20). *Al-Jazeera*. Retrieved from http://www.aljazeera.com/news/middlee ast/2010/10/201010201482298875.html

Egypt election: Hosni Mubarak's NDP sweeps second round (2010, December 7). *BBC*. Retrieved from http://www.bbc.com/news/world-middle-east-11935368

"Egypt: No acknowledgment or justice for mass protester killings: Set up a fact-finding committee as a first step." (2013, December 10). Retrieved from the Human Rights Watch website: https://www.hrw.org/news/2013/12/10/egypt-no-acknowledgment-or-justice-mass-protester-killings

"Egypt: Protesters' blood on the military leadership's hands: Violence, delays in transfer of power fuels protesters' rage." (2011, November 22). Retrieved from the Human Rights Watch Website: https://www.hrw.org/news/2011/11/22/egypt-protesters-blood-military-leaderships-hands

Egypt referendum strongly backs constitution changes. (2011, March 20). *BBC*. Retrieved from http://www.bbc.com/news/world-middle-east-12801125

Egypt voters back new constitution in referendum. (2012, December 25). *BBC*. Retrieved from http://www.bbc.com/news/world-middle-east-20842487

Egypt's Islamist parties win elections to parliament. (2012, January 21). *BBC*. Retrieved from http://www.bbc.com/news/world-middle-east-16665748

Egypt's Mubarak resigns after 30-year rule. (2011, February 11). *CNN*. Retrieved from http://www.cnn.com/2011/WORLD/africa/02/11/egypt.revolution/index.html

Egypt's Morsi assumes wide powers. (2012, November 23). *Al-Jazeera*. Retrieved from http://www.aljazeera.com/news/middleeast/2012/11/20121122161830842641.html

Egyptians vote in parliamentary elections amid fraud accusations. (2010, November 28). *CNN*. Retrieved from http://www.cnn.com/2010/WORLD/africa/11/28/egypt.elections/index.html

Eissa, A. (2015, October 19). Mohamed Mahmoud clashes: The day the few stood against the many. *Daily News Egypt*. Retrieved from https://dailynewsegypt.com/2015/11/19/mohamed-mahmoud-clashes-the-day-the-few-stood-against-the-many/

El-Ghobashy, M. (2012). The praxis of the Egyptian revolution. In *The journey to Tahrir Square: Revolution, protest and social change in Egypt*, J. Sowers & C. Toensing (Eds.), pp. 21–40. New York: Verso.

El Houdaiby, I. (2012). Islamism in and after Egypt's revolution. In *Arab Spring in Egypt: Revolution and beyond*. B. Korany & R. El-Mahdi (Eds.), pp. 125–152. Cairo, Egypt: The American University in Cairo Press.Elmasry, M. H. (2009). Death in the Middle East: An analysis of how the New York Times and Chicago Tribune framed killings in the second Palestinian intifada. *Journal of Middle East Media, 5*(1).

Elmasry, M. H. (2013, June 28). Unpacking anti-Muslim Brotherhood discourse. *Jadaliyya*. Retrieved from http://www.jadaliyya.com/Details/28855/Unpacking-Anti-Muslim-Brotherhood-Discourse

el-Nawawy, M., & Khamis, S. (2010). Collective identity in the virtual Islamic public sphere: Contemporary discourses in two Islamic websites. *The International Communication Gazette, 72*(3), 229–250.

el-Nawawy, M., & Khamis, S. (2012). Divergent identities in the virtual Islamic public sphere: A case study of the English discussion forum "Islamonline." *Journal of Arab & Muslim Media Research, 5*(1), 31–48.

el-Nawawy, M., & Khamis, S. (2013). *Egyptian Revolution 2.0: Political blogging, civic engagement and citizen journalism*. New York: Palgrave Macmillan.

el-Nawawy, M., & Khamis, S. (2009). *Islam dot Com: Contemporary Islamic discourses in cyberspace*. New York: Palgrave Macmillan.

Entman, R. (1993). Framing: towards clarification of a fractured paradigm. *Journal of Communication, 43*(4), 51–58.

Fact finding committee puts blame on security for Port Said tragedy. (2012, February 12). *Ahram online*. Retrieved from http://english.ahram.org.eg/NewsContent/1/64/34339/Egypt/Politics-/Fact-finding-committee-puts-blame-on-security-for-.aspx

Fadel, M. (2014, January 21). What killed Egyptian democracy? *Boston Review*. Retrieved from http://bostonreview.net/forum/mohammad-fadel-what-killed-egyptian-democracy

Fahmy, D. (2016). The Muslim Brotherhood: Between opposition and power. In *Egypt: beyond Tahrir Square*, E. Mohamed & B. Momani (Eds.), pp. 76–94. Bloomington: Indiana University Press.

Fahmy, M. (2012, February 2). Eyewitnesses: Police stood idle in Egypt football massacre. *CNN*. Retrieved from http://www.cnn.com/2012/02/02/world/africa/egypt-soccer-deaths-color/index.html

Fahmy, M. (2011, October 10). Prime minister says Egypt "scrambling" after at least 23 killed in clashes. *CNN*. Retrieved from http://www.cnn.com/2011/10/09/world/meast/egypt-protest-clashes/index.html

Fahmy, M., & Hanna, J. (2012, November 23). Egypt's Morsy grants himself more power. *CNN*. Retrieved from http://edition.cnn.com/videos/world/2012/11/22/idesk-morsy-egypt-delaration.cnn

Fairclough, N. (2003). *Analyzing discourse: Textual analysis for social science*. London: Routledge.

Fairclough, N. (1992). Discourse and text: Linguistic and intertextual analysis within discourse analysis. *Discourse & Society, 3*(2), 193–217.

Fayed, S., & Zayed, D. (2012, May 28). Egypt presidential election 2012: Mohammed Morsi, Ahmed Shafiq in run-off vote. *The Huffington Post.* Retrieved from http://www.huffingtonpost.com/2012/05/28/egypt-presidential-election-2012_n_1550483.html

Feldman, N. (2012, November 26). Egypt's Mursi turns tyrant to save democracy. *Bloomberg.* Retrieved from https://www.bloomberg.com/view/articles/2012-11-26/egypt-s-mursi-turns-tyrant-to-save-democracy

Fursich, E. (2009). In defense of textual analysis: Restoring a challenged method for journalism and media studies. *Journalism Studies, 10*(2), 238–252.

Gamson, W. A., & Modigliani, A. (1987). The changing culture of affirmative action. In R. G. Braungart & M. M. Braungart (Eds.), *Research in Political Sociology, 3,* 137–177.

Gamson, W. A., & Modigliani, A. (1989). Media discourse and public opinion on nuclear power: A constructionist approach. *American Journal of Sociology, 95*(1), 1–37.

Gardner, L. (2011). *The road to Tahrir Square: Egypt and the United States from the rise of Nasser to the fall of Mubarak.* New York: The New Press.

Geddes, B. (1996). *Politician's dilemma: Building state capacity in Latin America.* Berkeley, CA: University of California Press.

Ghoneim, W. (2012). *Revolution 2.0: The power of the people is greater than the people in power: A memoir.* Boston: Houghton Mifflin Harcourt.

Gitlin, T. (1980). *The whole world is watching: Mass media in the making and unmaking of the new left.* Berkeley, CA: University of California Press.

Goffman, E. (1974). *Frame analysis: An essay on the organization of experience.* Cambridge, MA: Harvard University Press.

Golan, G. J. (2013). The gates of op-ed diplomacy: Newspaper framing the 2011 Egyptian revolution. *The International Communication Gazette, 75*(4), 359–373.

Gunning, J., & Baron, I. Z. (2014). *Why occupy a square? People, protests and movements in the Egyptian revolution.* London: Oxford University Press.

Guzman, A. L. (2015). Evolution of news frames during the 2011 Egyptian revolution: Critical discourse analysis of Fox news's and CNN's framing of protesters, Mubarak, and the Muslim Brotherhood. *Journalism & Mass Communication Quarterly, 93*(1), 80–98.

Hafiz, A. (2008, December 13). Muslim Brotherhood websites. Retrieved from http://www.ikhwanweb.com/article.php?id=18865

Halse, R. (2012). The Muslim-American neighbor as terrorist: The representation of a Muslim family in 24. *Journal of Arab & Muslim Media Research, 5*(1), 3–18.

Hamdy, N., & Gomaa, E. (2012). Framing the Egyptian uprising in Arabic language newspapers and social media." *Journal of Communication, 62,* 195–211.

Hamid, S. (2014). *Temptations of power: Islamists & illiberal democracy in a new Middle East.* London: Oxford University Press.

Hamid, S. (2011, May/June). The rise of the Islamists: How Islamists will change politics, and vice versa. *Foreign Affairs, 90*(3), 40–47.

Hamza, K. (2009, June 16). Muslim Brotherhood's media, from the missionary to the political discourse. Retrieved from http://www.ikhwanweb.com/article.php?id=20546

Harris, C. P. (1964). *Nationalism and revolution in Egypt: The role of the Muslim Brotherhood.* The Hague: Mouton.

Hassan, A. F. (2015). *Media, revolution and politics in Egypt.* London: I.B. Tauris.

Hellyer, H.A. (2016). *A revolution undone: Egypt's road beyond revolt.* London: Oxford University Press.

Huber, E., & Dion, M. (2002). Revolution or contribution? Rational choice approaches in the study of Latin American politics." *Latin American Politics & Society, 44*(3), pp. 1–28.

Herrera, L. (2014). *Revolution in the age of social media: The Egyptian popular insurrection and the internet.* New York: Verso.

Human Rights Watch (2014). *All according to plan: The Rab'a massacre and mass killings of protesters in Egypt.* Retrieved from https://www.hrw.org/report/2014/08/12/all-according-plan/raba-massacre-and-mass-killings-protesters-egypt

Husaini, I. M. (1984). *Moslem Brethren.* Lahore, Pakistan: The Book House.

Hussein, A. (2012, August 13). Egypt defence chief Tantawi ousted in surprise shakeup. *The Guardian.* Retrieved from https://www.theguardian.com/world/2012/aug/12/egyptian-defence-chief-ousted-shakeup

Ibrahim, D. (2010). The Framing of Islam on network news following the September 11th attacks. *International Communication Gazette, 72,* 111.

Ibrahim, E. (2012a, October 9). Justice denied: Egypt's Maspero massacre one year on. *Ahram Online.* Retrieved from http://english.ahram.org.eg/NewsContent/1/64/54821/Egypt/Politics-/Justice-denied-Egypts-Maspero-massacre-one-year-on.aspx

Ibrahim, E. (2012b, November 19). Mohamed Mahmoud, 1 year on: "A battle for dignity." *Ahram Online.* Retrieved from http://english.ahram.org.eg/NewsContent/1/64/58444/Egypt/Politics-/Mohamed-Mahmoud-clashes,--year-on-A-battle-for-dig.aspx

Interactive: Full Egypt election results: One year after revolution, we examine the final tally of three rounds of parliamentary voting that began November 28. (2012, February 1). *Al-Jazeera.* Retrieved from http://www.aljazeera.com/indepth/interactive/2012/01/20121248225832718.html

Ikhwanweb.com. About us section. Retrieved from http://ikhwanweb.com/about.php

Iyengar, S. (1991). *Is Anyone responsible? How television frames political issues.* Chicago: University of Chicago Press.

Ketchley, N. (2017). *Egypt in a time of revolution: Contentious politics and the Arab Spring.* London: Cambridge University Press.

Khalifa, A. (2014, October 9). *Maspero: A Massacre Revisited.* Retrieved from the Tahrir Institute for Middle East Policy Website: https://timep.org/commentary/maspero-massacre-revisited/

Khalil, S. (2012, November 19). Egypt: The legacy of Mohammed Mahmoud Street. *BBC.* Retrieved from http://www.bbc.com/news/world-middle-east-20395260

Kirkpatrick, D., & Sanger, D. (2011, February 6). After first talks, Egypt opposition vows new protest. *New York Times*. Retrieved from http://www.nytimes.com/2011/02/07/world/middleeast/07egypt.html?pagewanted=all

Kirkpatrick, D. (2012a, January 21). Islamists win 70 % of seats in the Egyptian parliament. *New York Times*. Retrieved from http://www.nytimes.com/2012/01/22/world/middleeast/muslim-brotherhood-wins-47-of-egypt-assembly-seats.html?mcubz=0

Kirkpatrick, D. (2012b, February 4). As clashes continue, Egypt soccer riot becomes metaphor for government failure. *New York Times*. Retrieved from http://www.nytimes.com/2012/02/04/world/middleeast/egypt-2-protesters-killed-in-fury-over-soccer-riot-deaths.html?mcubz=0

Kirkpatrick, D. (2012c, June 24). Named Egypt's winner, Islamist makes history. *New York Times*. Retrieved from http://www.nytimes.com/2012/06/25/world/middleeast/mohamed-morsi-of-muslim-brotherhood-declared-as-egypts-president.html?mcubz=0

Kirkpatrick, D. (2012d, November 24). Egyptian judges challenge Morsi over new power. *New York Times*. Retrieved from http://www.nytimes.com/2012/11/25/world/middleeast/morsi-urged-to-retract-edict-to-bypass-judges-in-egypt.html?mcubz=0

Kirkpatrick, D., & El Sheikh, M. (2012, November 22). Citing deadlock, Egypt's leader seizes new power and plans Mubarak retrial. *New York Times*. Retrieved from http://www.nytimes.com/2012/11/23/world/middleeast/egypts-president-morsi-gives-himself-new-powers.html?mcubz=0

Kirkpatrick, D., & Fahim, K. (2012, December 15). Egypt Islamists expect approval of constitution. *New York Times*. Retrieved from http://www.nytimes.com/2012/12/16/world/middleeast/egypt-draft-constitution-vote.html?mcubz=0

Korany, B. (2012). Egypt and beyond: The Arab Spring, the new pan-Arabism, and the challenges of transition. In *Arab Spring in Egypt: Revolution and beyond*, B. Korany & R. El-Mahdi (Eds.), pp. 271–291. Cairo, Egypt: The American University in Cairo Press.

Korany, B., & El-Mahdi, R. (2012). The protesting Middle East. In *Arab Spring in Egypt: Revolution and beyond*. B. Korany & R. El-Mahdi (Eds.), pp. 7–15. Cairo, Egypt: The American University in Cairo Press.

Lesch, A. M. (2012). Concentrated power breeds corruption, repression, and resistance. In *Arab Spring in Egypt: Revolution and beyond*, B. Korany & R. El-Mahdi (Eds.), pp. 17–42. Cairo, Egypt: The American University in Cairo Press.

Lia, B. (1998). *The society of the Muslim Brothers in Egypt: The rise of an Islamic mass movement 1928-1942*. New York: Ithaca Press.

Lim, M. (2012). Click, cabs, and coffee houses: Social media and oppositional movements in Egypt, 2004-2011. *Journal of Communication, 62*, 231–248.

Lyon, A., & Elyan, T. (2012, December 9). Egypt's opposition rejects constitutional referendum. *Reuters*. Retrieved from http://www.reuters.com/article/us-egypt-politics/egypts-opposition-rejects-constitutional-referendum-idUSBRE8B30GP20121209

MacFarquhar, N. (2011, March 20). Egyptian voters approve constitutional changes. *New York Times*. Retrieved from http://www.nytimes.com/2011/03/21/world/middleeast/21egypt.html?mcubz=0

McKee, A. (2006). *Textual analysis: A beginner's guide*. London: Sage Publications.

Melkote, S. R. (2009). News framing during a time of impending war: An examination of coverage in *New York Times* prior to the 2003 Iraq war. *International Communication Gazette, 71*(7), 547–559.

Michael, M. (2011, March 21). Egypt: Constitution changes pass in referendum. *The Washington Post.* Retrieved from http://www.washingtonpost.com/wp-dyn/content/article/2011/03/20/AR2011032001465.html

Mitchell, R. P. (1993). *The society of the Muslim Brothers.* Orig. 1966. New York: Oxford University Press.

Mohamed Morsi signs Egypt's new constitution into law. (2012, December 26). *The Guardian.* Retrieved from https://www.theguardian.com/world/2012/dec/26/mohamed-morsi-egypt-constitution-law

Momani, B., & Mohamed, E. (2016). Introduction. In *Egypt beyond Tahrir Square*, B. Momani & E. Mohamed (Eds.), pp. 1–27. Bloomington: Indiana University Press.

Monier, E. I., & Ranko, A. (2013). The fall of the Muslim Brotherhood: Implications for Egypt. *Middle East Policy, 20*, 111–123.

Noueihed, L., & Warren, A. (2013). *The battle for the Arab Spring: Revolution, counter-revolution and the making of a new era.* New Haven, CT: Yale University Press.

Osman, T. (2013). *Egypt on the brink: From Nasser to the Muslim Brotherhood.* New Haven, CT: Yale University Press.

Ostrom, E. (1998) A behavioral approach to the rational choice theory of collective action. *American Political Science Review, 92*(1), 1–22.

Pan, Z., & Kosicki, G. M. (1993). Framing analysis: An approach to news discourse. *Political Communication, 10*, 55–75.

Pasha, T. (2011). *Islamists in the headlines: Critical discourse analysis of the representation of the Muslim Brotherhood in Egyptian newspapers.* PhD Dissertation. The University of Utah.

Peterson, M. A. (2015). Re-envisioning Tahrir: The changing meanings of Tahrir Square in Egypt's ongoing revolution. In *Revolutionary Egypt: Connecting domestic and international struggles*, R. Abou-El-Fadl (Ed.), pp. 64–82. London: Routledge

Pargeter, A. (2013). *The Muslim Brotherhood: From opposition to power.* London: Saqi Books.

Protests erupt across Egypt after presidential decree. (2012, November 23). *The Guardian.* Retrieved from https://www.theguardian.com/world/2012/nov/23/protests-egypt-presidential-decree

Putnam, R. D. (1996, December 1). The strange disappearance of civic America. *The American Prospect, 7*(24). Retrieved from http://www.prospect.org/print-friendly/print/V7/24/putnam-r.html

Q&A: Egypt constitution crisis. (2012, December 24). *BBC.* Retrieved from http://www.bbc.com/news/world-middle-east-20554079

Q&A: Egypt's constitutional referendum. (2011, March 17). *BBC.* Retrieved from http://www.bbc.com/news/world-middle-east-12763313

Q&A: Egypt's parliamentary election. (2010, November 24). *BBC.* Retrieved from http://www.bbc.com/news/world-middle-east-11803687

Q&A: Egypt's parliamentary election. (2011, November 24). *BBC*. Retrieved from http://www.bbc.com/news/world-middle-east-15874070

Rougier, B., & Lacroix, S. (2016). *Egypt's Revolutions: Politics, religion, and social movements*. New York: Palgrave Macmillan.

Ryan, M. (2004). Framing the war against terrorism: US newspaper editorials and military action in Afghanistan. *Gazette, 66*(5), 363–382.

Ryzova, L. (2011, November 29). The battle of Cairo's Muhammad Mahmoud street. *Al-Jazeera*. Retrieved from http://www.aljazeera.com/indepth/opin ion/2011/11/201111288494638419.html

Scheufele, D. (1999). Framing as a theory of media effects. *Journal of Communication, 49*(1), 103–122.

Scott, J. (2000). Rational choice theory. In *Understanding contemporary society: Theories of the present*, G. Browning, A. Halcli, & F. Webster (Eds). Thousand Oaks, CA: Sage.

Semetko, P. M., & Valkenburg, P. M. (2000). Framing European politics: A content analysis of press and television news. *Journal of Communication, 50*(2), 93–109.

Shadid, A., & Kirkpatrick, D. (2011, January 30). Opposition rallies to El-Baradei as military reinforces in Cairo. *New York Times*. Retrieved from https://mobile.nytimes.com/2011/01/31/world/middleeast/31-egypt.html?mcubz=0

Shalaby, E. (2013, January 29). Morsy agrees to form committee to review constitutional articles. *Daily News Egypt*. Retrieved from https://dailynewsegypt.com/2013/01/29/morsy-agrees-to-form-committee-to-review-constitutional-articles/

Shehata, D. (2012). The power of workers in Egypt's 2011 uprising. In *Arab Spring in Egypt: Revolution and beyond*. B. Korany & R. El-Mahdi (Eds.), pp. 83–103. Cairo, Egypt: The American University in Cairo Press.

Shehata, S., & Stacher, J. (2012). The Muslim Brothers in Mubarak's last decade. In *The journey to Tahrir Square: Revolution, protest and social change in Egypt*, J. Sowers & C. Toensing (Eds.), pp. 160–177. New York: Verso.

Shenker, J. (2011, November 21). Egypt protests: New street battles erupt in Tahrir Square. *The Guardian*. Retrieved from https://www.theguardian.com/world/2011/nov/21/egypt-protests-erupt-tahrir-square

Shenker, J. (2016). *The Egyptians: A radical history of Egypt's unfinished revolution*. New York: The New Press.

Shokr, A. (2012). The eighteen days of Tahrir. In J. Sowers & C. Toensing (Eds.), *The journey to Tahrir Square: Revolution, protest and social change in Egypt*, pp. 41–46. New York: Verso.

Sullivan, D. J., & Abed-Kotob, S. (1999). *Islam in contemporary Egypt: Civil society vs. the state*. Lynne Rienner Publishers.

Tadros, M. (2012). *The Muslim Brotherhood in contemporary Egypt: Democracy redefined or confined?* London: Routledge.

Tankard, James W., Jr. (2001). The empirical approach to the study of media framing. In *Framing public life: Perspectives on media and our understanding of the social world*, Stephen D. Reese, Oscar H. Gandy, & August E. Grant (Eds.). Mahwah, NJ: Lawrence Erlbaum Associates.

The Muslim Brotherhood in flux: As Egypt's vote nears, the largest opposition group has ignored allies' boycott calls and will run candidates. (2010, November 21). *Al-Jazeera*. Retrieved from http://www.aljazeera.com/inde pth/2010/11/2010111681527837704.html

Timeline: Egypt's revolution: A chronicle of the revolution that ended the three-decade-long presidency of Hosni Mubarak. (2011, February 14). *Al-Jazeera*. Retrieved from http://www.aljazeera.com/news/middleeast/2011/01/201112515334871490.html

Two dozen protesters against death sentences in Port Said stadium massacre case detained. (2017, March 1). *Ahram Online*. Retrieved from http://english.ahram. org.eg/NewsContent/1/64/259085/Egypt/Politics-/Prosecutors-detain-two-dozen-in-Port-Said-protesti.aspx

Tuchman, G. (1978). *Making news*. New York: Free Press.

Tversky, A., & Kahneman, D. (1981). The framing of decisions and the psychology of choice. *Science, 211*(4481), 453–458.

Valkenburg, P. M., Semetko, H. A., & De Vreese, C. H. (1999). "The effects of news frames on readers' thoughts and recall." *Communication Research, 26*(5), 550–569.

Van Dijk, T. A. (1988). *News as discourse*. London: Lawrence Erlbaum Associates, Publishers.

Van Dijk, T. A. (1993). Principles of critical discourse analysis. *Discourse & Society, 4*(2), 249–283.

Van Dijk, T. A. (1998). The study of discourse. In *Discourse as structure and process.* T. A. Van Dijk (Ed.), pp. 1–34. London: Sage Publications.

Vatikiotis, P. J. (1991). *The history of modern Egypt: From Muhammad Ali to Mubarak.* Baltimore: The Johns Hopkins University Press.

Wedeman, B., & Greene, A. (2012, May 23). Election day: "Finally Egypt is born." *CNN*. Retrieved from http://www.cnn.com/2012/05/23/world/africa/egypt-elections/index.html

Wellman, B., Haase, A. Q., Witte, J., & Hampton, K. (2001). Does the internet increase, decrease, or supplement social capital? Social networks, participation, and community commitment. *American Behavioral Scientist, 45*(3), 436–455.

Wickham, C. R. (2011). The Muslim Brotherhood and democratic transition in Egypt. *Middle East Law and Governance, 3*, 204–223.

Wickham, C. R. (2013). *The Muslim Brotherhood: Evolution of an Islamist Movement*. Princeton, NJ: Princeton University Press.

Zhang, W., & Chia, S. (2006, September 3). The effects of mass media use and social capital on civic political participation. *Communication Studies, 57*(3), 277–297.

Index

www.ingramcontent.com/pod-product-compliance
Lightning Source LLC
Chambersburg PA
CBHW021819270326
41932CB00007B/248